The Voting Rights War

The Voting Rights War

The NAACP and the
Ongoing Struggle for Justice

Gloria J. Browne-Marshall

Foreword by Rev. Dr. C.T. Vivian

ROWMAN & LITTLEFIELD
Lanham • Boulder • New York • London

Published by Rowman & Littlefield
A wholly owned subsidiary of The Rowman & Littlefield Publishing Group, Inc.
4501 Forbes Boulevard, Suite 200, Lanham, Maryland 20706
www.rowman.com

Unit A, Whitacre Mews, 26-34 Stannary Street, London SE11 4AB,
United Kingdom

British Library Cataloguing in Publication Information Available

Library of Congress Cataloging-in-Publication Data

Names: Browne-Marshall, Gloria J., author.
Title: The voting rights war : the NAACP and the ongoing struggle for justice /
    Gloria J. Browne-Marshall.
Description: Lanham : Rowman & Littlefield, [2016] | Includes bibliographical
    references and index.
Identifiers: LCCN 2016018581 (print) | LCCN 2016019726 (ebook) | ISBN
    9781442266896 (hardback : alkaline paper) | ISBN 9781442266902 (electronic)
Subjects: LCSH: African Americans—Suffrage—History. | African Americans—
    Civil rights—History. | African Americans—Politics and government. |
    National Association for the Advancement of Colored People—History. |
    Social justice—United States—History. | United States—Race relations—
    History. | BISAC: LAW / Civil Rights. | HISTORY / United States / 20th
    Century. | SOCIAL SCIENCE / Sociology / General.
Classification: LCC JK1924 .B76 2016 (print) | LCC JK1924 (ebook) | DDC
    364.6/208996073—dc23
LC record available at https://lccn.loc.gov/2016018581

♾™ The paper used in this publication meets the minimum requirements of
American National Standard for Information Sciences—Permanence of Paper
for Printed Library Materials, ANSI/NISO Z39.48-1992.

Printed in the United States of America

To All
Voting Rights Martyrs

Contents

Foreword

I've been here a long time and seen a lot of things. At ninety-two years old, it seems my entire adult life has been spent in The Movement for civil and human rights so that all would obtain equal treatment under law. As a teenager I was the vice president of the NAACP branch in Peoria, Illinois. We led protests that opened up the Caterpillar Tractor plant to African Americans. It was a big deal back then when all the businesses were segregated. The churches were segregated. The schools were segregated.

During World War II, before civil rights laws, I graduated from the American Baptist Theological Seminary and became part owner of a religious newspaper in Nashville, Tennessee, on behalf of a student movement. But, if racist white people didn't like what you wrote they tried to drive you out of business and even out of town. Power only came with the vote. The vote meant equality. It gave us power to choose our elected leaders and power to make demands. When Black folks are cheated out of their right as a citizen to vote, then everybody in this country has been cheated. Our fight was made even harder when the Supreme Court allowed money to replace the vote. Now, the rich want greater control over the masses. No matter their race or color, what power the poor may have threatens the rich. That is as old as time but Americans live in a democracy. Nonviolent direct action can give average citizens needed power.

If we lose, America will not remain a democracy. That vote is a voice. The vote is a weapon we can use. It's an opportunity to say something to the rich you could not otherwise say. It's the tool to make change in this country. It's not the best tool, but it's the only tool we've got. Since it's not a perfect tool I understand the disillusionment and impatience of young people, the disenfranchised, overburdened people, and those folks who stopped believing it could ever be fair. I have spent nearly one hundred years on God's earth fighting for freedom by using nonviolent protest. And I believe the vote has made the difference. People around the world watched us rise up and fight for our freedom. Then, they wanted to fight for theirs too. If you aren't ready to fight for a full democracy then you won't get it. That fight is ongoing and it is a war. I have seen the casualties and the victories.

The Voting Rights Act was a major victory. But, this fight over power is ongoing. Rich people want to give an illusion of shared power with the poor. But, making it harder to vote is not sharing power. Making the poor choose between food and the ballot is wrong. I want people to know their history and understand how much has been achieved despite restrictions and meager resources. Dr. Martin Luther King, Jr., moved mountains with nonviolence. Before Martin and the preachers led The Movement, it was the sleeping-car porters who were the civil rights leaders. I believe politicians will be the next leaders of The Movement. We've had great people with few resources do amazing things. There is still work to be done and battles to be fought. A democracy takes work, especially now.

Rev. Dr. C.T. Vivian
Recipient, The Presidential Medal of Freedom

Timeline of
Selected Events and Cases

1607	The Jamestown Colony is founded by King James I of England.
1619	Twenty Africans from Angola arrive in Jamestown Colony.
1620	The *Mayflower* lands in Massachusetts.
1654	African children must take status of mother, losing the right to vote if enslaved.
1689	Adapted from English laws, Connecticut requires voters to own property, be of good character, and be twenty-one years old. Other American colonies pass similar laws.
1739	The Stono slave rebellion takes place in South Carolina.
1762	Free Blacks, mulattoes, women, Native Americans, Jews, and Catholics are prohibited from voting in many, but not all, American colonies.
1768	The first known Black politician, Wentworth Cheswell, is elected to public office as a New Hampshire town constable.
1776	Voting in all colonies requires property ownership, being at least twenty-one years old, and residency.
1789	The US Constitution is ratified; article 1, section 2, clause 2 counts Africans in America as three-fifths of a person because the House of Representatives is based on population.
	Under Article 1, section 2, clause 1, states decide qualifications to vote for US representatives.
1790	States impose property ownership requirements to vote.
1807	New Jersey's constitution is changed from including women and people of color to restricting the vote to White men only.

1821	New York's constitution requires property ownership of $250 for men of color to vote, but not White men.
1848	The First Women's Rights Convention takes place in Seneca Falls, New York. No Black women are invited to attend. Frederick Douglass attends.
	Frederick Douglass, orator, author and former slave, is nominated for vice president of the United States by the Liberal Party, becoming America's first Black presidential nominee.
1850	The property ownership requirement is eliminated to increase the number of White male voters among poor immigrants from Europe.
1855	Connecticut establishes a literacy test to exclude Irish Catholic voters.
1857	In *Dred Scott v. Sanford*, the US Supreme court rules that Africans in America have no rights under the US Constitution.
1859	Frederick Douglass writes an article titled "The Ballot and the Bullet."
1861	The Civil War between the Union and Confederacy begins.
1863	President Abraham Lincoln delivers the Emancipation Proclamation, freeing enslaved persons in the Confederate states.
1865	African Americans fight for their freedom in the Civil War.
	Congress ratifies the Thirteenth Amendment, abolishing slavery and indentured servitude, except as punishment for a crime. All enslaved persons are freed from bondage.
	President Abraham Lincoln is assassinated.
	The Civil War ends.
1866	Congress passes the Civil Rights Act of 1866, giving all persons born in the United States citizenship, without regard to race, color, or previous condition of servitude.
1867	Congress passes the Reconstruction Act of 1867. Former Confederate states must add voting rights for African Americans to their constitutions.
	General Oliver O. Howard founds a college for Blacks in Washington, D.C.
1868	Congress ratifies the Fourteenth Amendment, giving African Americans citizenship and the constitutional guarantees of equal protection, privileges and immunities, and due process.
	In Vineland, New Jersey, 172 women are allowed to vote for president.
1869	Howard Law School is founded to train Black lawyers to protect the legal rights of the African American community.

The first Black political appointee, Ebenezer D. Bassett, is named minister resident to Haiti by President Ulysses S. Grant.

1870   Black men receive the right to vote under the Fifteenth Amendment: "The right of citizens of the United States to vote shall not be denied or abridged by the United States or by any state on account of race, color, or previous condition of servitude." Congress has the power to enforce it.

David Strother, of El Paso, Texas, is the first Black voter to cast a ballot under the Fifteenth Amendment.

Hiram Revels, of Mississippi, becomes the first Black member of the US Senate.

Joseph H. Rainey becomes the first Black member of the US House of Representatives.

1871   Congress passes an Enforcement Act, providing criminal penalties for interfering with Black voting rights granted by the Fifteenth Amendment.

1872   Frederick Douglass is placed on the Equal Rights ticket as nominee for US vice president as the running mate of the first female to run for US president, Victoria Woodhull.

1873   A White mob attacks Black Republicans in a dispute over the presidential election, murdering more than three hundred Blacks in a Louisiana race riot known as the Colfax Massacre.

In the *Slaughterhouse* cases, the Supreme Court rules that the Fourteenth Amendment is limited to state action, not private discrimination or individual acts of racial violence.

1874   Blanche Kelso Bruce, a Republican from Mississippi, is the first Black politician elected to a full term in the Senate.

1875   Congress passes the Civil Rights Act of 1875, making racial discrimination in hotels, theaters, public transportation, and jury selection illegal.

The Supreme Court rules that a state can deny a citizen the right to vote in *Minor v. Happersett*, a case brought by Virginia Minor, a White suffragette.

1876   The White murderers of the Colfax Massacre convicted of killing Black voters are set free by a Supreme Court ruling overturning federal protections, in *U.S. v. Cruikshank*.

1877   Reconstruction ends. President Rutherford Hayes withdraws the federal army protecting Blacks from violence in the former Confederate South.

1883   The Supreme Court strikes down the parts of the Civil Rights Act of 1875 that prohibit discrimination in private cabs, trains, hotels, and restaurants.

1884   The Supreme Court upholds the convictions under the En-
          forcement Act of 1870 of Jasper Yarbrough and seven other
          Whites in Fulton County, Georgia, who assaulted Berry Saun-
          ders, a Black man, for voting.
1888   Frederick Douglass receives one Republican delegate vote for
          president, making Douglass the first Black major party candi-
          date for president.
1889   Florida passes a poll tax law to restrict Black voters.
1890   Mississippi's state legislative scheme, "the Mississippi Plan,"
          adds poll taxes and literacy tests to eliminate Black voters.
          South Carolina, Louisiana, North Carolina, Alabama, Virginia,
          Georgia, and Oklahoma pass laws requiring poll taxes and
          literacy tests, and a grandfather clause, based on the Missis-
          sippi Plan.
1895   Charles Hamilton Houston is born. He will graduate from
          Harvard Law School, become the first dean of Howard Law
          School (for Blacks), and teach dozens of civil rights attorneys.
          Houston will become the first legal director of the NAACP and
          will be known as the "architect of civil rights legal strategy."
          Booker T. Washington, president of Tuskegee Institute, for-
          merly enslaved, gives the "Atlanta Compromise" speech, sup-
          porting racial segregation and Black economic independence.
1896   The Supreme Court upholds Louisiana's Separate Car Act,
          which segregates Blacks on local trains, in a decision written
          by Justice Henry Brown. The "separate but equal" doctrine
          is established in this case, *Plessy v. Ferguson*, resulting in na-
          tionwide violence and discrimination against people of color,
          especially Blacks.
          Louisiana has more than 130,000 registered Black voters prior
          to the *Plessy* decision.
          "Grandfather clause" laws are passed across the South, requir-
          ing potential voters to have a relative who voted prior to pas-
          sage of the Fifteenth Amendment.
          The National Association of Colored Women is founded.
1900   Louisiana's Black registered voters drop to fewer than six
          thousand.
          Race riots erupt in New York City and New Orleans.
1903   The Supreme Court rules in *Giles v. Harris* that Alabama can
          take away voting rights for a lifetime based on missing a
          single registration deadline, despite Whites refusing to register
          Blacks when they arrived on the designated day.

1904   George Edwin Taylor, African American newspaper owner, graduate of Wayland University, and Wisconsin Union leader, runs for president of the United States.

1905   W. E. B. DuBois leads a conference in Niagara Falls, Canada, to discuss how to challenge discrimination resulting from the Supreme Court's *Plessy* decision.

1906   White supremacists use the Democratic National Convention to create ways to further disenfranchise Black voters.

1908   The Springfield Riot, which erupts in the town known for Abraham Lincoln, makes national news as White immigrants attack Blacks, burn Black businesses and homes, and lynch a wealthy Black resident. More than forty Black families are left homeless.

1909   In January, six people (five of whom are White) meet in New York City to discuss racism against Black Americans.

On February 12, 1909, President Abraham Lincoln's birthday, a group of activists, led by Mary White Ovington, put out the "Lincoln Day Call" for a national conference on the "Negro question."

The NAACP, founded first as the National Negro Committee, is formed from those who answered "The Lincoln Day Call" and some members of DuBois's Niagara Movement.

1910   Voter disfranchisement is the theme of the Second Conference of the National Negro Committee, at which it adopts the name National Association for the Advancement of Colored People. Black attorneys make up less than 1 percent of all lawyers in America.

Moorfield Storey, a White constitutional lawyer, becomes the first president of the NAACP. Dr. W. E. B. DuBois is the only Black person in the NAACP's leadership.

W. E. B. DuBois, NAACP director of publications and research, creates *The Crisis* magazine, the official journal of the NAACP. Sixty-seven Blacks lynched.

1911   Representative William Henry, of Massachusetts, becomes the first Black assistant US attorney general.

1913   The Seventeenth Amendment gives voters the power to elect US senators.

President Woodrow Wilson segregates all federal government offices.

Alice Paul, leader of the North American Women Suffrage Association, will not allow Black women to join her protest for
women's voting rights in Washington, D.C.

1914   The NAACP challenge of Black women's exclusion from a
Women Suffrage Association parade results in an integrated
protest for women's rights.

The American Bar Association votes to exclude Black attorneys.

1915   NAACP lawyers work with the US attorney's office to successfully challenge Oklahoma's grandfather clause in its first case
before the Supreme Court, *Guinn and Beal v. United States*.

The Supreme Court rules that grandfather clauses are unconstitutional, but upholds literacy tests, if they are given without
racial bias.

The NAACP leads protests against the film *Birth of a Nation*,
based on the book *The Clansman: An Historical Romance of the
Ku Klux Klan*, in which White actors depict Black politicians as
lewd and criminals.

President Woodrow Wilson praises *Birth of a Nation* and shows
the film at the White House, despite NAACP protests.

1917   Race riots erupt in East St. Louis, Illinois; Houston, Texas; and
Chester, Pennsylvania.

The NAACP successfully lobbies for Blacks to be commis-
sioned as officers in World War I.

The NAACP leads ten thousand protesters in the "Silent Protest Parade" against lynching and mob violence down Fifth
Avenue in New York City.

1919   The NAACP publishes "Thirty Years of Lynching in the
United States: 1889–1918."

The "Red Summer" is filled with race riots in Elaine, Arkansas;
Chicago; Gregg County, Texas; Washington, D.C.; Knoxville,
Tennessee; Longview, Texas; Omaha, Nebraska; and twenty-
six other towns in the South and North.

1920   Women gain the right to vote with passage of the Twentieth
Amendment.

Black women voters become targets of terrorism.

The NAACP fails to save the life of Sergeant Edgar Caldwell,
a Black man, who is executed for killing a White man in self-
defense in Alabama.

James Weldon Johnson (1871–1938), lawyer, activist, and
writer of "Lift Every Voice and Sing," becomes the executive
secretary (leader) of the NAACP.

1921	Race riots destroy the Black community in Tulsa, Oklahoma.
1923	The NAACP successfully challenges the exclusion of Blacks from jury trials in the Supreme Court case *Moore v. Dempsey*, which arose from Arkansas's race riots in Elaine.
	Race riots destroy the Black community in Rosewood, Florida.
1927	The Supreme Court strikes down "White-only" Democratic primaries in the Texas case *Nixon v. Herndon*. But efforts against Black voters continue.
1928	The NAACP and local Black political clubs begin to challenge White-only Democratic Party membership, in *West v. Bliley* (Virginia), *H. O. Good v. Thomas Johnson* (Florida), and *Robinson v. Holman* (Arkansas).
	Oscar DePriest (D-IL) is elected to Congress. He is the first Black in Congress since George White (R-NC) in 1901.
1930	The NAACP successfully blocks the Supreme Court nomination of John Parker, an avowed racist.
1935	Charles Hamilton Houston leads the legal committee of the NAACP to victory in *University v. Murray*, an equal education case.
	The Costigan-Wagner Anti-Lynching bill is defeated in the US Senate despite national support and vigorous lobbying by the NAACP.
1936	The NAACP begins to raise a national defense fund for civil rights litigation.
1939	The NAACP Legal Defense Fund, Inc. (LDF) is formed as a separate organization from the NAACP for financial and legal reasons. It is led by Thurgood Marshall.
	Louisiana has fewer than three thousand registered Black voters.
1940	Elbert Williams, charter member of the Brownsville NAACP branch (Tennessee), is arrested for planning a voting rights meeting and found murdered three days later.
1942	The Geyer Anti-Poll Tax bill is defeated in the US Senate, despite lobbying by the NAACP.
	Race riots destroy Black communities in St. Louis, Missouri; Beaumont, Texas; Philadelphia; Baltimore; Indianapolis, Indiana; Harlem, New York; Mobile, Alabama; Los Angeles; Detroit; and Columbia, Tennessee.
1944	America enters World War II with a racially segregated military.

The Supreme Court rules that states cannot exclude Blacks from voting in a Democratic primary in *Smith v. Allwright*, striking down Texas's Whites-only primaries. But efforts to disenfranchise Black voters continue.

DuBois returns to the NAACP as director of special research after a ten-year absence.

The NAACP participates in the Supreme Court desegregation case *Mendez v. Westminster*.

1947   W. E. B. DuBois and Walter White, NAACP executive secretary, present "An Appeal to the World" to the United Nations Commission on Human Rights.

Harry Truman becomes the first US president to address the NAACP.

President Truman appoints the Committee on Civil Rights, which recommends repeal of the poll tax in a report titled *To Secure These Rights*.

1948   President Harry Truman signs Executive Order 9981, desegregating America's military, and Executive Order 9980, governing fair employment, in response to pressure from the NAACP and labor organizer A. Philip Randolph's Double V campaign: victory overseas and victory at home.

Black voters play a key role in President Truman's reelection.

Isaac B. Nixon is killed for attempting to vote in Georgia.

The Supreme Court upholds the challenge by the NAACP and George A. Elmore to South Carolina's Democratic primary, which had been re-created as all-White private clubs to exclude Blacks, in *Rice v. Elmore*.

The NAACP successfully challenges an oath forcing Black voters to pledge allegiance to the Democratic Party principles of racial segregation and state's rights in South Carolina, in *Brown v. Baskin*.

W. E. B. DuBois is terminated from the NAACP.

1951   NAACP activists Harry and Harriette Moore are killed on Christmas Day by a bomb exploding under their Florida home.

1952   Charlotta A. Bass of the Progressive Party is the first Black woman to run for vice president.

In Louisiana, more than 130,000 Blacks are registered voters.

1954   NAACP LDF attorney Thurgood Marshall, with a team of NAACP attorneys, successfully challenges segregated public schools, resulting in the famous Supreme Court decision in *Brown v. The Board of Education of Topeka, Kansas*.

The White Citizens Council is formed in Mississippi and then across the South to oppose desegregation and Black political participation.

1955   The NAACP investigates the lynching of Emmett Till, fourteen, who is kidnapped in Mississippi, tortured, and killed. His body is found in the Tallahatchie River.

Rosa Parks, NAACP secretary and youth council advisor, is arrested for refusing to give her seat on a public bus in Montgomery, Alabama, to a White male passenger.

Reverend George Lee is killed because he encouraged Blacks to vote.

Lamar Smith is shot dead in front of the courthouse lawn in broad daylight because he organized Black voters.

1956   The Montgomery bus boycott, led by Rev. Dr. Martin Luther King Jr., ends with the Supreme Court decision in *Browder v. Gayle* after 361 days.

Alabama sues the NAACP, demanding its membership lists and forbidding the organization to work within the state, in *NAACP v. Alabama*. A similar case, *Bates v. Little Rock*, is brought against the NAACP in Arkansas, resulting in years of litigation and near bankruptcy for the NAACP.

Louisiana has more than 161,000 registered Black voters.

A Southern Manifesto, opposing civil rights for Blacks, is signed by almost all members of the US Congress in the South.

1957   Congress passes the Civil Rights Act of 1957, giving the US attorney general the power to sue on behalf of citizens and creating the US Commission on Civil Rights.

The NAACP Legal Defense Fund becomes completely independent from the NAACP.

Martin Luther King Jr., Ella Baker, and others create the Southern Christian Leadership Conference (SCLC) in Georgia.

1958   Arson is the cause of a fire that burns down the suburban home of Pennsylvania NAACP branch president George Raymond.

1959   Requiring literacy tests for voting is upheld by the Supreme Court in *Lassiter v. Northampton County Board of Elections*.

Martin Luther King Jr., president of SCLC, speaks to the NAACP Convention on its fiftieth anniversary. It is the first time Dr. King has addressed the NAACP.

Firebombs are thrown into the home of Arkansas NAACP branch secretary Daisy Bates, again. Bates, a leader of the Central High Nine desegregation group, had refused to give the NAACP membership list to Little Rock prosecutors.

1960   Congress passes the Civil Rights Act of 1960, giving the De-
           partment of Justice power to investigate voter discrimination
           and gather statistics on voting.
           The NAACP LDF and local lawyers successfully challenge
           Alabama's racially gerrymandered voting districts in the Su-
           preme Court case *Gomillion v. Lightfoot.*
           Ella Baker, a civil rights activist, creates the Student Non-
           Violent Coordinating Committee (SNCC) in Raleigh, North
           Carolina, to protest segregation laws.
1961   The Twenty-third Amendment grants Washington, D.C., resi-
           dents the right to vote in US presidential elections for the first
           time.
           The Voter Education Project (VEP) is created by Attorney
           General Robert Kennedy under President John Kennedy's
           administration.
           James Farmer creates the Congress of Racial Equality (CORE)
           in Chicago.
           Herbert Lee is killed by a White state legislator after he helped
           Robert Moses register Blacks to vote in Mississippi.
           A "tent city" in Tennessee houses entire Black families who
           were evicted from their farms for registering to vote and
           forced to live in tents.
1962   The NAACP LDF challenges Tennessee voting districts, which
           are apportioned for federal elections based on 1901 segrega-
           tion laws, in *Baker v. Carr.*
1963   Medgar Evers, a voting rights leader, is assassinated in front of
           his Mississippi home.
           The March on Washington for Jobs and Freedom brings over
           250,000 protesters to Washington, D.C., where Rev. Dr. Martin
           Luther King Jr. gives his famous "I Have a Dream" speech.
1964   The Twenty-fourth Amendment, abolishing payment of poll
           taxes to vote in federal elections, is ratified.
           Student activists James Chaney, Andrew Goodman, and Mi-
           chael Schwermer are murdered for registering Black voters in
           Mississippi.
           Fannie Lou Hamer, a voting rights activist, testifies to racism
           in the Democratic Party during a televised speech at the Demo-
           cratic National Convention.
           The Supreme Court rules that states cannot require a candi-
           date's race be stated on a ballot.

Reverend Dr. Martin Luther King Jr. is awarded the Nobel Peace Prize.

Congress passes the 1964 Civil Rights Act.

Louis Allen, murder witness in the Herbert Lee case of 1961, is killed.

Malcolm X, born Malcolm Little and also known as El-Hajj Malik El-Shabazz (1925–1965), gives speech titled "The Ballot or the Bullet."

The NAACP wins its fourth appeal in *NAACP v. Alabama*, the 1956 case forbidding the organization from doing business in Alabama unless it gives up its membership lists.

The Supreme Court rules in favor of nearly equal-sized voting districts in *Reynolds v. Sims*. The Court rules that voting is a fundamental right.

1965   Members of SCLC and SNCC leading peaceful voting rights protesters are attacked by state troopers while crossing the Edmund Pettus Bridge in Selma, Alabama, on what becomes known as "Bloody Sunday."

Jimmie Lee Jackson, twenty-six, a member of SCLC, is killed by Alabama state troopers.

Reverend James Reeb, a White voting rights supporter, is beaten to death in Selma after the second attempt to march across the Edmund Pettus Bridge protesting for voting rights.

Viola Liuzzo, a White voting rights volunteer, is murdered in Selma, Alabama.

The Voting Rights Act of 1965 is passed by Congress. The act is only intended to last five years, unless reauthorized.

Jonathan Daniels, a White voting rights worker in Alabama, is killed by a deputy sheriff, who claims Daniels attempted to escape from jail.

1966   The Supreme Court upholds the Voting Rights Act in *South Carolina v. Katzenbach*.

Vernon Ferdinand Dahmer, president of the Forrest County NAACP branch, dies from burns in the firebombing of his Mississippi home following his offer to pay any poll tax for those who could not afford it.

The Supreme Court strikes down the poll tax, finding that there is no connection between the ability to pay taxes and voting, in *Harper v. Virginia Board of Elections*.

xxii   *Timeline of Selected Events and Cases*

The Lowndes County Freedom Organization forms the Black Panther Party, a political party of local Black politicians who will run against the oppressive White establishment in "Bloody Lowndes" County, Alabama.

A "tent city" in Alabama houses Black farmers evicted for registering to vote.

Edward W. Brooke (R-MA) is elected to the US Senate. He is the first Black US senator since Reconstruction.

1967   Former NAACP attorney Thurgood Marshall is nominated to the US Supreme Court by President Lyndon Johnson and becomes the first African American Supreme Court justice.

Wharlest Jackson, the Mississippi NAACP treasurer, is killed when a bomb explodes in his car.

1968   Reverend Dr. Martin Luther King Jr. is assassinated in Memphis, Tennessee.

The "Young Turks" of the NAACP demand a Black Power program more focused on urban Black political, economic, and education issues.

Shirley Chisholm, a Democrat from New York, becomes the first Black woman elected to the US House of Representatives.

Louisiana has more than 350,000 registered Black voters.

1969   NAACP attorneys successfully represent Adam Clayton Powell Jr. in the defense of his seat in the House of Representatives, in *Powell v. McCormack*.

The NAACP successfully opposes the nomination of Clement F. Haynsworth, a vocal racist, to the US Supreme Court.

1970   The Voting Rights Act is extended by President Richard Nixon.

The NAACP successfully opposes the Supreme Court nomination of G. Harrold Carswell, a racist.

The Supreme Court rules against Oregon's literacy tests in *Oregon v. Mitchell*.

1971   The Twenty-sixth Amendment changes the voting age to eighteen years old.

The Congressional Black Caucus is founded by thirteen US Representatives.

Firebombs destroy the home of Tennessee NAACP branch president James Mapp.

1972   Representative Shirley Chisholm is the first African American from a major political party to run for president.

1975   President Gerald Ford signs the reauthorization of the Voting Rights Act, with a provision eliminating all literacy tests and adding language protections for Latinos and other non-English-speaking voters.

1976   As a reprisal for boycotting segregated White businesses in Mississippi, those businesses sue the NAACP, and a court orders the NAACP to pay $1.25 million.

1977   The NAACP LDF successfully defends redistricting in Brooklyn, New York, in *United Jewish Organizations v. Carey*.

1978   The Supreme Court rules for the White plaintiff in its first "reverse discrimination" case, *Regents of the University of California v. Bakke*.

1979   The NAACP National Board of Directors revokes permission for the NAACP Legal Defense Fund, Inc. to use the initials NAACP.

         Michigan high school principals are given authority to register students to vote under a law developed by the NAACP.

1980   The Supreme Court rules against African American voters in the *Mobile v. Bolden* vote dilution case, requiring proof of intent to discriminate.

1982   The Voting Rights Act is reauthorized by Congress and signed into law by President Ronald Reagan, with a provision eliminating the *Mobile v. Bolden* proof of intent requirement.

1984   Rev. Jesse Jackson (D-IL) runs for US president.

1985   L. Douglas Wilder (D-VA) elected lieutenant governor.

1986   The Supreme Court upholds discriminatory effect as a test, allowing North Carolina Black voters to bring a vote dilution case under section 2 of the Voting Rights Act, but the court adds three required elements, in *Thornburg v. Gingles*.

1989   L. Douglas Wilder (D-VA) is the first elected Black governor in the United States.

         A mail bomb explodes in the NAACP office in Atlanta, Georgia. Civil rights attorney Robert Robinson is killed by a mail bomb in Savannah, Georgia.

         NAACP president Benjamin Hooks leads more than 100,000 protesters on a Silent March on Washington, D.C.

1990   The NAACP unsuccessfully opposes the nomination of David Souter to the US Supreme Court.

         The NAACP launches a redistricting project in twenty-three states.

1991   The NAACP unsuccessfully challenges the nomination of Clarence Thomas who replaces Thurgood Marshall on the US Supreme Court.

1992   Carol Moseley Braun, from Illinois, is the first Black woman to be elected to the US Senate and the first Black person in the Senate since the Reconstruction era.

1993   The Supreme Court strikes down the creation of majority Black districts in *Shaw v. Reno*. Justice O'Connor calls them "political apartheid."

          Congress passes the National Voter Registration Act to expand political participation through voter registration while renewing a driver's license or motor vehicle registration.

1994   The Supreme Court rules against the Georgia NAACP's claims of violation based on commission size in *Holder v. Hall*. Justice Thomas wants the Voting Rights Act to apply only to minority access to the vote and not voting districts.

1996   The Supreme Court rules against Georgia's redistricting plan as racial gerrymandering in violation of the Voting Rights Act, in *Miller v. Johnson*.

          The Supreme Court rules against racially gerrymandered congressional districts in Texas in *Bush v. Vera* and in North Carolina in *Shaw v. Hunt*.

1999   Advancement Project, a community-based organization of lawyers, is founded as the next generation of civil rights law activism.

2000   The Supreme Court rules that Florida's vote recount in the contested presidential election is unconstitutional, resulting in the presidency of George W. Bush, in *Bush v. Gore*.

          Florida is the site of a public hearing and the "Count Every Vote" rally after hundreds of complaints are made about voter irregularities.

2001   The NAACP rally "A Day of Moral Outrage: Count the Vote" draws attention to voters purged from the rolls and disenfranchised in the national election.

2002   President George W. Bush signs the Help America Vote Act (HAVA) to upgrade voting machines and improve elections.

2005   Indiana passes a law requiring photo identification to vote.

          The NAACP leads "Keep the Vote Alive" in Atlanta, Georgia.

2006   The Voting Rights Act is reauthorized by Congress, signed into law by President George W. Bush, with an extension of twenty-five years.

Mayor-elect Gerald Washington is found dead three days before he was to become the first Black mayor of the majority White town of Westlake, Louisiana.

2008   Senator Barack Obama becomes the first African American president of the United States, winning 53 percent of the popular vote.

The Supreme Court upholds Indiana's driver's license photo identification requirement in *Crawford v. Marion County Elections Board*.

2009   Congress passes the Military and Overseas Voter Empowerment Act to assist voting by members of the military overseas and, some suspect, to increase conservative votes.

2010   The Supreme Court rules that restrictions on corporate campaign funds violate a corporation's free speech rights, in *Citizens United v. Federal Election Commission*.

2011   Voter identification laws are passed in Texas, Florida, and South Carolina.

2012   The NAACP successfully defends against those in New York State who wish to maintain prison gerrymandering, which counts inmate populations within local political districts, in *Little v. LATOR*.

2013   The Supreme Court finds section 4 of the 1965 Voting Rights Act unconstitutional in *Shelby County, Alabama v. Holder*, removing the federal preclearance for voter protection.

The Supreme Court rules that states cannot require proof of citizenship to register to vote, in *Arizona v. Inter-tribal Council of Arizona*.

The NAACP LDF files an amicus, or friend of the court, brief in support of the Inter-tribal Council of Arizona.

President Barack Obama elected to a second term, with 51 percent of the popular vote.

2014   In *Texas Conference of NAACP Branches et al. v. Steen* (consolidated with *Veasey v. Perry*), the most rigid photo identification law in America is upheld by the Supreme Court in Texas.

An NAACP delegation testifies at the United Nations about US felony disenfranchisement at a human rights conference in Geneva, Switzerland.

Louisiana has more than 900,000 Black registered voters.

2015   President Barack Obama and Rep. John Lewis cross the Edmund Pettus Bridge for the fiftieth commemoration of "Bloody Sunday" in Selma, remembering the hundreds of Black Americans beaten by Alabama state troopers for peacefully protesting the denial of their right to vote.
NAACP leads march for voting rights from Selma to Washington, D.C.
NAACP and Ohio voters successfully challenge limits on registration outlets and voting hours in *NAACP v. Husted.*
North Carolina State Conference of the NAACP v. McCrory challenges the registration restrictions passed hours after the Supreme Court struck down federal preclearance protections in *Shelby County v. Holder.*
The North Carolina NAACP successfully challenges the state's redistricting plan as racial gerrymandering in *Dickson v. Rucho.*

2016   Supreme Court Justice Antonin Scalia, a conservative who railed against the Voting Rights Act, dies.
An eight-member Supreme Court lets stand the 1964 victory in *Reynolds v. Sims.*
Thirty-six states enact photo identification laws.
In *Evenwel v. Abbott,* an evenly divided Court results in allowing all people to be counted in determining the number of representatives in congressional districts, as opposed to excluding nonvoters, children, immigrants, and the mentally ill. The NAACP LDF is amicus.
The Georgia NAACP and other civil rights groups join forces to challenge attempts by Georgia, Kansas, and Alabama to add proof of citizenship as a requirement to register to vote in federal elections when no such requirement exists, in *League of Women Voters v. Newby.*
The NAACP and NAACP LDF continue to challenge voter suppression tactics that unfairly purge voting rolls; reduce polling sites; increase felony disenfranchisement; enact rigid photo identification options; dilute voting power; add requirements to discourage voters; and create political districts that discriminate based on race, color, or ethnicity.
The NAACP leads a march in Washington, D.C., for fair voting laws. A thousand are arrested.

Introduction

Lift Every Voice and Sing, Till Earth and Heaven Ring.

—James Weldon Johnson, "Lift Every Voice and Sing" (1899)

African Americans have political power. For a hundred years the National Association for the Advancement of Colored People (NAACP) has been fighting against those who would diminish that power by law or terrorism. The voting rights struggle began as soon as the first Black became eligible to vote. The NAACP was born in 1909 from the flames of White mob violence, with a mission of political, social, and educational advancement.

Its first victory in the US Supreme Court was a voting rights case. Today the NAACP and NAACP Legal Defense Fund are in legal battles against vote dilution, unfair photo identification laws, and felony disenfranchisement. In 1915 the NAACP entered the fight by challenging the grandfather clause. The NAACP has fought longer for voting rights, brought more voting rights cases, and lost more members to violence than any other civil rights organization. It has been a war.

America's voting war, like all combat, has slain heroes, historic battles, and untold foot soldiers left lifeless on the battlefield. Like any war, this one has ultimately changed the political landscape of a nation. Exercising this simple right of every American citizen has cost untold African American lives. It remains an ongoing battle, with each era facing its own sacrifices, challenges, and legal controversies. Waged with weapons of protest and diplomacy, against terrorists in the night and lawyers in the courtroom, year after year, this voting rights war continues.

1

Currently the opponents' weapons of war are identification laws and money, while disenfranchisement makes those with felony convictions die a civil death as prisoners of war. In 1915 the voting rights war was waged against Black voters using weapons of that era: the grandfather clause, Jim Crow segregation laws, and terrorism.

Each insurgence into the hallowed ground of White supremacy has been met with sharp reprisals. But the brave men and women of the NAACP forced their way onto the political landscape that was guaranteed to them by the Constitution in 1789, taken from them by the US Supreme Court's *Dred Scott* decision in 1857, and then retrieved after the Civil War in 1870.

The war over voting rights is an ongoing struggle between Black self-determination and White supremacy. It is waged using different strategies but with the same ultimate goal: political power. In 1915 the NAACP's voting rights battle involved grandfather clauses and literacy tests. In 2015 the battle involved photo identification, redistricting, and felony disenfranchisement based on mass incarceration that began when slavery ended.

For over one hundred years the NAACP has forged a path toward full political inclusion despite bitter odds and oppression. Its members' courage is constant. From grandfather clauses to gerrymandering and all-White Democratic primaries to redistricting, each case proves the crucial role of the National Association for the Advancement of Colored People in the voting rights war.

With the vote, Blacks could control their destiny by electing sheriffs who would protect them from race-based attacks. Their votes could prevent government officials from taking their land, segregating their schools, criminalizing their behavior, excluding them from public places, and taking their lives without any consequences. The vote meant power: power to change a future overshadowed by growing terrorism by some Whites who struck relentlessly against Black progress.

Less than forty years after the first Black man entered the US Congress, murder and assault made exercising their right to vote a death wish. The NAACP is an interracial organization born of the slaughter of the 1908 Springfield Riot. It was revolutionary in its inception and has remained the most effective civil rights organization in America throughout much of the last hundred years.

There are those who have criticized its methods and deliberative process. However, in its early years, deluged with requests for assistance, with scant funding and limited staff the organization achieved miraculous progress. With success came expectations that could not have been met by any organization. Yet the NAACP has influenced American law more than any other single private organization. The US Justice Department is modeled on the methods of the NAACP and entered the fray of racial justice nearly a half century after the NAACP began doing the job alone.

In the early twentieth century White political leaders boasted about disenfranchising Black voters, and Ku Klux Klan members could shoot a Black voter in cold blood on the courthouse steps in broad daylight; it was a crime without any legal consequences. Now, legislatures quietly disenfranchise voters of color, and the criminal justice system incarcerates Blacks disproportionately, leaving them without a vote while incarcerated and disenfranchised after they are set free.

As a college student with a paper to write on African American history, I chose the NAACP. As I presented my paper to the class, a sense of ownership overcame me. My research opened my eyes and my mind to an organization that had done so much for my community and this country. Yet even then, most Americans had begun to take the work of this venerable organization for granted. It was the beginning of a relationship that continues to this day. I did not know then that I would become a civil rights attorney and work in the New York office of the NAACP Legal Defense and Education Fund, Inc. Outside of long days, constant travel, and interoffice intrigues, I did not bear the great weight of those civil rights activists and lawyers who came before me. I often think of the sacrifices made by those young, idealistic activists who risked their lives to change the world.

As African American political leaders rise to power and African American citizens exercise their rights under the Constitution, they demand more from their government than mere privileges. The inevitable backlash will occur as the ghost of White supremacy rises in opposition to self-determination. For there are many who still agree with the words of Chief Justice Roger B. Taney in the *Dred Scott* decision: "[I]t is too plain for argument, that [African Americans] have never been regarded as a part of the people . . . nor supposed to possess any political rights which the dominant race might not withhold or grant at their pleasure."[1] In every era, for over one hundred years, individuals have underestimated the determination of African Americans to have full inclusion as citizens of this country, despite discrimination and violence.

However, now too many Americans are taking their political power for granted. Remember the voting rights martyrs. They lost their lives. Be vigilant. We are still in a voting rights war.

1

~

Born of Bloodshed

Sing a song full of the faith that the dark past has taught us.

—James Weldon Johnson, "Lift Every Voice and Sing" (1899)

The Springfield Riot began with a lie. Blacks were murdered and terrorized because of that lie. But it was from those brutal days of death and destruction in an Illinois city made famous by President Abraham Lincoln that the National Association for the Advancement of Colored People (NAACP) was born.[1] Fearless, it entered a bloody battlefield with a mission to advance the rights of Blacks in America, especially the right to vote.

Lynch mobs were too often a part of life in the American South. The Springfield Riot of 1908, as violent as any southern lynch mob, signaled the need for immediate action. The NAACP was born of the fear that the South's bloody race war would come to the North, unless in the "spirit of the abolitionists . . . [we come] to treat the Negro on a plane of absolute political and social equality," as William English Walling wrote.[2] Walling, a Socialist, along with his wife, Anna Strunsky, a progressive, boarded a train for Springfield, Illinois, to personally investigate the brutality of the riot, detailed in headlines across the nation. Walling, shocked by the murderous mobs killing Blacks with impunity, asked in the abolitionist-founded *Independent* magazine, "[W]hat large and powerful body of citizens is ready to come to their aid?"[3]

The spread of lawless attacks upon the Negro, North, South and West—even in the Springfield made famous by Lincoln—often accompanied by revolting brutalities, sparing neither sex nor age nor youth.

5

Oswald Garrison Villard, *The Independent*, September 3, 1908[4]

In Springfield, for two long days White mobs torched homes, leaving hundreds of Black men, women, and children bloody and homeless. Whites, enraged by allegations of rape, lynched two elderly Black men. Smoldering wooden shells stood where Blacks once lived and did business. But the claims of rape were lies. No White woman had been raped by a Black man. Mabel Hallam, a married White woman, lied to cover up her affair with a married White man by accusing George Richardson, a Black man, of rape.

Her lie ignited already simmering racial tensions, which exploded into the Springfield Race Riot of 1908. Oswald Garrison Villard, grandson of antislavery abolitionist William Lloyd Garrison, and fellow newspaperman Henry Moskowitz met with social worker Mary White Ovington, a Brooklyn native (all three were White), to form an alliance to combat the increasing racial violence against Blacks. Villard wrote an impassioned plea to like-minded people to work to fight against racism and for the advancement of Black Americans. Their call was published on the one hundredth anniversary of Lincoln's birth. The "Lincoln's Birthday Call" on February 12, 1909,[5] published by Villard, would come to be recognized as the birth of the NAACP. More than 1,000 individuals were invited, and 150 accepted.[6]

During the Springfield Riot, two thousand Blacks were forced to flee the city of sixty thousand residents. It took nearly four thousand militiamen to restore order in Springfield.[7] Local newspapers had fed the rage of a bloodthirsty mob intent on revenge and already simmering from jealousy about Black advancement and fear of competition for jobs:

Dragged From Her Bed and Outraged by Negro.
Frenzied Mob Sweeps City Wreaking Bloody Vengeance for Negro's Heinous Crime.
The Illinois State Journal, August 15, 1908

On August 14, 1908, a White mob of more than five thousand went on a rampage, killing two Blacks and four Whites, destroying Black businesses, and setting fires that left forty Black families homeless. The animosity of poor Whites over Black progress drove mobs to ransack Black businesses, loot the homes of wealthy Blacks, and murder Whites whom they believed were friendly to Black positions.

Negro Assaults High-Tone Lady in a Most Prominent Neighborhood.
The Illinois Register, August 14, 1908

Whites gathered outside the Springfield jailhouse to lynch the suspected rapist, as well as another Black man being detained there. However, the two men had secretly been taken to safety by a White business owner. Cheated, the mob burned cars and destroyed the businesses of Whites who had helped the men escape death and for two days roamed the streets, destroying Black businesses and homes. The White woman recanted her story of rape, conceived to cover up an illicit affair with a White man, but it was too late. A wealthy Black man living in a prominent White community was dragged into the street and lynched by low-income Whites jealous of his wealth.

Before this riot, racial attacks against Blacks were rarely covered in White newspapers unless for sensationalism. Newspaper coverage was limited. Race riots led by White mobs may have been mentioned, but with little detail, especially when they took place in rural places or small southern towns. However, the Springfield Riot changed the way racial conflicts were reported. The level of property damage caused by White mobs; the location of Springfield, the capital of Illinois; and the violence of this riot grabbed national headlines and the attention of Blacks and Whites alike.

In Springfield, White immigrant workers suspected Blacks would try to take their jobs. Blacks had begun to arrive in the North after the Supreme Court legalized segregation in 1896, to escape Jim Crow terrorism, Black Code criminal laws, and political exclusion to join relatives in towns like Springfield, seeking jobs and peace and freedom. But their numbers were not yet large. White immigrants were resentful, although Black laborers worked the worst jobs for cheaper wages and longer hours. The conditions under which Blacks could find work were only a slightly better version of Jim Crow segregation found in the South.

INTERRACIAL ALLIES

Ironically, the bloody Springfield Riot, which erupted over an alleged interracial attack, would give birth to an interracial organization formed to protect the rights of Blacks. Slavery had created a complex web of relationships on plantations and among those who sought to crush the plantation system. The idea for an interracial organization was not unique. An organization comprised of Whites and Blacks, created for the purpose of defending and advancing the rights of Blacks, was deeply rooted in American abolitionist history.

Black abolitionists Frederick Douglass, Harriet Tubman, and Sojourner Truth belonged to White abolitionist organizations. However, the law forbade miscegenation (racial mixing), and there was open hostility toward any interracial group. Such groups were not always illegal in the North. However, racial mixing in a group was considered a prelude to possible romantic involvement and marriage, which was illegal. Frederick Douglass in fact married fellow abolitionist Helen Pitts, a White suffragette, after the death of his wife of forty-four years, Ann Murray Douglass, a free Black woman.

Discouraged in the North, interracial social groups, friendships, and non-employment-related meetings of any kind were untenable in the South. Interracial love relationships could result in a criminal fine and a sentence of hard labor in the penitentiary. In 1883 the US Supreme Court ruled against an interracial couple in *Pace v. Alabama*, the first Supreme Court case involving such a relationship.[8]

Marriage was only allowed within racial groups. It was illegal for any couple of any race to live together without being married in Alabama. Tony Pace, a Black man, was living with Mary J. Cox, a White woman. They were arrested and convicted of violating a statute prohibiting interracial cohabitation, or living under the same roof.

Under Alabama law:

> If any white person and any negro, or the descendent of any negro to the third generation, inclusive, though one ancestor of each generation was a white person, intermarry or live with each other, each of them must, on conviction, be imprisoned in the penitentiary or sentenced to hard labor for the county for not less than two nor more than seven years.[9]

Pace argued that the punishment he and Cox received was harsher than a White couple would have been given because they were in an interracial relationship.

A conviction for fornication without marriage between two Whites was punishable by a $100 fine and two years of hard labor or confinement in the state penitentiary, under section 4184 of Alabama law. But the Supreme Court supported a harsher sentence, because both the White woman and the Black male were given the same punishment. It was irrelevant that the tougher punishment would not have been given to two unmarried Whites living together. The Supreme Court's decision in the *Pace* case gave the states and American society in general a clear message that interracial relationships of any kind would not be tolerated. But its interracial membership made the NAACP especially unique and powerful.[10]

Pressure against interracial associations grew when the Supreme Court ruled in 1896 that the states could segregate the races in all social settings. The Supreme Court's decision in *Plessy v. Ferguson* opened the floodgates of racial animosity against African Americans, leading to the migration of Blacks from the South to the North and fostering a sense of lawlessness against Blacks nationwide that led to White mob violence like the Springfield Riot of 1908.[11]

THE NIAGARA MOVEMENT AND THE LINCOLN DAY CALL

Even before the Springfield Riot, William Edward Burghart DuBois, an intellectual and the first Black recipient of a Harvard doctorate in sociology, decided that action had to be taken against the wave of violence against and total disregard for the constitutional rights of Black Americans. DuBois was a northerner born into a middle-class Black family in Massachusetts. He had known integration as well as the sting of prejudice. But his experience was unlike those of southern Blacks, who lived with the constant fear of lynching as punishment for any attempt to achieve racial equality. As DuBois witnessed the backlash against Black freedoms, he devised an intellectual strategy.

In 1905 W. E. B. DuBois drafted his "Call" to men of goodwill to meet in Buffalo, New York, to draft a response. His group of Black intellectuals and White activists was refused accommodations by Buffalo hotels. On July 10, 1905, DuBois's meeting was held across the border in Canada near Niagara Falls, which resulted in the name the Niagara Movement.[12] The Niagara Movement was not limited to adult men. Of the women who joined the movement, the most notable were educator and journalist Ida B. Wells-Barnett and Mary White Ovington. Born into a White, once-wealthy family, Ovington was a social worker who had been taught that all people were equal. Working among the poor in New York City led her to investigate racial discrimination in that city. Her findings were published as *Half a Man: The Status of the Negro in New York*.[13]

Ida B. Wells-Barnett, the other woman who attended the Niagara Conference, had exposed the myth of White rape as the rationale for White lynch mobs' attacking Black communities and murdering Black men.[14] Chased out of Tennessee while investigating the lynching of her friends, Wells-Barnett knew that rape was not the reason they and most victims were killed. Unfounded rumors of rape, as would be the case in the Springfield Riot; jealousy; and the need to impose racial superiority were the true motives behind most lynchings. Race riots stemmed from rage over the progress of African Americans. Wells-Barnett was a suffragette who had fallen out with Francis Willard and other White leaders of the women's voting movement because their organizations were segregated, were openly hostile to Black women, did not believe in equal suffrage for all women, and had refused to acknowledge the growing violence against Blacks, especially Black men and boys.

DuBois's Niagara Movement included a Junior Niagara Movement for college students and youths. The following letter was sent to Junior Niagara members by Mason A. Hawkins of Baltimore, Maryland, treasurer of the movement and secretary of the Junior Niagara Movement; it shows the mission and passion of Niagara members:

The world spurns the coward who fears to try. Besides there is no telling what can be done by thoughtful, intelligent co-operation. . . . [A]t least in such an organization we can make the country know and realize that as men we will not, without protestation or an effort to obtain our own, allow others to take what rightfully belongs to us. . . . [t]he objects of the Niagara Movement [are]: (a) Freedom of speech and criticism. (b) An unfettered an unsubsidized press. (c) Manhood suffrage. (d) Abolition of caste d[i]stinctions based simply on race and color. (e) The recognition of the principle of human brotherhood as a practical present creed. (f) The recognition of the highest and best human training as the monopoly of no class or race. (g) A belief in the dignity of labor. (h) United effort to realize these ideals under wise and courageous leadership. The Niagara Movement represents[,] I might say, the final attitude to which every courageous, race-loving, self-respecting, intelligent Negro has been driven. After waiting many years following the line of least resistance, during which we have been deprived by our ruthless enemies of many rights and privileges, we have come to the decision to stand hard and fast by all the rights and privileges pertaining to us as American citizens. These principles have been fully set forth in the object of the Niagara Movement. For them we must contend in season and out of season; but always in a quiet, gentlemanly way. . . . [I]t is the wish of . . . the Niagara Movement that this movement should become rooted in the fertile minds and fearless hearts of our college students. We want you as college men to become deeply interested in the affairs which vitally concern our race. We have been out of college long enough to learn that the saddest mistake is to shut himself off while in school from the questions and conditions which are with difficulty and hardship being worked out by the race. . . . We want our college students to take a stand for the principles set down in the objects of the Niagara Movement. We want you to do so because it will make you fearless men useful to the race. . . . Develop and make yourselves strong for the leadership which will come to you! . . . [T]he future of our race depends to a large extent upon its college men. . . . [S]uch an attitude may cost you something. Everything worth having costs. But regardless of cost, whether you wish to or not, being as you are men of extraordinary training, having many talents, the race demands of you, its coming leaders, a wise, loyal, courageous, upright, manly attitude upon all questions of vital interest to the race.

Activist Mary Ovington, a descendant of abolitionists born in 1865, the year slavery ended, was also stunned by the ferocity of the Springfield Riot. She would be part of a majority call to arms: the Lincoln's Birthday Call. The symbolism of the mob violence taking place on Lincoln Day in Springfield, the town made famous by Abraham Lincoln, was not lost on her. As President Abraham Lincoln's one hundredth birthday drew near, activists met in January 1909 to determine their response to the Springfield mob. Ovington and fellow activists Dr. Henry Moskowitz and William English Walling, a wealthy southern gentleman and writer, decided to join forces with Black leaders DuBois, Mary Church Terrell, and Wells-Barnett and leader of the Black clergy Rev. William H. Brooks of the African Methodist Episcopal (AME) Church.

Together they would initiate the Lincoln Day Call to action. The invitation list was impressive. However, Booker T. Washington, the renowned president of Tuskegee Institute, was notably absent.[15] Washington was the most influential Black person in America. However, his stance on economic separation and independence as a strategy for Black advancement in the South conflicted with the northern view of Black full integration held by DuBois and other members of the committee. In addition, Washington had publicly criticized DuBois's Niagara Movement.[16] Ovington asked, "[C]ould we ignore the man who was unquestionably the most influential and the most famous Negro living?"[17] Yet they did.

Formed on February 12, 1909, by sixty progressive Whites and Blacks to be an "aggressive watchdog of Negro liberties," the group had been brought together in response to the murderous Springfield Riot of 1908. Silence about the oppression of Blacks had gone on too long. Conservatives and progressives with occupations in the ministry, social work, journalism, law, and education sat down together to pronounce their opposition to the silence surrounding racial attacks on Black Americans. Although Ovington was horrified when she read about the rampage through the streets of Springfield, her vision for Black citizens went well beyond living without fear of mob violence. She wanted Blacks to enjoy full participation in all aspects of American life. Tirelessly, she guided the meeting toward her vision of full inclusion.

These individuals came together as an interracial group to fight race discrimination. Their racial composition presented problems. Ovington noted that "the majority of the people launching the movement were white and therefore under suspicion. Were they going to be nam[b]y-pamby at the last, as so many whites before them had been, and counsel halfway measures? The resolutions [of the committee] demanded the ballot, the same education for colored as the white, and the enforcement of the Fourteenth and Fifteenth Amendments."[18]

The Lincoln Day statement sent a warning shot into the supremacists' nests in the US Supreme Court, US Congress, and state governments, with this declaration:

"The CALL"
A Lincoln Emancipation Conference
To Discuss Means for
Securing Political and Civil Equality
for the Negro

The celebration of the centennial of the birth of Abraham Lincoln widespread and grateful as it may be, will fail to justify itself if it takes no note and makes no recognition of the colored men and women to whom the great emancipator labored to assure freedom.

***

If Mr. Lincoln could revisit this country he would be disheartened by the nation's failure in this respect. He would learn that on January 1st, 1909, Georgia had rounded out a new oligarchy by disfranchising the negro after the manner of all the other Southern states. He would learn that the Supreme Court of the United States, designed to be a bulwark of American liberties, had failed to meet several opportunities to pass squarely upon this disfranchisement of millions by laws avowedly discriminatory and openly enforced in such manner that white men may vote and black men be without a vote in their government; he would discover, there, that taxation without representation is the lot of millions of wealth-producing American citizens, in whose hands rests the economic progress and welfare of an entire section of the country.[19]

The Lincoln's Birthday Call marks the entry of the NAACP onto the battlefield for justice under law.

The NAACP chose the right to vote as its primary goal. Advancement for Blacks meant political participation as elected officials at every level of government, with a choice of political party and the right to elect or defeat candidates without fear of violence. Walling recalled members of the Springfield mob shouting at Black victims, "Lincoln freed you, we show you where you belong."[20]

The bloody Springfield Riot meant that even for educated Blacks living comfortably in cities, the threat of mob violence and lynching was ever present. Although poverty was rife among Blacks and most Africans in America could trace their families back to enslavement, their ambition was palpable. So much had been promised by the Constitution, the North's victory in the Civil War, and the three post–Civil War amendments, but too little had become reality.

After slavery ended, when Blacks demanded and expected constitutional rights, former slaveholders had little reason to restrain their racist rage, and facing no criminal consequences, they let it loose. The murder of Black men, women, and children by mobs comprised of thousands of uncontrolled, bloodthirsty Whites, who hunted down and shot, hanged, and burned to death any Black person unfortunate enough to get caught, is a notorious part of American history. The riots in Springfield arose from decades of White mob violence against Blacks.

THE PLAN TO LIMIT BLACK POLITICAL POWER

After Reconstruction, southern states had adopted constitutions intended to limit the rising political power of Black voters and political leaders. Before the Mississippi Constitutional Convention of 1890, Blacks held some political power.[21] Hiram Revels, the first Black US senator, was from Mississippi, as was Blanche K. Bruce, the second Black US senator. John R. Lynch served in the Mississippi House of Representatives and was elected to the US House of Representatives. If there was any doubt that the true purpose of the convention was to deprive Blacks of political power, the words of James Kimble Vardaman, later governor of the state and a US senator, removed all doubt about why the state had voted to add a literacy test and poll tax: "There is no use to equivocate or lie about the matter. Mississippi's constitutional convention was held for no other purpose than to eliminate the nigger from politics; not the ignorant—but the nigger."[22] Vardaman believed the cold-blooded murder of Blacks to prevent them from progressing beyond menial labor was acceptable. "If it is necessary every negro in the State will be lynched; it will be done to maintain white supremacy," he wrote. Detractors like William Percy, the son of a political opponent, referred to the crowds attending a Vardaman rally as the type "that attend [religious] revivals and fight and fornicate in the bushes afterwards."[23]

The Mississippi Constitution of 1890 became the prototype for the South. It crushed the voting rights of the Black majority with poll taxes, which were required to be paid for two years; literacy tests requiring voters to read and interpret provisions from the constitution; and a list of crimes (theft, obtaining money or goods under false pretenses, perjury) that fit perfectly within a criminal justice system replete with Black Code laws that criminalized Blacks unfairly, resulting in criminal records that rendered them ineligible to vote, a civil death.

Henry Williams unsuccessfully challenged Mississippi's constitution when he appealed his murder indictment in 1898. For most grand and petit juries, the names of those who serve on them come from the voter rolls. The grand jury that had indicted Williams was comprised of all White men, because only White men were allowed to register to vote. Williams

argued that Blacks, who had been a majority of voters prior to the Mississippi Convention of 1890, were now precluded from voting and thus from
serving on his grand jury, which violated his constitutional right to a jury
of his peers. Williams stated:

> That the constitutional convention was composed of 134 members, only one
> of whom was a negro. That under prior laws there were 190,000 colored vot-
> ers and 69,000 white voters. The makers of the new constitution arbitrarily
> refused to submit it to the voters of the state for approval, but ordered it
> adopted, and an election to be held immediately under it, which election
> was held under the election ordinances of the said constitution in Novem-
> ber, 1891, and the legislature assembled in 1892, and enacted the statutes
> complained of, for the purpose to discriminate aforesaid, and but for that
> the "defendant's race would have been represented impartially on the grand
> jury which presented this indictment," and hence he is deprived of the equal
> protection of the laws of the state. It is further alleged that the state has not
> reduced its representation in congress, and generally for the reasons afore-
> said, and because the indictment should have been returned under the con-
> stitution of 1869 and statute of 1889, it is null and void. The motion concludes
> as follows: "Further, the defendant is a citizen of the United States, and, for
> the many reasons herein named, asks that the indictment be quashed, and he
> be recognized to appear at the next term of the court."

Justice Joseph McKenna wrote the US Supreme Court opinion upholding Williams's conviction. McKenna, a former US representative who had
been called unfit to serve on the court, ruled in favor of the segregationist
Mississippi Plan, allowing political disenfranchisement. The fate of Black
voters across the South was sealed.

Armed with favorable Supreme Court rulings in *Plessy* and *Williams*,
White southern Democrats flexed their renewed political muscle over
Blacks through the ballot and mob violence. The century that had wit-
nessed the freeing of Blacks from bondage ended with the Wilmington
Massacre. In Wilmington, North Carolina, in 1898, a riot began with
White rage against Black political power, which was called "Negro domi-
nation." A riot was deemed inevitable by some because:

> "The relations between the races were too strained for it to be avoided" since
> "matters had reached a point in Wilmington at which a conflict between the
> races was inevitable."
> *Wilmington Messenger,* November 15, 1898.

Black political power was wielded by Black Republicans as successfully
as by White Democrats. This ability to lobby, compromise, organize, and
vote as shrewdly as their counterparts enraged certain Whites, who trans-

formed into murderous mobs. "This is a white man's country and white men must control and govern it," stated the *North Carolina Democratic Handbook*.[24]

White Democrats controlled state politics in North Carolina. However, in the town of Wilmington, Blacks comprised the majority of the population and held most elected offices. Black political leadership in the majority Black town of Wilmington was tolerated. When a coalition of White and Black Republicans swept into state government, the Democrats launched a deadly racial campaign.

A speech by Rebecca Felton, a White racist suffragette from Georgia, illustrates the simmering hostility. Felton said, "If it requires lynching to protect a woman's dearest possession from ravening, drunken human beasts, then I say lynch a thousand negroes a week . . . if it is necessary." Her threat, published in the local newspaper, was rebuked by Black newspaperman Alexander Manley, owner of the Wilmington *Daily Record*. Racial tensions heightened. Democratic leader Daniel Schenck promised that the election of 1898 would "be the meanest, vilest, dirtiest campaign since 1876"; it led to the election of Rutherford B. Hayes as president and the removal of the federal troops that had been protecting Blacks in the South. Despite a vast Black majority, White Democrats stole the 1898 election and set out to punish Blacks and make Wilmington an example for all Black politicians who got out of their place.

On November 10, 1898, the riot began. Thousands of Whites stormed the streets in search of Manley and all Black politicians. They either had to leave town immediately or face death. Days later the coroner held fourteen inquests on murdered citizens, but more than sixty Blacks may have been murdered by White businessmen, lawyers, bankers, and politicians, who turned to mob violence to get their way in politics. The bodies of Black men, women, and children who had been bludgeoned to death were thrown into the Cape Fear River.

The Wilmington Massacre, like the Colfax Massacre in Louisiana in 1873, had at its roots White outrage over Black political power. Outgunned and outnumbered, Blacks were forced to retreat from public office or die. Black citizens like the two thousand in Wilmington, North Carolina, were chased from town, barely escaping with their lives, never to return. Duly elected Republican officials were removed from office at gunpoint and replaced by White Democrats chosen by a secret committee.

The twentieth century began with racial terrorism. Some 106 Blacks were lynched in 1900 and 105 in 1901. White rage, abetted by the failure of federal and state law enforcement agencies and prosecutors to act, meant that although Blacks might be free under law, they were not equal. In 1900 race riots erupted in New Orleans and New York City. In 1904 Springfield, Ohio, experienced the first of three race riots. In 1906 White mobs attacked Blacks in Greenburg, Indiana, and within weeks Blacks in Atlanta, Georgia, were attacked, with their body parts sold as souvenirs. Soldiers on an army base in Brownsville, Texas, were attacked. Whenever Blacks fought back in self-defense, hordes of Whites were quickly deputized by local authorities and allowed to kill at will. Discouraging Black progress was a key goal of mob violence.

After the Civil War the Fifteenth Amendment to the US Constitution gave Black men the right to vote in 1870. That amendment also gave Congress the power to create legislation to enforce those voting rights. The enforcement provision led to passage of federal civil rights laws. But the Constitution gave the power to determine who could vote to the states. The battle lines were formed. From here, every arsenal was used in the fight for White supremacy, whether between the states and the federal government, the North and South, or Blacks and Whites—terrorism, self-serving laws, and conservative courts would be constant obstacles to exercising the right to vote. States had the power.

Upon the rare occasion of a victory being gained for voting rights in the courts, southern legislatures would simply employ a new deceptive tactic to disenfranchise Black voters. At the Virginia Convention of 1906, Congressman Carter Glass stated, "We are here to discriminate to the very extremity of permissible action under the limitation of the Federal Constitution, with a view to the eliminating of every negro voter who can be gotten rid of legally, without materially impairing the numerical strength of the white electorate."[25]

Terrorism guaranteed White political supremacy when racism failed. Yet Blacks were blamed for starting the violence used against them. After the worst riots, if a commission investigated, as had occurred after the Springfield Riot, it had no authority to bring charges or compensate Blacks for their losses. Like lynching and night riders, these White mobs were effective weapons of vote suppression. They kept Blacks "in their place"—away from direct competition for jobs and outside of any active role in this democracy.

THE FOUNDING OF THE NAACP

Coming on the heels of ten years of mob violence, the Springfield Riot sent a bloody message of more terror to come. Therefore, African Americans decided they must fight for their freedom, in the North and the South, or risk being forced back into slavery. It was in light of this violence that W. E. B. DuBois added his name to the "Lincoln Day Call," gathering those who would join in the fight against racial oppression. Mary White Ovington understood the message of White mob violence, and wanted to send back a message of her own: Blacks would not have to fight alone.

The Lincoln Day Call was answered first with a National Negro Committee, which met at Henry Street Settlement on the Lower East Side of New York City in late May 1909.[26] Ovington knew that it was important that the Call be supported by people with a national reputation and published where it would gain the greatest visibility. Members of that conference of the National Negro Committee worked into the night, debating the "present evils, the voicing of protests, and the renewal of the struggle for civil and political liberty."[27]

It might have stepped onto the battlefield for racial justice under law on February 12, 1909, as a small group of determined progressives, but now, with sixty progressive Whites and Blacks, its mission was to become an "aggressive watchdog of Negro liberties." It would bring publicity to racism and denounce "the ever-growing oppression of our 10,000,000 colored fellow citizens." The group chose voting rights as a primary organizational goal. Advancement for Blacks required political participation. Political participation meant holding the perpetrators of racial violence accountable and forcing government leaders to protect the rights of Black citizens.

The group that began as the Niagara Movement continued until 1911. Then most of its members joined the NAACP. But William Monroe Trotter, an intellectual and journalist, as well as some other Niagara Movement members, refused to join the NAACP, arguing that having Whites, even Whites of goodwill, lead an organization for Black self-determination would ultimately undermine the goal of African American social, economic, and political independence. Instead, Trotter put his efforts into the National Negro Political League and National Equal Rights League.

The National Negro Committee officially became the National Association for the Advancement of Colored People in 1910. Led initially by a handful of White liberals, it would work to ensure the ability of Black Americans to elect officials at every level of government, with a choice of political party and the right to elect or defeat candidates, without fear of violence.[28] With the vote, Blacks could control their destiny by electing sheriffs who would protect them from race-based attacks. Their vote could prevent government officials from taking their land, segregating their schools, criminalizing their behavior, excluding them from public places, and taking their lives without any consequences.

Moorfield Storey, a thirty-two-year-old White, progressive lawyer, watched the treacherous journey of Africans in America from enslavement, to Civil War soldiers, to citizens begin to falter due to their own government's betrayal. As a well-respected Boston lawyer, he looked to the rights and protections promised by the Constitution and Congress.

Storey was not present at the first meeting of the National Negro Committee in New York City. Ovington had inadvertently left off his name from that first invitation. However, he too had been shocked by the racial violence that met every step of Black progress and the silence of White Americans. Later, in 1909 Storey, now sixty-four, brought his renown as a lawyer and his activist spirit to the National Negro Committee.[29]

Born in Boston in 1845, Moorfield Storey was an anti-imperialist and antiracist who learned at the feet of renowned reformer and US senator Charles Sumner, of Massachusetts. Sumner, the leader of the antislavery Republicans, had been beaten bloody on the Senate floor in 1856 by Representative Preston Brooks of South Carolina.[30] Senator Sumner fought to abolish slavery and give full political rights to African Americans. He wrote the first civil rights laws.

Moorfield Storey, a blue-blood American, had a deep family tradition of attacking racial discrimination even among his own political elite and those legally trained. In 1911, when the American Bar Association discovered the race of Assistant US Attorney General William H. Lewis, a Black former Massachusetts US representative and a graduate of Amherst College and Harvard Law School, it rescinded his membership. Although Storey's wife was dying, he took the time to challenge the nation's largest legal organization, stating, "If the Association sustains this action, I shall resign, and I hope my example will be followed by a large number of people."[31] Lewis was allowed to stay in the ABA. However, stating one's race became a requirement on the application form for the ABA. Perhaps Storey was motivated by the White elites in Kentucky who lynched a Black man inside the Opera House that very year; shooting the victim came with the price of the opera ticket.[32]

From a family of Puritans, Storey carried his conviction of equality onto the battlefield for racial justice. "I am firmly of the opinion that the most pressing political duty of every citizen today is to do what he can to secure for every citizen of the United States, whatever his race or color, equal standing before the law, equal political rights, and equal opportunity."[33] He could not have predicted that the next twenty years of his life would be spent in an almost military campaign against racial injustice as a civil rights leader.

In the early twentieth century, all civil rights organizations had a magazine or newsletter. Harvard-trained intellectual W. E. B. DuBois created a magazine to be the voice for the silent oppression under which Black Americans were made to suffer, *The Crisis*. DuBois was the only person of color in the initial leadership of the NAACP. To her lifelong regret, activist Ida B. Wells-Barnett left the group rather than confront what she considered DuBois's self-interested maneuverings, which resulted in his singular Black leadership position.

The enemy in this voting rights war was White supremacy. This multifaceted opponent to democracy was set on robbing Blacks of their political power using any available weapon, including murder. By the end of 1910, lynching had taken the lives of sixty-seven Blacks. Moorfield Storey had taken on the challenge of navigating the advancement of Black people through treacherous territory with little money, an unpaid staff, and no legal arsenal, against entrenched opposition with power in every American institution and a penchant for murder with impunity.

Storey, a former leader of the ABA, proudly said of the newly formed organization, whose future lay in his hands and whose path he would chart:

> The object of the National Association is to create an organization which will endeavor to smooth the path of the Negro race upward, and create a public opinion which will frown upon discrimination against their property rights, which will endeavor to see that they get in the courts the same justice that is given to their white neighbors, and that they are not discriminated against as they are now all over the country. We want to make race prejudice if we can as unfashionable as it is now fashionable. We want to arouse the better feelings of the white people, and broaden the sympathy which should be felt for the race to which we owe so much, and it seems that this is a field for our labor.[34]

Within four years this fledgling organization—born from the blood spilled by innocent Blacks in Springfield and the courage gained from a history of abolitionism and fighting White supremacists to gain freedom and self-determination—grew to have branches in nearly every city and became an internationally recognized champion for the rights of African Americans, known primarily by the initialism NAACP.

Moorfield Storey served the NAACP from 1910 until his death in 1929. He was the first NAACP attorney to argue a case in the US Supreme Court—*Guinn and Beal v. United States* (1915)—the association's first legal strike at White supremacy. The NAACP entered a deadly battleground to fight for the right of Black citizens to vote. The South had constructed a barricade of notorious laws enacted to disenfranchise Black voters. This first NAACP battle involved the "grandfather clause," a voting restriction based on a lingering stain of slavery.

2

⁓

Earning the Vote

Facing the rising sun of our new day begun.

—James Weldon Johnson, "Lift Every Voice and Sing" (1899)

Black Americans earned their right to vote. They were forced to fight for every single ballot. The vote meant power: power to change a future dimmed by growing terrorism from Whites, who struck relentlessly against Black progress. But the enemy underestimated the resilience learned through the oppression of enslavement.

Resilience, courage, and determination can be effective weapons in any protracted battle. They are necessary weapons in the war for voting rights. Slavery ended, but Blacks were still under the control of others. With the vote, they could control their destiny by electing local sheriffs who would protect them or dismissing those who did not. Their vote could prevent government officials from taking their land and reward those who supported their interests.

Public officials who stood for segregating their schools, criminalizing their behavior, excluding them from public places, and taking their lives without any consequences would have to face an angry Black electorate. The vote meant the power to change a future overshadowed by White supremacists, who fought relentlessly against Black progress. The vote was earned by free Black men during slavery and by all Black men five years after slavery ended.

BEFORE THE CIVIL WAR

To understand the frustration felt by African Americans, one must con-
sider their three-hundred-year quest for full political participation. In
1619 Africans arrived in the Virginia colony, before the landing of the
Mayflower in Massachusetts. A free Black couple in early colonial James-
town, Virginia, named Mary and Anthony Johnson, owned property and
had White and Black servants in the 1600s. To vote, the law required
land ownership. The Johnsons had earned their freedom and their land
but were cheated out of political participation, labeled illegal aliens by a
change in the law, and chased from their land in Virginia. They, like many
other Blacks in the 1600s, were denied the right to vote for or against the
laws that governed their lives and instituted slavery.

As the free African community grew in America, restricting the vote
to Whites only became imperative for those who believed in White supremacy over all other peoples. Tensions waxed and waned with changes
in laws and circumstances. Based on English law, the colonies required
property ownership to vote. Then the colony of Connecticut added good
character and a minimum age of twenty-one. Other American colonies
soon passed similar laws.

By 1762 free Blacks, mulattoes, women, Native Americans, Jews, and
Catholics were denied the franchise by law in the American colonies.
However, in 1768 Wentworth Cheswell was the first Black person elected
to public office, when he became a constable in New Hampshire.

Ironically, while America was fighting for its independence in 1776, the
requirements for voting in all colonies demanded property ownership,
being at least age twenty-one, and proven residency in a state. Vermont
ended slavery and sought to give Blacks the right to vote in 1777. When
the US Constitution was ratified in 1787, Africans counted as three-fifths
of a person, a compromise between the southern and northern states, for
determining the number of representatives to Congress each state would
get.[1] The framers of the Constitution decided to give the states the power
to decide the qualifications needed to vote.[2]

Certain White males with property could vote. Few White women
could vote. In the 1790s, as more immigrants from Europe arrived in
America, the states changed their laws to exclude them by imposing
property ownership requirements for voting. Discrimination against the
Black vote took place in the North as well as the South. In 1807 New Jersey's constitution was changed to exclude women and people of color,
restricting the vote to White men only.

In New York the federal election of 1813 was close. But the power of
three hundred Black voters changed the outcome, putting Federalists
back in office. Tammany Society members, who engaged in violence and

bribes to gain political advantage, saw this as a sign of the "dangerous importance of the Negro." The laws were changed. By 1821 New York State had restricted the voting franchise to Black men with the enactment of a constitutional amendment requiring a lengthy period of residence and property ownership of at least $250, a substantial amount, to vote. The number of Black voters dropped from more than 300 to 163 in 1821 and to 15 in 1824.[3] The financial requirement was only applied to "men of color," not White male voters.

In 1848 White women gathered at the first Women's Rights Convention in Seneca Falls, New York, to discuss their rights, including the right to vote. These "suffragettes," as they were called, included Frederick Douglass at this meeting. However, no Black women attended, and there is scant evident that any were invited. This discrimination by oppressed White suffragettes against oppressed Black suffragettes continued in the movement until 1920, when the US Constitution was amended, giving the right to vote to women.

As in New York, when Blacks became politically powerful or began to outnumber Whites, requirements for them to vote were made more difficult, while for Whites the requirements were loosened. The property ownership requirement was eliminated for Whites to increase the number of poor White male voters. In the South, enslaved Blacks were forced to leave the state once they gained their freedom through manumission; they were freed by the slaveholder or purchased their freedom. Discrimination against poor Whites continued, but was lifted when their votes were needed to defeat Black interests. In Connecticut, discrimination against Roman Catholics from Ireland led to the establishment of a literacy test in 1855 to exclude Irish Catholic voters. The test was used against Blacks as well.

In 1857 the US Supreme Court made a decision in *Dred Scott v. Sandford*[4] that helped catapult the country into the Civil War four years later. The court had previously ruled that the states could not enact laws saving escaped Blacks from bounty hunters, in *Prigg v. Pennsylvania*.[5] The Fugitive Slave Act of 1850 had made failing to report an escaped slave a federal crime. Now the court's ruling in *Dred Scott* inflamed the abolitionist movement to talk of war.

The high court denounced the Missouri Compromise as unconstitutional. Africans in America were "beings of an inferior order, and altogether unfit to associate with the white race, either in social or political relations, and so far inferior that they had no rights which the white man was bound to respect."[6] Africans in America were not citizens, despite first arriving in 1619, and could not bring cases in court.

Due to this Supreme Court decision, free Blacks lost their citizenship and the relatively few rights they had fought so long to exercise. They had no constitutional rights or protections. Regarding the right to vote, Chief Justice Taney, who wrote the infamous *Dred Scott* decision, said: "[I]t is too plain for argument, the [Blacks] have never been regarded as a part of the people . . . nor supposed to possess any political rights which the dominant race might not withhold or grant at their pleasure."[7] Before the *Dred Scott* decision, the rights of Blacks were essentially unrepresented in any government. They could vote based on state or local custom. Congressmen certainly did not represent the interests of enslaved persons. Millions of enslaved people gave political power to their state of residence based on population censuses, and states gained economic clout without providing any compensation or expressing any concern regarding the health or welfare of the enslaved, who had given the states every man-made resource.

Free Blacks lived guarded lives. While they were better off than their enslaved brothers and sisters, they led a tenuous life, facing the fear of being sold into slavery by treacherous bounty hunters; mob violence; night-riding bands of White hooligans intent on trouble; and poor White laborers, who jealously guarded their insecure economic position, with violence if necessary. Despite their protests, even free Blacks were virtually voiceless in federal, state, and local governments prior to the Civil War. They had limited access to political power, and too few Whites were willing to represent their interests in government before the war.

However, free Blacks played a role in politics even if their opinions were not welcomed or respected. In 1856 free Blacks in Boston passed a resolution in support of the Republican Party candidates John Fremont for president and William Dayton for vice president. In their resolution of support they criticized the Republican press for ignoring "the colored man's interest in the party, plainly show[ing] us that it is not an anti-slavery party; and while we are willing to unite with them to resist the aggressions of the Slave Power, we do not pledge ourselves to go further with the Republicans than the Republicans will go with us."[8]

Free Blacks were hard working and had an interest in their communities. However, the financial requirements to vote meant they needed wealth or highly paid stable employment. Even before the Civil War, Blacks had a deep belief in education as a means of securing their rights. Fannie M. Jackson Coppin was the first Black woman to graduate from Oberlin College, in Ohio, in 1865, and Edward Jones had graduated from Amherst College in 1826. But both were denied full employment due to discrimination and a fear of Black competition.

Black workers trained in skilled trades could not find work, because Whites refused to work alongside their "inferiors." Most important, many "white laborers feared competition from this great reservoir of black workers."[9] Terrorism was meant to keep African Americans as manual laborers. But White landowners were in need of cheap farm labor and feared that too much terrorism would drive Blacks out of the South to pursue opportunities up North. They wanted Black labor but not Black citizenship.

Although their taxes supported the public schools, the children of free Blacks were denied a public school education. Enslaved Blacks were forced to leave their home states as a condition of manumission, leaving their businesses behind to begin anew with nothing. Before the Civil War, freedom was a privilege, not a right. Northern states allowed certain liberties. A few slaveholders may have even educated their favored mulatto offspring.

There were colleges founded for free Blacks by White missionaries before the Civil War. What became known as Lincoln University was founded in 1854, and Wilberforce University was established in 1855. But for each story of White kindness during slavery, there were a thousand acts of horrific cruelty. The cruelty that had had certain limits during slavery because a slaveholder did not want to damage his property faced no such limits when White supremacists saw Blacks as competition for their political, economic, or social standing. But working a lifetime for free, under a brutal dictatorship of slavery, over eight generations earned Blacks the right to vote.

THE RIGHT TO VOTE AFTER THE CIVIL WAR

Bravery earned their right to vote. As in the Revolutionary War, when Crispus Attucks, a Black man, became the first casualty of war, free Black and enslaved battalions fought in the Civil War for the Union and their freedom. That freedom meant political rights as well as the privileges and immunities of citizenship. The Civil War ended in June 1865, a few months after the passage of the Thirteenth Amendment. Within three years, Blacks became citizens with equal protection and due process rights, reversing the Supreme Court's decision in *Dred Scott*.

Congress added an important section to the Fourteenth Amendment in 1868. Abolitionists and Republicans were well aware of the dangerous racism among certain southerners, who would attempt to prevent Blacks from voting. As a punishment, the number of eligible voters in a state found to violate the voting rights of Blacks would "be reduced in the proportion which the number of such male citizens shall bear to the whole number of male citizens twenty-one years of age in such State."[10]

Since the consequences would affect all elected officials, this powerful section of the Constitution, which would allow a reduction in all eligible voters by the number of Black voters denied their right to vote, has been threatened but never applied.

The Fifteenth Amendment was ratified in 1870—five years after President Lincoln died from an assassin's bullet on April 15, 1865, a month before the capture of Confederate president Jefferson Davis on May 10, 1865. About 179,000 Black soldiers served in the Union army, and 19,000 served in the navy. Nearly 40,000 Black soldiers died in the war.[11] Black soldiers comprised 10 percent of the Union army, not counting the nonenlisted personnel, such as cooks, horsemen, and orderlies. Harriet Tubman, the famous leader of escaped slaves, was a spy for the Union army during the Civil War.

In 1870, only a month after passage of the Fifteenth Amendment, an African American minister in Mississippi named Hiram Rhodes Revels became the first Black US senator. Born in 1827 in Fayetteville, North Carolina, to a family of free Blacks, Revels first worked as a barber before becoming an ordained minister in the African Methodist Episcopal (AME) Church.

For Reverend Revels, the AME Church offered dignity and religious training to aspiring Black clergy and congregants. The church was based on Black self-determination. Founded by Richard Allen and Absalom Jones, the AME grew out of a protest by Black worshipers, who walked out of the predominantly White, segregated St. George Methodist Church in 1787, and it remains an established denomination for African Americans worldwide.

After fighting for the Union in the Civil War at the Battle of Vicksburg, Reverend Revels moved to Mississippi. He became known for his fiery oration and intelligence. In 1868 he was elected alderman. However, violence against Black political progress and Black politicians began early in his career. Although the Fourteenth Amendment to the US Constitution had guaranteed Blacks equality under law in 1868, in reality equality would often ring hollow. White mob violence was a constant reminder of that refrain in the *Dred Scott* decision: a Black man had no rights a White man was bound to respect. The brutal New Orleans Riot and the Meridian Riot of 1871 highlighted the need for federal legislation and troops to back up the amendment. These, and many other race riots in which thousands of Whites tore Blacks from their homes, lynched men, raped women, and burned businesses, were predecessors to the infamous Springfield Riot of 1908.

Thirty-four Blacks and three Whites were killed in the New Orleans Riot, which is more accurately described as a massacre. On July 30, 1866, former Confederate soldiers and police officers shot unarmed Blacks attending Louisiana's constitutional convention to decide Reconstruction policies and whether Black men would gain the right to vote. When the men emerged from the meeting hall holding white flags of surrender, they were gunned down.

Federal troops were called in, but they arrived too late. In Meridian, Mississippi, Blacks were arrested under the Ku Klux Klan Act of 1871. During the trial, conservative Democrats and Klansmen shot the Republican judge and several Blacks in the courtroom. No one was convicted for these crimes. The Meridian Riot resulted in conservative Democrats gaining control of Mississippi and suppressing the Black vote through terrorism.

President Andrew Johnson's Reconstruction plan failed to stop the violence against Blacks, intentionally or negligently. Congress enacted a Reconstruction plan that sent federal troops into the war-torn South, providing a level of military protection for Blacks, coupled with the Civil Rights Acts of 1866 and 1870 and leading to the passage of the Ku Klux Klan Act in 1871. Due to the violence and opposition to Blacks' political, economic, and social progress, it took courage to be a Black voter or politician.

After the riots in Meridian and New Orleans, Congress responded by enacting civil rights legislation. Under the Enforcement Act of 1870, anyone convicted of conspiring to deprive Blacks of their right to vote or equal protection rights faced a $5,000 fine and six years in prison. But these laws required local prosecutors to bring charges and local police to make arrests, and local prosecutors, law enforcement personnel, and politicians were often members of the Ku Klux Klan.

Despite the threat of violence to his Black and White supporters, Revels was appointed to serve in the Mississippi State Senate as a Republican. Then, with growing Republican support, he was urged to take the US Senate seat vacated by the legendary Jefferson Davis, the defeated president of the Confederacy. He accepted.

Senator Revels held political office before he actually gained the right to vote. On February 3, 1870, Congress ratified the Fifteenth Amendment, which reads: "The right of citizens of the United States to vote shall not be denied or abridged by the United States or by any state on account of race, color, or previous condition of servitude." Then Congress was given the power to enforce this legislation, through the enforcement clause.

The Supreme Court would determine how much Congress could enforce voting rights for Black Americans, and with which legal weapons. In 1884 the US Supreme Court upheld the convictions of Jasper Yarbrough and seven other Whites in Fulton County, Georgia, who had assaulted Berry Saunders, a Black man, for voting. In *Ex parte Yarbrough*, one of the few times a criminal penalty was upheld, Yarbrough and his co-conspirators received two years of hard labor in a New York State prison in Albany.

The Supreme Court upheld their sentences and found that under the Fifteenth Amendment the federal government has a role in protecting the voting rights of citizens, even if the majority of that power belongs to the states.[12] The court relied on the Enforcement Act of 1870. But that was one case among thousands of acts of unimpeded racial violence nationwide.

Debates over the legal place of Blacks in American society, referred to as the "Negro question," filled the parlors of Whites and their academic conferences. The Fifteenth Amendment had passed the House of Representatives 144–44 and the Senate 39–13. However, the debate over whether Blacks were indeed worthy of the right to vote continued into the twenty-first century. White supremacy requires that only White voters have a role in determining the future of America, from the smallest school board election to the presidency.

Senator Hiram Revels served only one year. Reportedly, he did not resign due to the constant hostility he faced. But since he lived under constant death threats, discrimination, and ridicule, it was an understandable decision when another leadership opportunity was presented. Revels had made history and opened the door for others. He then became president of Alcorn Agricultural and Mechanical College in Mississippi, founded to educate newly freed Blacks. He remained at Alcorn College until his death in 1901.

Senator Revels opened the doors of political participation for Blacks, and one in particular: a former enslaved African, Joseph Hayne Rainey, a Republican, who was born in Georgetown, South Carolina. Congressman Rainey served as the first Black US representative, from 1870 until 1879. Congressman Rainey was an advocate for civil rights. He served on standing committees for Freedman Affairs, Indian Affairs, and Invalid Pensions.[13]

During the Civil War, Rainey had been forced to work for the Confederate army digging ditches, until he escaped to Bermuda, where he became a wealthy businessman. Rainey returned to South Carolina after the war and started his political career as a census taker in Charleston, South Carolina, in 1869. He then served in the state senate in 1870, where he became chair of the finance committee. First appointed by the Republican Party to fill the seat of a "disgraced" White politician, Benjamin F. Whittemore, Rainey was later voted into office, becoming the first African American elected to Congress in 1870, where he represented both Black and White constituents.

"I tell you that the Negro will never rest until he gets his rights," Rainey said, standing on the floor of Congress in 1873, the first African American to ever speak in Congress.[14] "We ask [for civil rights] because we know it is proper, not because we want to deprive any other class of the rights and immunities they enjoy, but because they are granted to us by the law of the land." During his tenure as a congressman, Representative Rainey watched the federal government remove troops from the South and saw the dilution of political progress made by free and newly freed Blacks. While Blacks viewed their achievements with pride, a growing number of Whites saw only a threat worthy of the most brutal acts of violence.[15]

Representative Rainey also witnessed the rise of the Ku Klux Klan and acts of terrorism against Blacks. Federal legislation such as the Ku Klux Klan Act, signed by President Ulysses S. Grant in 1871, gave authority to federal agents to uphold post–Civil War protections because it was understood that local prosecutors and law enforcement officers in the South would not protect the rights of African Americans. As chair of the Committee on Freedman's Affairs, Rainey worked tirelessly to assist newly freed slaves to find their place in the political, economic, and social life of this country, despite threats and the betrayals of White northern presidential hopefuls, who shamelessly sought the White southern vote at the expense of protecting the constitutional rights of African Americans.[16]

In 1865 Andrew Johnson, who succeeded President Abraham Lincoln after Lincoln's assassination, began to show his disdain for Reconstruction as it pertained to federal protection for Black political rights. President Johnson focused on bringing the eleven states that had seceded from the Union back into the United States. He vetoed the first, second, and third Reconstruction Acts. But Congress overrode the veto and passed this legislation, providing funding for the federal government to assist newly freed slaves and for the military might to protect Black rights in the South.

By 1866 the Freedman's Bureau had begun assisting African Americans. Underfunded and poorly staffed, this fledgling government bureau quickly became the target for imagined embezzling plots, scandals, and political ridicule. Most of the criticisms were based on racial animus rather than financial mismanagement.[17] Under this withering weight, the Freedman's Bureau could not live up to its promise. Progressive White Republicans sincerely sought to use the Freedman's Bureau to right the wrongs of slavery. But Democratic conservatives rebelled against any agency, law, or social efforts toward egalitarianism—anything that would make Blacks equal to Whites economically, socially, or politically. Politicians reduced funding for the Freedman's Bureau. White newspapers ridiculed it. Terrorists sought to kill that Black man in Congress who championed it: Representative Rainey.

Rainey faced dangers in Washington, D.C., and in his home state of South Carolina. The Red Shirts, a notorious club of White supremacists, lay in wait to kill him. "When myself and my colleagues shall leave these Halls and turn our footsteps toward our southern homes, we know not that the assassin may await our coming, as marked for his vengeance," he said.[18] In 1876 Dixiecrats, the conservative Democrats who arose from the ashes of the fallen South, rose in opposition to the Freedman's Bureau. Enraged and seeking revenge for their defeat in the Civil War, the Dixiecrats took power across the South, leaving only Louisiana, Florida, and South Carolina in Republican hands.

Murderous Whites turned the political tide again. In 1876 a parade of Black soldiers celebrating July 4 were gunned down by Whites in the streets of Hamburg, South Carolina. Requesting justice for the "Hamburg Massacre," as it became known, Rainey found none in the federal government and knew there would be none in South Carolina. He lost the next election to Samuel Cox, a conservative Democrat. Like Hiram Revels, while in office Rainey received death threats, but they did not deter him from seeking other political positions after leaving Congress in 1879.[19] Politics has always been a war of attrition, or decreasing the other side's army until it can be crushed. African Americans were voted out of office by Whites, and Black voters who wanted to vote for Black candidates were terrorized from going to the polls.

Soon the fate of all African Americans rested in the hands of two men seeking the presidency. A disputed election between Republican Rutherford B. Hayes and Democrat Samuel J. Tilden led to that infamous compromise with the Dixiecrats that left Blacks political castaways.[20] The South would support Hayes for president. In exchange, conservative Democrats gained absolute control over their Black citizens, without any further interference from the federal government.

The Civil War had destroyed a southern culture of aristocracy built on slave labor. After the war, Bedford Forrest gathered with other Confederate soldiers to remember life in the South before Blacks were free and the Confederacy fell into ruin. Returning Blacks to subservience became the mission of the organization known as the Ku Klux Klan (KKK). A concerted goal of the KKK was reinstituting Black servility through terrorism. With the withdrawal of federal troops, Klansmen would no longer dream about lost White dominance; they would re-create it.

Terrorizing people of color, especially African Americans; introducing segregationist laws; and working to defeat any civil rights legislation had begun even before slavery officially ended. President Abraham Lincoln was aware that freed Blacks would demand the franchise. "Mr. Lincoln has been quoted as saying that he was not in sympathy with giving the right of franchise to the negro."[21] The Black vote had been hotly contested in Congress along with the issue of "Negro emancipation."[22] Freedom meant voting. For every political step forward, there was a backlash of segregationist laws, bloodshed, and terror. White Americans of goodwill, although there were relatively few, were bloodied as well. For others, Blacks were the enemy in a war to maintain White political supremacy. As in too many American political contests, the rights of Blacks were bargained away in political side deals with supremacists, and they were left to suffer the horrific consequences.

In the contested presidential election of 1876, neither Republican Rutherford B. Hayes nor Democratic Samuel Tilden had a clear victory. To acquire Democratic votes from politically powerful Whites in the South, Hayes made an agreement to withdraw federal troops from the South, who were protecting the lives, property, and legal rights of people only ten years out of slavery, in exchange for the electoral votes he needed to gain the presidency.

Most progressive Whites and former abolitionists turned their backs on Black citizens and supported the Hayes bargain. Even *The Independent*, a weekly newspaper edited and published by abolitionists, wrote: "We know this is a sad state of things . . . [but] the Negro must fight his own battle, win his own elevation, prove his own manhood, and accredit his own citizenship."[23] The era known as Reconstruction ended when President Hayes withdrew all federal troops in 1877, as promised. Blacks were on their own, unprotected, but not helpless. They fought against oppression despite the failure of law enforcement to defend them and of the courts to fully protect their rights.

FIGHTING BACK BEFORE THE CIVIL WAR

Blacks in America have a history of fighting against racial oppression, alone when necessary, and most often. During slavery Africans in America, who had no rights of personhood under law but were moveable property, or chattel, protested against oppression and sought justice in slave tribunals when possible. Free Blacks lobbied federal, state, and local governments. Formerly enslaved Blacks, like Frederick Douglass, protested against slavery and lobbied for legislation to allow escaped Blacks to become legally free.

The *Ethiopian Manifesto, Issued in Defence of the Blackman's Rights, in the Scale of Universal Freedom*, published by Robert Alexander Young in 1829, was a brash protest against the evils of slaveholding: "Hearken, therefore, oh! Slaveholder, thou task inflicter against the rights of men, the day is at hand, nay the hour draweth nigh, when poverty shall appear to thee a blessing, if it but restore to thy fellow-man his rights," wrote Young. That twentieth-century fictionalized image of cowardly Blacks shaking in fear of reprisal in the face of White supremacy was untrue even during slavery. Protest literature, newspapers, and books were published, and full conferences attended by hundreds were held to demand legal rights for the enslaved and the free.

David Walker, another Black fiery orator who drafted petitions against slavery, wrote the famous *Walker's Appeal* and circulated petitions seeking Black unity against oppression. In *Walker's Appeal* he mused: "Can our condition be any worse?—Can it be more mean and abject? If there are any changes, will they not be for the better, though they may appear for the worst at first?"²⁴ Whether escaping slavery despite the risk of death or fighting for their freedom in a slave uprising, the history of Blacks' protests for their rights demonstrates that the roots of Black activism ran deep even before the birth of the Niagara Movement and the National Association for the Advancement of Colored People.

When the Fugitive Slave Act was passed by Congress in 1850, Blacks and progressive Whites fought against this slave law through protest and abolitionism. This act granted far-reaching authority to slave owners and bounty hunters to hunt down and return escaped slaves. Free Blacks, some of whom were fugitives, met in Cazenovia, New York, to propose their own strategies to prevent a return to slavery. The convention members spoke of the dreaded bounty hunters, who kidnapped free Blacks who were not fugitives and sold them into slavery. Even without the right to vote, free and fugitive Blacks attending the convention drafted militant resolutions opposing the federal and state laws.

One such resolution opposing racial oppression was adopted at a meeting in Springfield, Massachusetts, in 1850:

> 2. Resolved, That we will repudiate all and every law that has for its object the oppression of any human being, or seeks to assign us degrading positions. And, whereas, we hold to the declaration of the poet, "that he who would be free, himself must strike the blow," and that resistance to tyrants is obedience to God, therefore,
> 3. Resolved, That we do welcome to our doors everyone who feels and claims for himself the position of a man, and has broken from the Southern house of bondage, and that we feel ourselves justified in using every means which the God of love has placed in our power to sustain our liberty.²⁵

The Fugitive Slave Act of 1850 made Whites responsible for turning in any escaped slave about whom they had direct or indirect knowledge. Unintentionally, this act brought the White and Black abolitionists closer together and drove Whites who had been tepid about slavery into the opposition ranks. The law forced Whites to take a side. In the North, many sided with the abolitionists. Both Blacks and Whites defied the Fugitive Slave Laws.

Certain Whites went even further and gave their lives to end slavery. John Brown sacrificed his life and that of his sons to liberate Africans enslaved in America. In June 1859 John Brown, a White abolitionist, broke into an armory in Harpers Ferry, Virginia. Brown planned to arm Blacks and mobilize a national slave revolt. Accompanied by twenty-one men, including his son, fifteen other Whites, and five Blacks, Brown successfully entered the armory. However, the alert was sounded. In town, as thousands of militia surrounded the armory, Brown surrendered. His son was killed. A trial resulted in a verdict of treason. John Brown was sentenced to death by hanging.

John Brown believed a violent protest was necessary to end the grip of slavery in America. On the date of his execution, Brown stated: "Now, if it is deemed necessary that I should forfeit my life for the furtherance of the ends of justice, and mingle my blood further with the blood of my children and with the blood of millions in this slave country whose rights are disregarded by wicked, cruel, and unjust enactments, I submit; so let it be done!" Many still believe John Brown was insane because he was willing to give his life for enslaved African Americans. Like Mary White Ovington, Oswald Villard, and William English Walling, the sacrifice of John Brown is a precursor to the racially integrated fight for social justice that would be the hallmark of the NAACP. A small band of Whites willingly placed their lives and livelihoods in harm's way for the sake of racial equality under law.

Legal strategies and court cases were also a long-standing part of the fight for racial justice. Enslaved Africans had sued for their freedom in slave courts. The case of Dred and Harriett Scott is renowned. Their quest for freedom by filing a lawsuit was rebuffed by the US Supreme Court, which ruled that Blacks "had no rights which the white man was bound to respect."[26] But as early as 1654, in the Virginia colony, Elizabeth Key, a mulatto, had sued for her freedom, with a White attorney representing her claim in court. African Americans were never afraid to access the court system. Key lobbied the local government, and a law was passed allowing her to be free; however, another law was passed that made slaves of the children of any enslaved woman.

Africans in America, whether enslaved or free, were quite aware of the political process, so much so that Delaware passed laws keeping all enslaved Blacks away from polling places, because lawmakers did not want Blacks to witness democracy and become disenchanted with their positions and get ideas about freedom.[27] As early as 1859, Frederick Douglass wrote a voting rights article titled "The Ballot and the Bullet." Frustrated by the slow-pace of White abolitionists, Douglass thunders:

If speech alone could have abolished slavery, the work would have been done long ago. What we want is an anti-slavery government, in harmony with our anti-slavery speech, one which will give effect to our words, and translate them into acts. For this, the ballot is needed, and if this will not be heard and heeded, then the bullet. We have had cant enough, and are sick of it. When anti-slavery laws are wanted, anti-slavery men should vote for them; and when a slave is to be snatched from the hand of a kidnapper, physical force is needed, and he who gives it proves himself a more useful anti-slavery man than he who refuses to give it, and contents himself by talking of a "sword of the spirit."[28]

This theme will be repeated in 1964 by Malcolm.

With the assistance of thousands of African soldiers, the Civil War ended. Slavery was abolished in 1865. Frederick Douglass wrote "Slavery is not abolished until the black man has the ballot. While the Legislatures of the South retain the right to pass laws making any discrimination between black and white, slavery still lives there. " Equal protection was granted by the Fourteenth Amendment of the US Constitution in 1868. The question of voting rights for Africans was almost as controversial as ending slavery.

Once again, the great orator Frederick Douglass, in "What the Black Man Wants," speaks to the issue with these resounding words:

> I hold that women, as well as men, have the right to vote, and my heart and my voice go with the movement to extend suffrage to woman.
> . . . This war, let it be long or let it be short, let it cost much or let it cost little . . . shall not cease until every freedman at the South has the right to vote.
> . . . We may be asked, I say, why we want it. I will tell you why we want it. We want it because it is our right, first of all. No class of men can, without insulting their own nature, be content with any deprivation of their rights. We want it again, as a means for educating our race. Men are so constituted that they derive their conviction of their own possibilities largely from the estimate formed of them by others. If nothing is expected of a people, that people will find it difficult to contradict that expectation. By depriving us of suffrage, you affirm our incapacity to form an intelligent judgment respecting public men and public measures; you declare before the world that we are unfit to exercise the elective franchise, and by this means lead us to undervalue ourselves, to put a low estimate upon ourselves, and to feel that we have no possibilities like other men. Again, I want the elective franchise, for one, as a colored man, because ours is a peculiar government, based upon a peculiar idea, and that idea is universal suffrage.
> . . . It is said that we are ignorant; I admit it. But if we know enough to be hung, we know enough to vote. If the Negro knows enough to pay taxes to support the government, he knows enough to vote; taxation and representation should go together. If he knows enough to shoulder a musket and fight for the flag, fight for the government, he knows enough to vote. If he knows as much when he is sober as an Irishman knows when drunk, he knows enough to vote, on good American principles.[29]

Voting rights were given only to Black men in the Fifteenth Amendment in 1870. However, as in New York prior to the Civil War, when Black men began to use their voting rights, the fight became more brutal, and the law was used to undermine their voting strength. Then African Americans were sacrificed in 1877 for the sake of White political expediency and saving a fragile union. The deep, festering animosity against African Americans for having gained full citizenship by law triggered a war for White supremacy intent on forcing Blacks back into a class of lifelong labor.

The Civil War had been as much about the Confederate States demanding the power to maintain slavery to support a farm-based economy as about the North seeking to move the nation toward industrialization. The horrific institution of forced labor under penalty of torture and death, known as slavery, was a by-product of two competing economies: industrialization and farming. Abolitionists fought for the end of the despicable institution of slavery despite the economic pressures.

POLITICAL PROGRESS AFTER THE CIVIL WAR

Once abolished, slavery was soon replaced with the convict lease system. Using the criminal justice system, and relying on the Thirteenth Amendment, slavery was abolished except as punishment for a crime. Worn out by war, few White activists were willing to put on battle armament again in the name of true freedom for African Americans. Some freedom was better than none at all. The children of White abolitionists looked on in horror as voting rights and equal protection were undermined by mounting segregation laws.

Blacks sued. They relied on the Civil Rights Acts of 1866, 1870, and 1871, passed by Congress after slavery ended and meant to protect the freedom of Blacks to travel, purchase property, use restaurants, ride in trains, and sit in the front of the theater, as well as the right to vote under the Fifteenth Amendment. But they found no relief at the Supreme Court, which ruled that the federal government could only protect Blacks from state laws and not from White individuals who discriminated by segregating Blacks or refusing to sell them a first-class ticket in *The Civil Rights Cases* of 1883.[30] The Supreme Court upheld state laws intended to limit Black voter rights and defended the right of business owners to discriminate based on race.

Congress created the US Bureau of Refugees, Freedmen and Abandoned Lands, known as the Freedmen's Bureau, shortly after the war. The Freedman's Bureau had a mission to assist newly freed Blacks in their transition into American society, but it was always underfunded and burdened with false accusations of financial double-dealing. More than four million former enslaved persons relied on the Freedman's Bureau's meager budget and a staff of about nine hundred, most of whom meant well but were facing a nearly impossible task.

The bureau provided food and medical care, legalized marriages, found lost relatives sold during slavery, built schools and colleges, and assisted Black veterans. When General Oliver Howard was dismissed as president of the Freedman's Bureau and the budget was cut in half, its demise soon followed. Forced to close in 1872 under pressure from conservative southerners, it left Blacks on their own.

As Black political participation soared, White fears mounted. Blacks could boast of federal, state, and local political participation. But in 1876 a compromise between the Republicans and Democrats following a disputed presidential election resulted in the election of Rutherford B. Hayes. President Hayes gained office by promising to remove all federal troops protecting Blacks in the South. His rise to power was the end of a short-lived period of first-class citizenship for African Americans. Blacks would not enjoy that level of freedom again for nearly a hundred years.

In 1877, Reconstruction ended and federal troops who had guarded Black freedoms in the South were taken away. African Americans remained resilient despite terrorism from all sides. Teachers, doctors, business owners, inventors, and farmers carved freedom out of oppression and created as close to first-class citizenship as possible. They had been promised forty acres and a mule with which to gain a foothold in the American economy. But President Andrew Johnson had vetoed that provision. Now, with President Hayes removing the few remaining federal troops, each attempt by Blacks to exercise their political rights was met with violence.

Relying on the power of an education, Blacks built primary schools and hired teachers. Tuskegee Institute was founded on July 4, 1881, in Tuskegee, Alabama, by Booker T. Washington, who had been born into slavery. The Howard Normal and Theological School for the Education of Teachers and Preachers was founded in 1867 and became Howard University, located in Washington, D.C.

Attorneys were needed to fight the discriminatory laws enacted to oppress African Americans on every level. In 1869 the leaders of Howard University recognized the need to train Black lawyers to protect and advance their newly gained rights and defend against abuses by the criminal justice system through Black Codes. Under the Thirteenth Amendment, slavery was abolished, except as punishment for a crime. W. E. B. DuBois wrote:

[T]he South believed an educated Negro to be a dangerous Negro. And the South was not wholly wrong; for education among all kinds of men always has had, and always will have, an element of danger and revolution, of dissatisfaction and discontent. Nevertheless, men strive to know. It was some inkling of this paradox, even in the unquiet days of the Bureau, that allayed an opposition to human training, which still to-day lies smoldering, but not flaming. Fisk, Atlanta, Howard, and Hampton were founded in these days, and nearly $6,000,000 was expended in five years for educational work, $750,000 of which came from the freedmen themselves.[31]

For decades Black leaders, activists, and regular citizens held off lynch mobs and White legislators who sought to re-enslave them. The federal government's relatively small reinforcements fell away early and arrived late in the war for voting rights.

Blacks organized. Activists had been creating organizations long before slavery ended. The Prince Hall Masons, the New York City and County Suffrage Committee of Colored Citizens, the Pennsylvania Freemen, and the Colored Conventions Movement were founded before the Civil War. After the war Blacks created clubs and committees that supplemented the vital role of churches in serving the needs of their homeless, illiterate, elderly, and orphaned.

The Supreme Court had ruled that the Constitution offered no protection against discrimination by individuals. In 1889 Florida passed a poll tax law to prevent Blacks from voting. In 1890 Mississippi passed the Mississippi Plan, laws adding poll taxes and literacy tests to prevent Blacks and poor Whites from voting. South Carolina, Louisiana, North Carolina, Alabama, Virginia, Georgia, and Oklahoma passed laws adding poll taxes, grandfather clauses, and literacy tests to voting registration requirements, based on the Mississippi Plan.

As Blacks reeled from this political apocalypse, Booker T. Washington, the most famous Black man in America, president of Tuskegee Institute, and a formerly enslaved person, gave his famous "Atlanta Compromise" speech in 1895.[32] In his autobiography, *Up From Slavery*, he writes of the apprehension he felt when he received the request to speak on behalf of the Black race.[33] He knew there would be criticism from all sides, especially the Black integrationist and intellectual W. E. B. DuBois.

Washington spoke of racial segregation and Black economic independence: "In all things that are purely social we can be as separate as the fingers, yet one as the hand in all things essential to mutual progress."[34] But he did add: "There is no escape through law of man or God from the inevitable: The laws of changeless justice bind Oppressor with oppressed."[35] Less than a year later the US Supreme Court ruled in *Plessy v. Ferguson* that states can segregate the races in all social settings, establishing "separate but equal."[36] In 1898 the US Supreme Court upheld literacy tests in *Williams v. Mississippi*.[37]

Before the *Plessy* decision, Louisiana had more than 130,000 registered Black voters. By 1900, after *Plessy* was enforced, the number of Black registered voters in Louisiana dropped to fewer than 6,000. Then, in 1903, the Supreme Court ruled in *Giles v. Harris* that Alabama could take away voting rights for a lifetime based on missing one single voter registration deadline, even though the White registrar refused to register Jackson W. Giles when he and other Blacks arrived well in advance of the designated day.[38]

The Supreme Court ruled that Giles had not shown the required minimum of $2,000 in monetary damages for a lawsuit. The liberal justice Learned Hand wrote that the court would not "supervise the voting in that State by officers of the court," which was exactly what was needed to secure Black voting rights. In Wisconsin in 1904, George Edwin Taylor, a Black newspaper owner, graduate of Wayland University, and Wisconsin Union leader, made an unsuccessful bid for president of the United States.[39]

Taylor proposed extraordinary, visionary legislation. His National Labor Party created its own platform for the presidency, demanding the following:

> *Suffrage.*—universal suffrage "which does not discriminate against any reputable citizen on account of color or condition;"
> *Citizenship.*—"Secured Constitutional rights for all citizens."
> *Lynch Law.*—indemnified to the next of kin and restitution for property destroyed by lynch mobs.
> *Pensions for Ex-Slaves:* "We firmly believe that the ex-slave, who served the country for 246 years, filling the lap of the nation with wealth by their labor, should be pensioned from the overflowing treasury of the country."
> *American Citizens Deprived of Self-Government.*—The people of the District of Columbia should receive the right to vote.

Like Jackson Giles with his challenge to Alabama voting laws, it was a courageous but futile shot against a legal and terroristic barrage by the court, Congress, and the states, all intent on undermining Black political power. This group and hundreds of other Blacks did all they could do with the scant tools and resources available to them.

When W. E. B. DuBois led the Niagara Movement, there was Black activism taking place across the country. Black women formed the National Association of Colored Women's Clubs in 1896 as a clearinghouse for the hundreds of clubs founded to meet the needs of their children and advocate on behalf of their communities. The Frederick Douglass Club, founded in 1906, was one of the few interracial women's clubs in the country. Black lawyers, although few in number, courageously represented Black interests before the Civil War and throughout the era of *Plessy.*[40] Therefore, when the NAACP was formed in 1909, as a racially integrated, White-led organization fighting for African American rights, it did not find Blacks idly waiting for a savior. Black Americans cut a path out of the wilderness, having been given nothing by their government in exchange for hundreds of years of free labor and military service. They had earned the right to vote. The NAACP became an ally to access this elusive right. Other groups would assist in this challenging endeavor, including the Communist Party.[41]

Since Black Americans persisted in their fight for self-determination after the Supreme Court ruled that they had no rights a White man should respect, they had no intention of allowing White supremacists to determine their political destiny half a century after slavery had ended. If the right to vote would not be given to them freely, they would fight for it. The NAACP was a willing ally in this life or death battle.

3

⌣

First Victory:
The Grandfather Clause

Sing a song full of the hope that the present has brought us.

—James Weldon Johnson, "Lift Every Voice and Sing" (1899)

Black families hoped for a better life. But letters from threatened African Americans in Texas, Florida, and Tennessee begged for legal assistance from the NAACP because to simply register to vote was deemed an act of aggression by some Whites, who would retaliate with acts of physical assault, rape, and even murder. Citizens were embattled: "like we are in a war." Letters from hundreds desperately seeking the assistance of the NAACP reveal the daily burdens suffered in the war for voting rights. Of the nine million Blacks in America in the early 1900s, nearly eight million lived in the states that had fought to keep slavery. White supremacy was the objective of every law that touched the lives of Black citizens. Since the US Supreme Court had ruled in favor of this supremacy, progressives viewed Congress, not the court, as a possible ally in their fight for racial justice.

In 1896 the Supreme Court, controlled by southerners, ruled in *Plessy v. Ferguson* that racial segregation was the law of the land. This was a Louisiana case brought by Homer Plessy, a civil rights activist in New Orleans. He challenged the Separate Car Act of 1890, which segregated the races on intrastate railroad cars. Black nurses caring for White women's children could sit in the White-only cars, but not Black paying customers like Homer Plessy. An octoroon who could pass for White, Plessy was convicted of violating the law. Despite warnings of failure, he pressed his case all the way to the Supreme Court, which denied his claim under both the Thirteenth and Fourteenth Amendments. The court ruled that states could pass laws segregating the races.[1]

LEGAL DISCRIMINATION

Segregation was the law of the land. The Supreme Court had turned its back on justice and embraced White supremacy. Congress refused to pass the antilynching law introduced by George White, the last Black member of Congress left from the days of Reconstruction. Lynching was a constant threat for Blacks seeking to exercise their constitutional rights as citizens or to defend themselves as human beings. An article in the *New York Tribune* on April 24, 1899, describes the lynching of a Black man, Sam Hose, and the desecration of his corpse by the mob, who cut off pieces to sell:

> Sam Hose (a Negro who committed two of the basest acts known to crime) was burned at the stake in a public road, one and a half miles from here. Before the torch was applied to the pyre, the Negro was deprived of his ears, fingers and other portions of his body with surprising fortitude. Before the body was cool, it was cut to pieces, the bones were crushed into small bits and even the tree upon which the wretch met his fate was torn up and disposed of as souvenirs. The Negro's heart was cut in several pieces, as was his liver. Those unable to obtain the ghastly relics directly, paid more fortunate possessors extravagant sums for them. Small pieces of bone went for 25 cents and a bit of the liver, crisply cooked, for 10 cents.

It was in this state of heinous violence that the young NAACP first looked to the Supreme Court for justice, only to be disappointed.

In 1907 Pink Franklin, a Black man, killed Henry Valentine, a White constable. Franklin's death row appeal was the NAACP's first attempt to argue a case before the US Supreme Court. Peonage was a form of slave labor, and it was against the law. But in South Carolina, that didn't matter. Unfair labor contracts, once signed, brought criminal consequences for any Black man or woman who refused to work under slavery conditions. Pink Franklin refused.

For decades White businessmen in need of cheap labor tricked illiterate farmers like Franklin into signing contracts for slave wages. The contracts had criminal consequences if the laborers stopped showing up for work. The Supreme Court had upheld the conviction of a Black man for failing to fulfill an unfair sharecropper contract in the two cases of *Bailey v. Alabama*.[2] Bailey argued that Alabama's law was a form of slavery and forced him into involuntary servitude. Even the US attorney general took his side. And Justice Oliver Wendell Holmes Jr., writing for the court, stated that peonage was against the law. But the contract was not.

Pink Franklin had an outstanding warrant for failing to work under his labor contract with a local White landholder, Jake Thomas, and South Carolina constable Henry Valentine meant to collect this runaway laborer. The warrant was issued by a magistrate who happened to be Henry Valentine's brother. Franklin, twenty-two years old, shot and killed Valentine when he barged into Franklin's home, where he lived with his wife, Patsy, at 3:00 a.m. on July 29, 1907. Valentine had knocked down the door, meaning to take Franklin by surprise. But that night, when Valentine kicked open the door and shot into the house, Pink Franklin returned fire. Both men were wounded, but Valentine died of his wounds.

In those days, a Black man who killed a White person, even in self-defense, would either be lynched by a mob or be found guilty by an all-White jury and executed. The right of self-defense had been taken away from Blacks during the early days of slavery and had never been given back in full. Peonage, nearly slavery, had been outlawed as unconstitutional. But in South Carolina landowners like Thomas continued to trick Blacks into signing illegal labor contracts, and constables like Valentine and magistrates like his brother enforced them. Pink Franklin had every right to resist apprehension under a law that had been repealed.

Although they escaped a lynch mob, Pink and Patsy Franklin were tried for murder, on September 9, 1907. South Carolina's case against Pink and Patsy Franklin became the NAACP's first case, handled by two well-respected Black lawyers, Jacob Moorer and John Adams from South Carolina. The prosecutor argued that Pinky's wound was self-inflicted. The NAACP lawyers challenged the fairness of the all-White jury. Franklin did not know the officer had a warrant. The jury sentenced Pink to death by hanging. Patsy was found not guilty.

The NAACP appealed to the South Carolina Supreme Court. That court upheld Franklin's death sentence. Moorer and Adams asked the US Supreme Court to review Franklin's case, but the court refused to hear the appeal. It would not overturn Franklin's conviction. The NAACP turned to lobbying political power brokers. With the help of dozens of petitions, one thousand signatures from mostly Black citizens from across the state, and a personal letter from then president William Howard Taft, Franklin's death sentence was finally commuted to life in prison by Governor Martin Ansel in 1911.

The NAACP refused to give up on Franklin. Repeated pleas for mercy were finally answered. Pink Franklin was serving hard labor on a South Carolina chain gang when Governor Richard Manning gave Franklin a full pardon. Although Franklin's life was eventually spared, this case had been a defeat in the courtroom. A White man would not have been convicted for protecting his own home.

CHALLENGING THE GRANDFATHER CLAUSE

After the poor result in the Pink Franklin case, the NAACP realized it needed to form a legal committee. Moorfield Storey would chair it. Storey was a wealthy White attorney like Albion Tourgee, who had represented Homer Plessy in the fight for racial justice. The future was unknown for the millions of Black Americans who lived with privileges that could be taken away by unjust race laws. When Storey became president of the NAACP in 1911 and attorney of record in the first case to defeat the grandfather clause, he was relying on a belief that the courts, not Congress, held the key to racial justice. Nine justices might prove easier to persuade than a Congress controlled by hundreds of southern Democrats. The chance to prove his theory came with the case *Guinn and Beal v. United States* in 1915. The NAACP decided to challenge the grandfather clause, believing that this would be its first legal victory and a decisive victory for voting rights. Given the *Plessy* decision, this belief demonstrated how little the federal, state, and local governments offered in securing basic constitutional rights for Black Americans.

The grandfather clause took many forms. It was so called because if a Black man's grandfather had not been eligible to vote in 1865, his descendants were not eligible to vote in 1915. Laws required that a family member would have been able to vote at the time of or have served in the Civil War or have voted in another country; this excluded millions of potential Black voters, who could not vote because they or their predecessors had been enslaved or prohibited due to the racism of the *Dred Scott* decision. These laws did not state outright that they applied only to a certain race, but the intention was well known. Slavery had ended in 1865, and Black men did not gain the right to vote until 1870, with passage of the Fifteenth Amendment.

The grandfather clause did not apply to most European immigrants. However, Native Americans also could not vote, because they were not considered citizens. And Asians were precluded from voting under a federal law called the Chinese Exclusion Act (1882). A Supreme Court case ruling in favor of Chinese Americans facing discrimination in *Yick Wo v. Hopkins* held out hope for African Americans.[3] All people of color were targets of oppression and terror, including assault, arson, and lynching. However, grandfather clauses were specifically created for Americans of African descent.

Oklahoma used the phrase voted for "some form of government" to allow Irish immigrants or any Whites emigrating from Europe who became citizens to have the right to vote because they or their grandfathers could have voted in Europe. But African Americans who were born in America could never gain the right to vote, because their enslaved grandparents were not allowed to vote, and even free Blacks with property were not able to vote. Racial divisions became more entrenched after the Supreme Court ruled that racially separate could be equal in *Plessy v. Ferguson* (1896). The court stated that there was supposed to be a "distinction between laws interfering with the equality of the negro and those requiring the separation of the two races in schools, theatres."[4] Social separation was somehow not intended to interfere with political rights or privileges of citizenship. However, segregation was the state's prerogative, and second-class citizenship allowed states to fashion laws to bolster and protect White supremacy.

Whites understood the clear message of *Plessy*: Blacks were outside of the protection of the law. Violence met Blacks who wanted to vote or run for office and those who were already in office. The Ku Klux Klan and other terrorist organizations, government officials, judges, prosecutors, and discriminatory voting laws served to greatly diminish the access of Blacks to political power. In 1896 in Louisiana, the site of the *Plessy* case, 130,344 African Americans were registered to vote. But by 1900, after the *Plessy* case, only 5,320 registered Black voters remained.

Blacks in Louisiana watched their early triumphs disappear. Political gains, like Lieutenant Governor Pinckney Benton Stewart Pinchback serving as governor of the state for one month, from December 1872 to January 1873, turned to bitter sorrow. In 1873, on Easter Sunday, in what became known as the Colfax Massacre, more than one hundred Blacks were gunned down by a White militia because they attended a meeting to discuss strategies to defend Republican politicians. The US Supreme Court would later rule in favor of that militia. Later that same year, in the Coushatta Massacre, thirty Black and White Republicans were gunned down by White militia, who claimed the group was planning an uprising.

By 1913 the NAACP had a growing list of request for assistance as White supremacists fought to maintain complete control of Black Americans. The association chose to join an Oklahoma case challenging the grandfather clause. This voting rights case involved a criminal punishment for the violators, Frank Guinn and J. J. Beal. These two White farmers, working as election registrars, refused to allow Black citizens in Oklahoma to vote. Guinn and his co-conspirator, Beal, were arrested for violating the Fifteenth Amendment and the civil rights laws that enforced it.

When the territory of Oklahoma sought to join the Union as an official state, it promised to treat its African American residents equally under the law. In 1907, as a condition of statehood, Oklahoma put in its constitution a clause that promised it would be free of racial discrimination. But soon after it received statehood, Oklahoma amended its constitution to require suffrage and literacy tests in order to disfranchise Blacks.

The state imposed a literacy test, in which a person had to read and write out sections of the Oklahoma constitution. This requirement only applied to persons who, on or prior to January 1, 1866, had been entitled to vote in the United States or under some form of government. Oklahoma's legislature chose 1866 because some Blacks could vote in 1867. Congress had granted Blacks in Washington, D.C., the vote, as well as those African Americans in the western territories, under the Territorial Suffrage Act.[5]

Based on the testimony at trial, J. A. Harris, chair of the Oklahoma Republican Committee, admitted that "election inspectors had received orders to permit no man to vote who was colored." Blacks were predominantly Republican. Conservative Democrats or Dixiecrats were winning elections because Blacks were excluded from the polls. Violence and sometimes lynching followed Blacks who pushed for their right to vote. They sought help from the US attorney general's office and Republican president William H. Taft.

THE CASE: *GUINN AND BEAL V. UNITED STATES*

They received it. The NAACP was arguing as a friend of the court, or amicus. The issue in this particular grandfather clause case is as much about the facts of the case itself as about the law passed in Oklahoma to exclude Blacks from voting. These are the facts presented at trial and reviewed by the Supreme Court:

> The precinct election board was constituted by the county election board, composed of J. J. Beal, inspector, Frank Guinn, judge, and C. W. Stephenson, clerk. Mr. Stephenson was a colored man, he had served in the township as trustee and ex officio assessor for 4 years, had been justice of the peace for 8 years, and postmaster for more than 12 years, and had served on the election board with both of the defendants in prior years. Both of the defendants must have known that he complied with all the requirements of the grandfather clause, even if it had been valid, and Beal said to Stephenson: "I know you can read and write just as good as I can." But they excluded him from his position in the board, at least temporarily, and until after he offered to vote, and his vote was received by the board. They, although well knowing he was entitled to vote, rejected his vote the first two times he offered to vote, and never restored him to the election board. They finally allowed him to vote without any showing. Their action in excluding him from the election board was lawless. The same reason existed for excluding themselves, as they also had to make a showing that they could read and write any section of the state Constitution, or that they or their ancestors were within the exceptions of the grandfather clause, if any showing was necessary by Stephenson. There was exactly the same reason for excluding the whole board that there was to exclude Stephenson.
>
> Mr. Beal excluded from voting, apparently with the approval of Mr. Guinn, J. Hilyard, a colored man, who was a graduate of Alcorn A. & M. College, Mississippi, of Lincoln University, Pennsylvania, and the Bryant

& Stratton Institution at Buffalo, N.Y. He was at the time, and had been for three or four years, principal of the Cimarron Industrial Institute, located in the very township where the election was held, and where one of the defendants had lived 22 years and the other 19. There is not the slightest room for doubt as to whether he could vote, even under the grandfather clause, if valid. There seems no room for doubt that the defendants knew that fact.

Mr. G. I. Curran, a colored man, testified that his grandfather was Tommy Curran, was an Irishman and voted. Mr. Curran had been a member of the Legislature for that county, and had been deputy United States Marshal. He would have been entitled to vote on his ancestry, and also because of his ability to read and write, and these facts must have been known to the defendants; but he was excluded from voting.

Oliver Andrews, a colored man, applied to vote, and he was interrogated as to his ancestry, and could not rightfully vote if the grandfather clause had been valid upon his ancestry. He then asked "if I can vote if I can read and write the Constitution?" and was told without examination, "No, you can't read or write at all; go on out."

Thomas Pettis, a colored man, applied to vote. He was interrogated as to his ancestry, and, not being able to qualify upon that, he was not given the opportunity to qualify under the educational test. Told he could not vote, he testified he could read and write the Constitution.

T. J. Adkins, a colored man, swore he was the son of a white man. If this was true, and the grandfather clause was valid, he was entitled to vote on his ancestry. Notwithstanding this fact, he was told he must take the educational test. When he came to write a section of the Constitution, he missed a couple of words, and himself called the inspector's attention to that fact, and was told: "You might as well stop; you won't pass."

After some 40 or 50 negroes had been rejected, because they failed to qualify under the grandfather clause, upon the advice of three citizens of the county, John P. Bradley, Jr., J. A. Banker, and Harvey Utterback, who came to the voting place and advised the negroes to offer to read and write any section of the Constitution, eight or more of the negroes went back to the polls and made this offer, although no one was voting and no one voted at the election after that time. Though more than half an hour elapsed before the polls closed, Mr. Beal announced that they had tried to vote earlier in the day, as they had, and had failed to qualify, and did not think they were entitled to another test or another opportunity. He then called Mr. Guinn, who was also deputy sheriff, and he came to the door, and, without specifying who he was talking to, the persons attempting to vote or the three gentlemen who were advising them, said: "Get back, you sons of bitches; if you don't get back, I will have every one of you arrested."[6]

The US attorneys John Embry and William R. Gregg of the Justice Department had Guinn and Beal arrested for violating federal law. As J. A. Harris said, "Election inspectors had received orders to permit no man to vote who was colored, and the orders were carried out in practically all portions of the State." Although President Taft was a Republican, he needed southern voters to win his bid for reelection. He did not want the men to be indicted, because that could anger Whites and mean the loss of southern votes. Embry defied the president's wishes and pressed for an indictment of Beal and Guinn, under the federal Civil Rights Acts of 1866 and 1870, which made it a crime to deprive someone of his or her rights under the Constitution and federal law.

Judge John H. Cotteral presided over the case. Judge Cotteral was a legal pioneer in Oklahoma. Although he had "read the law," he had no formal legal education or a college degree, but he was well respected by his peers and would rise to the rank of appellate judge. On September 29, 1911, Guinn and Beal were found guilty in the District Court for the Western District of Oklahoma.

At last embattled Black voters had a victory. Frank Guinn and J. J. Beal had been found guilty of violating the rights of Black voters. Judge Cotterall had explained to the jury: "[I]f [Guinn and Beal] knew or believed those colored persons were entitled to vote and their purpose was to unfairly and fraudulently deny the right of suffrage to them . . . on account of their race and color, then their purpose was a corrupt one, and they cannot be shielded by their official positions."[7] The victory came at the hands of an all-White jury.

Guinn and Beal appealed. First they argued that as public officials they had followed Oklahoma law and did not know it was illegal to prevent Blacks from voting. A three-judge appellate court set out the facts of discriminatory conduct against Blacks, who were eligible to vote even under the laws created to stop them. The trial court revealed that Guinn had accused Beal of misleading him and creating the scheme. On appeal, the court found:

> Mr. Guinn was as much a member of the election board as Mr. Beal, and except in the case of Mr. Stephenson never dissented from anything Mr. Beal did. There was abundant evidence, even assuming that they both thought the grandfather clause of the Constitution was valid, that they had formed a conspiracy to prevent colored persons within its exceptions, or who were able to comply with its terms from voting, and there is no error shown, and the case is affirmed.[8]

After losing that appeal, Guinn and Beal asked the US Supreme Court to reverse their convictions. This time they based their argument on states' rights: Oklahoma had the right to fix standards for voting, and this power was not taken away by the Fifteenth Amendment. The NAACP had lobbied the US attorney general's office to bring the case, and now it wanted to make sure the court understood how laws like the "grandfather clause" undermined the rights of African Americans and American democracy.

The attorney general's office allowed Moorfield Storey to join the case as a friend of the court, or amicus. Storey submitted the first NAACP brief ever accepted by the Supreme Court. This case began the close, sometimes tumultuous, relationship between the US attorney's office and the NAACP. It would take decades for the federal government to recognize the need to have an agency of lawyers specifically trained to protect the constitutional rights of people of color. For its first fifty years, the NAACP was the primary legal watchdog for all African Americans.

In his brief, Moorfield Storey told of the harmful history of the "grandfather clause." He used this opportunity to educate the court about the ongoing struggle for voting rights. In 1915 the Supreme Court ruled in *Guinn and Beal v. United States* that Oklahoma's grandfather clause was discriminatory and violated the Fifteenth Amendment of the US Constitution. The convictions of the two men were upheld. The unanimous decision was written by Chief Justice Edward Douglass White, a Louisiana Democrat who did not agree with Reconstruction. Historian Robert Highsaw wrote that Justice White initially sought to "oust Louisiana's Reconstruction government and return control of Louisiana to the white population."[9] Yet he led the court to its unanimous decisions in *Guinn* and *Myers v. Anderson* (1915), a voting case involving a 1908 Maryland law with a grandfather clause[10] that created three classifications for voting. One voter category was for those who could vote prior to January 1, 1868. Of course Blacks obtained the right to vote after that date.

In *Guinn v. United States*, the NAACP had indirectly won its first voting rights victory. Although as amicus the NAACP had been considered a friend of the court and not a true party in the case, the organization had successfully lobbied the US attorney to take the case. Storey had been allowed to argue before the court, in no small way probably persuading Chief Justice Edward Douglass White to rule in favor of the Fifteenth Amendment over Oklahoma's blatantly unconstitutional states' rights claim.

Chief Justice White was a known conservative, born on a sugar plantation near Thibodaux, Lafourche Parish, Louisiana, the youngest of five children. His father, Edward Douglass White Sr., was the governor of Louisiana and a congressman. His grandfather, Dr. James White, was a US representative, physician, and judge.[11] The young Edward White Jr. served with the Confederacy. But as an Irish Catholic, he may have identified with the outsider. It was quite unusual to have a man of Storey's stature, a former leader of the now segregated American Bar Association, arguing a case as amicus on the side of Negro voting rights. White must have respected Storey's pedigree, legal skill, and passion for the cause of racial justice.[12]

OVERTURNING "SEPARATE AND UNEQUAL"

The triumph in *Guinn* led Moorfield Storey to create an ad hoc legal committee. With this victory, letters from oppressed Blacks pleading for assistance poured into the committee's offices at 20 Vesey Street, across from the centuries-old Trinity Church in Manhattan. A strategy of protest, lobbying for legislation, and litigation was forming. Storey knew that to be successful, the NAACP would have to find lawyers in the South. They had to be well trained, smart, and brave. Lawyers and staff members, most of whom were Black, traveled by train into the deep South; they understood the danger. Many NAACP workers lived in New York but were originally from the South. They knew White supremacists viewed segregation as a way of life to be defended by law or murder, assault, and rape. No person of color was safe, and White advocates for racial justice could be killed as well. But for Blacks, one false move would result in death by lynching.

The letter below illustrates the members' dedication to the NAACP's despite the constant danger. James Weldon Johnson, NAACP assistant secretary, wrote the lyrics for "Lift Every Voice," the Negro national anthem, based on personal experience seeing the blood of the slaughtered. He wrote about lynching in Florida, used to keep Blacks from the polls, in "Election by Terror in Florida," published by the *New Republic*.

December 27, 1920
The New Republic
421 West 21st Street
New York City, NY
Attention: Mr. Alvin Johnson
My dear Mr. Johnson
I return to you enclosed, corrected proof of the article, "Election by Terror in Florida."
In the contributor's box you can say that I am a graduate of Atlanta University, have done newspaper and magazine work, and have investigated thirty-six lynchings and five race riots in the past three years.
Very truly yours,
Assistant Secretary

NAACP attorney Charles Hamilton Houston was brilliant, handsome, and driven to end legal segregation. He swore to give his life to defeating racial segregation. As a privileged Black child growing up in the segregated shadows of the Capitol dome, he knew the words of liberty spoken by politicians in Washington, D.C., were only skin deep.

His father was a successful attorney. Houston graduated from Amherst College and Harvard Law School. While at Harvard, he was the first African American asked to join the coveted *Harvard Law Review*. Yet no White law firm would hire him. He returned to Washington and worked at his father's law firm. It was not the rejection by White law firms but the seething racism Houston faced while fighting for his country in World War I that drove him to dedicate his life to defeating the "separate but equal" doctrine of *Plessy v. Ferguson*. Charles Hamilton Houston was an officer in the US army serving during World War I (1914–1918).

Houston wrote: "The hate and scorn showered on us Negro officers by our fellow Americans convinced me that there was no sense in my dying for a world ruled by them. I made up my mind that if I got through this war, I would study law and use my time fighting for men who could not strike back."[13] And he did. Although Houston had graduated from Harvard Law School and was appointed the first Black editor of the *Harvard Law Review*, he knew that racial oppression could not be escaped through economic class. His desire to strike a death blow against the laws that allowed oppression required him to learn everything necessary to challenge *Plessy v. Ferguson*. He returned to practice law in Washington.

The NAACP needed his legal skills, and Houston needed a bigger platform. Together they would counter the onslaught of segregationist laws mounting against Black Americans. Houston would become the architect of the legal cases supporting the twentieth-century civil rights movement. He became known as "the man who killed Jim Crow" and the architect of the civil rights legal strategy. "Houston played a role in nearly every civil rights case before the Supreme Court between 1930 and *Brown v. Board of Education*."[14]

The racial discrimination Houston and all people of color faced in America could be traced directly back to *Plessy v. Ferguson*. As discussed previously, in Louisiana, Homer Plessy, a Black civil rights activist and businessman, refused to accept legalized segregation. The Separate Car Act of 1890, a newly enacted state law, segregated the seating on the intrastate railroad train by race. Based on this act, Blacks were relegated to the filthy front cars of the local railroad. Homer Plessy joined with others to draft a strategy to defeat the law. *Plessy v. Ferguson* placed the issue of state-imposed segregation before the US Supreme Court.

The *Plessy* case also meant to drive a wedge between White and Black alliances. Plessy, a proud Black man, a Creole, who could pass for White and claimed to be seven-eighths White, sat in the White-only section of the train as an act of defiance. He had watched the backlash against Black economic, social, and political progress that came when Reconstruction ended in 1877. He chose to challenge Louisiana's 1890 Separate Car Act, which restricted each race to a specific railroad car. Like the Mississippi Plan of voter disenfranchisement, southern states were enacting racial segregation to further marginalize Blacks. On June 7, 1892, Homer Plessy purchased a first-class ticket on the East Louisiana Railway line and sat in the railroad car designated for Whites.

Under the law, conductors on the trains (all of whom were White) had to remove any interloper or themselves risk jail and a fine. In this way, a

White conductor who did not want to follow the segregation law would be arrested for failing to call the police on any Black person who defied it. In the case at hand, the conductor asked Plessy to move to the "Negro-only" car. When he refused, Plessy was dragged away by the police, arrested, and placed in the Orleans Parish jail for violating Louisiana's segregation law. But Homer Plessy and a band of civil rights activists intended to appeal his arrest to the US Supreme Court, even in the face of possible defeat.

The Supreme Court was controlled by segregationists. Earlier decisions challenging state segregation laws had led to dismal results. *The Civil Rights Cases* filed by Blacks challenging discrimination in access to theaters, restaurants, and local transportation resulted in the Supreme Court ruling that the federal government could not protect Blacks against private individual discrimination. Earlier, in the *Cruikshank* case of 1875, one of the few cases in which the state had convicted Whites for the cold-blooded murder of Blacks, the Supreme Court had overturned the convictions. Chief Justice Melville W. Fuller was a Democrat and noted for interpreting the Constitution strictly, especially regarding race matters. He handed the task of writing the *Plessy* decision to Justice Henry Brown, a known segregationist and advocate for states' rights.

When Plessy appealed the decision, arguing that the act violated his Thirteenth and Fourteenth Amendment rights, he was represented by a White civil rights attorney, Albion W. Tourgee. Tourgee had been a businessman, journalist, and wealthy novelist when he took on the segregationists in Louisiana.[15] A lawyer and former judge, he championed the cause of racial equality even when it meant a loss of career opportunities and possibly risking his life. He argued that segregating public transportation placed a badge of inferiority on Blacks. Although Plessy was warned against appealing his case to the Supreme Court, he and Tourgee would not be deterred. A successful argument needed five votes. But since the court was controlled by a southern majority, the plaintiff only received one. Justice Henry Billings Brown delivered the now infamous opinion, in which Plessy's claims of discrimination were soundly defeated.

The court dismissed Plessy's argument that a badge of inferiority would be placed on Blacks segregated from the general population, stating: "If one race be inferior to the other socially, the Constitution of the United States cannot put them upon the same plane."[16] Every aspect of American life was affected by this ruling. The states were given the power to legislate social interaction between the races. The *Plessy v. Ferguson* opinion instituted the "separate but equal" doctrine, which imposed on the country an Americanized version of apartheid. In hypocritical rhetoric, the court stated:

A law which implies merely a legal distinction between the white and colored races—a distinction which is founded in the color of the two races and which must always exist so long as white men are distinguished from the other race by color—has no tendency to destroy the legal equality of the two races. . . . The object of the [Fourteenth Amendment] was undoubtedly to enforce the absolute equality of the two races before the law, but in the nature of things it could not have been intended to abolish distinctions based upon color, or to enforce social, as distinguished from political equality, or a commingling of the two races upon terms unsatisfactory to either.[17]

Justice John Marshall Harlan's dissent, like the dissent in *Dred Scott*, confirmed that there had always been a relatively small number of Whites willing to withstand social ostracism, threats, and assault to do what was just. Justice Harlan spoke directly to the racial hierarchy sanctioned by the *Plessy* majority: "In view of the Constitution, in the eye of the law, there is in this country no superior, dominant, ruling class of citizens. There is no caste here. *Our Constitution is color-blind*, and neither knows nor tolerates classes among citizens." He continued, "In my opinion, the judgment this day rendered will, in time, prove to be quite as pernicious as the decision made by this tribunal in the *Dred Scott* case."[18] This one case, *Plessy v. Ferguson*, began an onslaught that went well past segregation. Since segregation was now established by the highest court in the country, it would have to be overturned by an act of Congress, which was impossible at that time because it was under the conservative control of legislators from both the South and the North.

Plessy v. Ferguson would have to die in the high court that had given birth to it. Lawyers would have to carve a path through deadly terrain to reach this court again, and once there, place a stake in the heart of "separate but equal." Segregation took hold of American culture, then spread blood deep into every crevice. Terrorism followed, giving rise to murder with impunity by civilians as well as law enforcement officials. *Plessy v. Ferguson* heralded a disastrous period for all those who believed in American democracy.

Houston vowed to defeat segregation. His strategy was simple but brilliant. He turned a doctrine meant for racial oppression into a tool against the oppressor. Under Houston's strategy, a state would have to provide Black qualified students with entry into White-only colleges or pay to build them a separate but equal school. Houston trained a team of NAACP lawyers and local attorneys in the South to argue appellate cases. Few attorneys knew how to take a case to the US Supreme Court. Victory in the Supreme Court became the weapon needed to defeat Jim Crow segregation. Nothing would stop Houston from creating a team of brilliant legal minds fixed on the Supreme Court.

Charles Hamilton Houston saw himself as a social engineer who could use his legal prowess to change American society. He asserted, "Any lawyer who did not see himself as a social engineer is a parasite to society." With each case he placed African Americans a step closer to gaining the constitutional rights denied them by the Supreme Court in *Plessy*. When Houston taught Black law students to be specialists in civil rights litigation, from trial to the appellate courts, he was changing the entire practice of law. Appellate practice would never be the same.

It was highly unusual for lawyers of any race to view the practice of law as anything other than an occupation. It was a respected profession in most communities, but few attorneys in the early twentieth century practiced law with the idea of using cases to change the fabric of American society. Houston knew the US Supreme Court could in effect create the law of the land and thus change American society with one legal decision. He was determined to bring the case that would change America.

Thurgood Marshall and Robert L. Carter were students under Houston at Howard Law School. It was a night school in a dank basement when Houston arrived; he envisioned a training ground for civil rights attorneys who would spread across the country, litigating race cases all the way to the Supreme Court. He would train them to build a strategy and create a foundation of legal precedent that would eventually overturn *Plessy v. Ferguson*. The need for Black lawyers in the fight for full constitutional inclusion was understood early; thus the founding of Howard Law School in 1869. Protests and lobbying alone would prove insufficient.

The NAACP believed that with the end of legalized segregation, the murder of Blacks with impunity, and denial of their rights under law would end. The organization pushed steadily on all fronts: litigation, legislation, and protest. On July 28, 1917, the NAACP led a protest against the lynching and race riots that were destroying Black communities and taking Black lives without any legal consequences for the perpetrators. According to historian Winston James, "You have black troops going off to fight [in World I in Europe] to make the world safe for democracy in April and in July you have black people being murdered in the most wanton and barbaric manner in East St. Louis; children being thrown back into flaming houses, people being boarded up in their houses before they're torched so that they couldn't escape. So even by American standards, East St. Louis was a horror."[19]

On that day in 1917, in response to an NAACP call for action, more than ten thousand people marched in a "silent protest parade" against lynching. No one spoke. They marched side by side, in silence, down Fifth Avenue in New York City. Only the sound of shoes hitting the sidewalk could be heard. They marched to protest the East St. Louis, Illinois, riots, in which White factory workers who resented the hiring of Blacks attacked them with clubs and burned Black homes and businesses, leaving six thousand homeless; at least forty Blacks and eight Whites were killed. Blacks controlled very little without the right to vote. Police officers did not arrest Whites for killing or assaulting Blacks. Prosecutors would not press charges in state courts or seek indictments. Politicians would not fire police officers and prosecutors who failed to provide governmental services to Black communities. The victory in *Guinn v. Beal* in 1915 had placed the NAACP one step closer to controlling the laws and law enforcers who governed their communities, terrorized, or ignored them. It was time for the NAACP to return to the Supreme Court.

As mentioned previously, the NAACP had not been an official party in the *Guinn* case, just amicus; the US attorney general had led the case. Moorfield Storey was anxious to access the power of the Supreme Court as a full participant, standing his ground and arguing a case shaped by him. If he succeeded, the NAACP could wield that legal ruling as a weapon to combat racial injustice nationwide. In 1917, Storey chose a Louisville, Kentucky, case brought to him by the NAACP chapter there.

In Kentucky, African American William Warley, age thirty-three, was a postal worker and editor of the *Louisville News*. He used his newspaper to fight for voting rights and speak out against segregated street cars and unequal public schools. Warley was also president of the Louisville Chapter of the NAACP. He wanted to challenge the housing discrimination law passed by the Louisville City Council. As in *Plessy v. Ferguson*, Louisville based its segregation laws on maintaining the peace by separating the races. It was thought that violence would erupt if Blacks were allowed to reside next to Whites.

Moorfield Storey took the case, *Buchanan v. Warley* (1917), with an eye toward the US Supreme Court. He joined with local attorney Clayton B. Blakely to challenge Kentucky's segregation law. This would be the first US Supreme Court case challenging racial discrimination in housing and a strike against the court's segregation ruling in *Plessy v. Ferguson*. Unlike the Pink Franklin case, this time it would be a clear victory for the NAACP.

Kentucky law prohibited homes in White neighborhoods being sold by Whites to people of color. The NAACP chapter, led by Warley, had White allies who also opposed the law. The challenge needed to be creative, because *Plessy v. Ferguson* had legalized segregation in every area of American life. A White realtor named Charles Buchanan entered into an agreement to sell his Louisville property, located on the corner of 37th Avenue and Pflanz Street, a White neighborhood, to William Warley.[20]

The sale agreement contained a clause that allowed Warley to void the sale if he was unable to occupy the home due to Louisville's segregation laws. Blacks could not live on a residential block that was occupied by a majority of White residents. They could work in constructing homes for Whites, but were prohibited from living in a home on a street with a majority of White residents. Whites could not sell land to Blacks if the Black purchasers intended to build a residence on a block occupied by a majority of White residents.

Under certain exceptions, Black servants and employees could work and live within the homes of Whites on the block. However, the law was enacted to "prevent conflict and ill-feeling between the white and colored races . . . and to preserve the public peace and promote the general welfare, by making reasonable provisions requiring, as far as practicable, the use of separate blocks, for residences, places of abode, and places of assembly by white and colored people respectively."[21] As the number of Blacks in the community grew, concerned White neighbors sought enforcement of the law against Warley. They did not know that William Warley was a member of the NAACP. He had arranged to buy the property from Charles Buchanan in order to challenge Kentucky's housing segregation law.

Warley had been told he could not occupy the property he planned to purchase. He then refused to pay Buchanan the full amount for the land. Buchanan sued Warley for breach of contract, arguing that the Louisville segregation law prevented him from completing the sale of his property to Warley and violated his rights under the Fourteenth Amendment of the US Constitution.

The City of Louisville countered that its law separating the races was legal under *Plessy v. Ferguson*'s "separate but equal" ruling. The city also argued that it needed to protect citizens against violence. To protect the general public welfare from violence, the races had to be separated; violence would erupt if the races lived in close proximity to one another. The city argued that its law was not racist or discriminatory because it also prevented Whites from living in neighborhoods where Blacks lived. As expected, Kentucky's courts found in favor of the City of Louisville.

Moorfield Storey appealed to the US Supreme Court. The issue before the high court was whether the City of Louisville could prevent a White seller from selling his property to a Black buyer based solely on the race of the buyer, given the Thirteenth Amendment, which abolished slavery, and the Fourteenth Amendment, which provided for full citizenship and equal protection and guaranteed due process as well as privileges and immunities. Congress had also passed laws to protect the rights of Blacks to buy and sell property, knowing that states would try to interfere with those rights. Storey based the appeal on the federal laws passed after the Civil War, and the Civil Rights Acts of 1866 and 1870.

He argued that "were such a restriction upheld, an attempt to segregate Irish from Jews, foreign from native citizens, Catholics from Protestants, would be as justifiable."[22] The law forced Blacks to live only in the parts of town that Whites refused to occupy. They were relegated to reside near waste dumps, with poor sanitation, and far from city services.

The Civil Rights Act of 1866 states: "All citizens of the United States shall have the same right, in every state and territory, as is enjoyed by white citizens thereof to inherit, purchase, lease, sell, hold and convey real and personal property." The Civil Rights Act of 1870 states: "All persons within the jurisdiction of the United States shall have the same right in every state and territory to make and enforce contracts." The US Congress passed these federal laws to protect the privileges and immunities and due-process rights of Blacks against discrimination by the states.

The Supreme Court found in favor of Buchanan. The court held that the City of Louisville's housing segregation law interfered with the conveyance of property to a Black purchaser. In addition, the property rights of Buchanan were violated. Therefore, the law was an unconstitutional restriction in violation of the Civil Rights Acts and the Fourteenth Amendment. *Buchanan v. Warley* remains a landmark case in the struggle for access to housing.

The Supreme Court supported "the civil right of a white man to dispose of his property if he saw fit to do so to a person of color *and* of a colored person to make such disposition to a white person."[23] Segregation in housing continued after *Buchanan*, because restrictive covenants, or private agreements prohibiting the sale of homes to people of color, were used to prevent Blacks from moving into White neighborhoods. But in *Buchanan v. Warley* the court ruled against government discrimination against Black home buyers: "Colored persons are citizens of the United States and have the right to purchase property and enjoy and use the same without laws discriminating against them solely on account of color."[24]

Surprisingly, in another case, Chief Justice White, who was still on the court, had voted against Tennessee's segregationist housing law. This prior ruling instilled hope that Justice White might strike down the race-based grandfather clause and rule in favor of the NAACP and US attorney general. As in *Guinn* and *Myers*, White played a positive role in marking a new relationship between civil rights advocates and the high court. However, he had ruled in favor of oppressive literacy tests and poll taxes in *Henry Williams v. Mississippi* in 1898.[25] Clear evidence of Mississippi's intent to disenfranchise Black voters was ignored by the court because the effect was not established.

James Kimble and other Mississippi politicians openly voiced the purpose of Mississippi's Constitutional Convention in 1890: to add literacy tests and poll tax requirements would eliminate Blacks from politics. Yet the same Supreme Court had ruled in favor of Mississippi and against the voting rights of Black citizens. The *Buchanan* victory was instrumental in galvanizing financial contributions and membership. Morale was lifted. Litigation, not just in defense of injustice, as in the Pink Franklin case, but in an affirmative move to defeat racist laws, gained a foothold within the NAACP.

The NAACP had gained a great strategic and legal victory in *Buchanan*. The states had been allowed to create qualifications for voting as long as they were not discriminatory on their face, and the NAACP would have to prove discriminatory application of voting qualifications. Despite a road strewn with more obstacles and few friends, the NAACP had reason to be proud. Its pride in this success at the Supreme Court was felt nationwide. The *Buchanan* ruling gave millions of Blacks a much-needed boost to morale during this era of diabolical injustice.

THE NAACP STRATEGY

Morale is a decisive factor in war. It is important for both the commander and the foot soldier. The NAACP needed to show that it could achieve a string of successes. Some critics have claimed that this single victory was hollow and inconsequential because it did not provide any alternatives to America's housing segregation laws.[26] But litigation, legislation, and protest are all needed to create systemic change. The NAACP was litigating cases while its branches conducted protests and its lobbyists began to focus on preventing the passage of detrimental legislation and encouraging protections against discrimination. The Black community, which had placed its trust and hope in this organization, needed to know that their confidence was well founded.

Blacks who confronted implicit racism based on discriminatory state housing laws could now rely on the NAACP's victory in *Buchanan* as a weapon, where none had existed previously. In a nation of sustained racial violence, *Buchanan* provided a glimmer of hope that a higher governmental power would step in between the state and the Black home buyer. Importantly, propaganda is an essential part of warfare. It was necessary to show White supremacists a view of Black Americans as financially powerful enough to reach the highest court, smart enough to engage the court, and courageous enough to challenge racial discrimination in that court.

Whites who wanted to assist the NAACP could look to the crucial role that Charles Buchanan, a White man of goodwill, played in bringing this case to court. "I cannot help thinking it is the most important decision that has been made since the *Dred Scott* case," Moorfield Storey said of this case.[27] In fits and starts, a civil rights strategy of litigation, legislation, and protest was gaining ground. The organization was most successful when all three elements were in play. But litigation was costly and relied on a branch's expertise, dedication, and availability. Not all attorneys would follow the lead of the NAACP. They were dependent on whoever practiced law in a particular town. A local lawyer would have to make an investment not only of time, taken from other clients, but also of personal funds.

Waco Texas, September 14, 1918
   Sec. of NAACP,
   New York, USA

   Dear Sir
   The colored people in this part attempted to vote in the democratic primary election, which was held on or about July 27, last. We were prohibited from having any part in this election, but not because we were not willing to take the democratic oath, but on the grounds that we were Negro. We desire to test this matter to the limits of the courts and win what we go after.
   Any suggestions you may offer will be very highly appreciated. It would mean much for the N.A.A.C.P. and more for us if you would take the matter up and allow us to finance it through you. Please advise me at once what you think about it and the amount of money that will be necessary to prosecute the case should you take it up.
   Sincerely,
   R.H. Hines[28]

The NAACP could pay very little to local attorneys working on its cases. Its own staff members were underpaid. Cries for help poured into the small office in waves, from farmers to city folks, seeking assistance in cases from voting and racial assaults to death penalty appeals and discriminatory teacher salaries. The need was far greater than any organization could address. Its ability to do so much for so many with so little was nearly miraculous.

October 5, 1918
   Dear Mr. Hines
   We have your letter and are much interested in what you write concerning the colored people not being able to vote in your city. I am expecting to see the chairman of our legal committee today and will write you in a few days just what it is possible for the Association to do in this matter.
   We have branches in five Texas cities—Beaumont El Paso Fort Worth Houston San Antonio—we could do much more effective work on this case if we had a branch in Waco. I trust you may be able to interest the colored people of Waco in forming a branch of the Association there.
   Sincerely yours,
   Secretary

Money was a constant issue for the NAACP. It was needed to finance litigation, maintain the office in New York City, publish *The Crisis*, pay staff, and promote its work. Fund-raising from wealthy White patrons, and of course NAACP membership dues from working-class Black communities, were pivotal to the survival of the organization throughout its history. A lack of funds meant a potential lawsuit or appeal would be whittled down to an investigation. An investigation that required paying for travel by train down South would instead become the NAACP requesting well-respected community members in the town where help was requested to send it documents or newspaper clippings substantiating their claims of discrimination. This evidence, in turn, could be used by the NAACP in letters to the president, a governor, or members of Congress, demanding an end to that particular discriminatory law or conduct.

Supplemental Memorandum to Mr. R.H. Hines, Waco, Texas
Subject: Refusal to Allow Colored People to Register in Democratic Primaries

Since dictating the enclosed letter I have consulted the Chairman of our Legal Committee. Our suggestion is this: That since the complaint you made could probably be made in other Texas communities, and is therefore a statewide disability of colored people, if the action taken by your state-wide local election officials is any criterion, of what would happen elsewhere unless successfully combated as at Houston (see printed matter enclosed), we would recommend that it be fought by the joint action of as many branches of the NAACP that will join in the fight. In practice it may be best to bring your legal action in the locality where success seems most certain. One cause of failure for Negroes to win, in some cases, is that poor lawyers are engaged. The lawyer would better be a local man of standing at the bar and of knowledge of the law, of course.

I am giving you the names of secretaries of our Texas branches. In addition, Mrs. Mary B. Talbert (colored) of Buffalo, NY, will probably be in Waco in the next ten days, speaking on behalf of the Fourth Liberty Loan. She could help in regard to a branch organization, if you wish to move in that direction.

When she has completed her Liberty Loan work she plans to begin an organizing tour for the N.A.A.C.P. in Texas.

I am sending you a few samples of literature of which more may be had if you are interested. My idea is, of course, that the National Office is too far away to be of direct service and therefore the joint action of the branches is best in the registration fight. The National Office will advise all that is possible and be helpful in any way we can.

Secretary

Lobbying Congress to prevent or to repeal racist laws and working to push passage of federal legislation to protect the rights of African

Americans meant having a continuous presence in Washington, D.C. In 1913, when New York, Michigan, and Kansas introduced antimiscegenation bills, the NAACP voted to hire a Washington lobbyist.[29] As early as 1914, the Washington bureau began publishing a "Civil Rights Legislative Report Card" to inform the membership about how their congressional representatives were voting on civil rights issues.[30] The NAACP hired a Washington lobbyist to work on securing antilynching legislation. Changing federal legislation meant national change. After all, it was federal civil rights laws that had protected African Americans when slavery ended. The federal government knew the states could not be trusted to defend the rights of Blacks, especially in the South. Under the NAACP's watchful eye, swift action could be taken to address congressmen bent on passing laws to harm the advancement of Black Americans, even if the action was only an open letter to the newspaper.

Protest became not only an effective tool but also a more affordable one. The members of the community were actively engaged in their own liberation by writing letters to politicians, filing petitions, and placing themselves in harm's way, demanding their rights in the face of violence by marching with signs declaring their right to vote. Protest put pressure on governments and shamed individuals who had the power to bring about change for African Americans but hid behind cowardice, reliance on tradition, or fear of being ostracized.

Using litigation, legislation, and protest, the NAACP had developed a strategy for challenging entrenched racism, although it seemed that for every step forward there was a lynching or a new law to remind the organization just how difficult the road to true freedom would be. The NAACP's mission to advance the rights of Blacks was clear, even if how long it would take to successfully fulfill that mission was not.

W. E. B. DuBois wrote in the NAACP magazine *The Crisis* that the *Buchanan* case was "breaking the backbone of segregation." But thirty-six Blacks were lynched that year, and despite the NAACP's victory against the grandfather clause in the *Guinn* case, the Supreme Court had allowed the states to require literacy tests and poll taxes. States did little to end intimidation at polling places. In most states, White and Black voter lists were maintained in separate books. Laws allowed those who had served in the Civil War, most of whom were White and proslavery, to be exempted from paying any poll taxes. While tens of thousands of Blacks served in the Civil War, their descendants were not exempted from poll taxes. The local White sheriff or election official determined who was exempted from paying the poll tax and the type of test questions needed to prove a citizen literate enough to vote.

Most Blacks across the South were still denied their right to register to vote. The next battle in this war for voting rights had to be voter registration. It would be deadly work.

Orlando FL 28 Oct. [1920]
   Mr. W.R. O'Neal
   City,

   Sir:
   While stopping in your beautiful little city this week I was informed that you were of the habit of going out among the negroes of Orlando and delivering lectures, explaining to them just how to become citizens, and how to assert their rights.
   If you are familiar with days of reconstruction that followed in the wake of the Civil War, you will recall that the "Scalawags" of the North and the Republicans of the south, proceeded very much the same as you are proceeding, to instill into the negro the idea of social equality. You will also remember that these things forced the loyal citizens of the south to organize clans of determined men who pledged themselves to maintain white supremacy and to safeguard our women and children.
   And now if you are a scholar, you know that history repeats itself, and that he who resorts to your kind of a game is handling edged tools. We shall always enjoy WHITE SUPREMACY in this country and he who interferes must face the consequences.
   GRAND MASTER FLORIDA KLUCK KLUKS

The threatening letter above was sent to a W. R. O'Neal, a White attorney working on behalf of voting rights for Blacks in Orlando, Florida. A copy was also sent to Judge Jonathan M. Cheney, also White. "You may accept this as a fitting message to you" was an added warning on the letter sent to Judge Cheney. A copy of this letter was also sent to the local Ku Klux Klan chapter with this request: "[W]atch these two."
   No one was safe. The NAACP had deepened its counterattacks in the South. The enemy was fighting back—hard. Blacks needed to vote for sheriffs, judges, prosecutors, and school board members. They needed to be able to run for office. The right to vote meant nothing if Blacks were prohibited from voting in the local primaries. A "Whites-only" primary was the law enforced with terror across the South. Democrats controlled the South. Political control had been given to the South by President Hayes in 1877, and the tradition continued, including absolute control over Black citizens. Republicans could not win a general election, so the primary decided the outcome. Only White voters could vote in Democratic primaries.
   Leaders of the NAACP knew that defeating White-only primaries must be their next target in the war for voting rights.

4

~

White-Only Primaries

Yet with a steady beat, Have not our weary feet
Come to the place for which our fathers sighed?

—James Weldon Johnson, "Lift Every Voice and Sing" (1899)

These deaths symbolize the ultimate sacrifice made by all voting rights martyrs. On June 12, 1963, NAACP voting rights leader Medgar Evers, thirty-seven, was murdered when a rifle bullet struck him in the back while he was standing in front of his home in Jackson, Mississippi. Evers, a World War II veteran, had wanted to become a lawyer. But he was denied admission to the University of Mississippi Law School because he was Black.

As field secretary for the Mississippi branch of the NAACP, Evers was leading a statewide voter registration campaign. He was also leading a protest against discrimination practiced in downtown Jackson department stores and working to desegregate the University of Mississippi. Evers joined the NAACP in December 1954. By 1955, he was the youngest man on a nine-man "death list." The list was reduced to eight when Rev. George T. Lee was gunned down in Beloni, Mississippi, after refusing to take his name off of a voter registration list. Said Evers then, "you don't have time to be afraid." Of Mississippi, Evers said: "A Negro cannot live here or die here in peace as long as things remain as they are."[1]

In the Freedom Summer of 1964, Andrew Goodman and Michael Schwerner from New York City and James Chaney from Meridian, Mississippi, were working with the Congress of Race Equality (CORE) in Neshoba County, Mississippi. They were there to help Blacks register to vote. On the night of June 21, 1964, Goodman, Schwerner, and Chaney were abducted while driving on a country road to investigate the burning of the Mount Zion Methodist Church. They were arrested by Deputy Sheriff Cecil Price for allegedly speeding, and after paying a fine, they were allowed to leave. But that was a ruse. When they drove through a remote area, two cars filled with Klansmen stopped them.

That was the last time they were seen alive. Some forty-four days later, an informant revealed where their bodies could be found. Buried in an earthen dam, those three students had been tortured, shot, and dismembered. National outrage over these murders led to the passage of the Civil Rights Act in August 1964. In 2005 Edgar Ray Killen, an itinerant Baptist minister, was convicted of orchestrating this depravity.

Viola Liuzzo, thirty-nine, was among the many female victims of terrorism, assault, and murder perpetrated against voting rights workers. A member of the Detroit NAACP branch, Liuzzo, a White mother of five, drove to Alabama after learning of the carnage on the Edmund Pettus Bridge. On March 25, 1965, following Dr. King's successful protest march from Selma to Montgomery, Liuzzo was shot and killed by three Klan members while driving Leroy Jerome Moton, nineteen, a Black SCLC member, back to Selma. Liuzzo died at the scene. Moton survived by pretending to be dead.

The death of these martyrs and the horrific "Bloody Sunday" televised attack on them by Alabama state troopers provided the impetus for those Americans of goodwill who had stood on the sidelines of this war to finally enter the fray.

FIGHTING FOR SELF-DETERMINATION

Life, liberty, and the pursuit of happiness. For the NAACP, the war for voting rights was part of a mighty struggle for Black Americans' self-determination: the right to chart their own course in human history. The enemy was a White supremacy created in slavery, with tentacles reaching into every aspect of American life. It was now a life and death struggle for the future of millions of Black families.

Voting was an act of self-determination as well as self-governance. After centuries of enslavement and the Supreme Court's wretched *Plessy* segregation decision in 1896, too many Whites in the twentieth century truly believed that Black Americans were not yet ready to vote. The same sentiment was felt about women, regardless of race, for different reasons. Blacks were still considered to have mere privileges and no rights a White man need respect, as the Supreme Court had ruled in *Dred Scott* in 1857. Black lives could be taken without criminal consequences, and Black children undereducated to maintain a perpetual labor class.

There were among communities in both North and South virulent racists who believed Blacks to be undeserving of self-determination and, move important, political power over the affairs of Whites. Those beliefs fed a fear of "Negro domination" and sparked much of the violence aimed at preventing Black Americans from ever attaining political status worthy of their voting numbers and acumen. It was assumed that Blacks in positions of power would act as viciously against White progress as many Whites in public office had acted against Blacks.

Historically, the brutal attacks that met Blacks who attempted to register to vote were meant to send a message. The attackers were often led by the very men hired to conduct voter registration. Yet even in the face of this intimidation, Blacks sought help from the NAACP, at further risk of their lives. As the following letter indicates, too often, for Black Americans, bloodshed accompanied any attempt to vote:

Hon. Moorfield Storey 1918
    Boston, Mass
    Dear Sir
    I regret to have to report for your consideration that on the seventh day inst, that being the first Monday of the month and under the statute of this state, the various registration office are required to be open for any and all citizens who qualify under the Constitution and statu[t]e laws.
    I am reliably informed that one Greenfield preacher applied under the statute laws and was registered. He thereupon returned to his home and brought his son to be registered, and another minister accompanied him. By the time they reached the Court House where the registration was in progress about one dozen Negroes had appeared to be registered. This was more than the white members of that community cared to stand whereupon they set upon the first minister who been previously registered during the day a crowd held him while another man took his pistol put it right aside his head and fired making a serious wound. The other minister was knocked down and beaten unmercifully. And every Negro who had appeared to be registered was driven from the Court House by the peaceful citizenry of that community.
    I am handing you under enclosure a few copies of the Southern Indicator which contains an article written by one of the ministers who received the harsh treatment. Both were ordered to leave the county at once. I am informed that the man who was shot is in a hospital in Washington, D.C., the whereabouts of the other minister, I have not learned as of yet.

I think that the National Association for Colored People by judiciously proceeding as they always do, might be able to send a representative there and get all of these facts, first hand.

Blacks in the South were lynched for attempting to join the Democratic Party. After Reconstruction, when conservative Democrats were given free rein in the Deep South by northern presidents in exchange for southern White votes, the number of lynchings and other attacks against Blacks increased during voter registration and elections. But they would not go quietly into disenfranchisement.

Upon entering office, President Woodrow Wilson, a Democrat and segregationist, yet labeled a political progressive, segregated the White House and all federal agencies. Originally from Virginia, Wilson rose to be governor of his adopted state of New Jersey and then US president, from 1913 to 1921. He declared war on Germany during World War I in the name of freedom, but refused to allow Blacks to enlist as soldiers. During Wilson's two terms, there would be no friend of the Black community in the White House. Although Blacks had voted for the academic, Wilson refused to address their concerns about injustice.[2] An infamous encounter between President Wilson and the Niagara Movement's Monroe Trotter defines the administration's view about race relations.[3]

Monroe Trotter, the son of a slave, graduated magna cum laude and Phi Beta Kappa from Harvard University in 1895. He rejected membership in the NAACP because he did not believe that Whites should lead an advocacy organization with a mission of Black self-determination. He founded the newspaper *The Boston Guardian*. In response to Wilson's racially conservative policies, Monroe Trotter led a delegation to the White House to discuss the needs of Blacks generally and desegregating the federal offices that Wilson had recently segregated, in particular. Their 1914 encounter made front-page news. The NAACP's magazine, *The Crisis*, reported the meeting:

> *Mr. Monroe Trotter.* Mr. President, we are here to renew our protest against the segregation of colored employees in the departments of our National Government. We [had] appealed to you to undo this race segregation in accord with your duty as President and with your pre-election pledges to colored American voters. We stated that such segregation was a public humiliation and degradation, and entirely unmerited and far-reaching in its injurious effects. . . .
>
> *President Woodrow Wilson.* The white people of the country, as well as I, wish to see the colored people progress, and admire the progress they have already made, and want to see them continue along independent lines. There is, however, a great prejudice against colored people. . . . It will take one hundred years to eradicate this prejudice, and we must deal with it as practical men. Segregation is not humiliating, but a benefit, and ought to be so regarded by you gentlemen. If your organization goes out and tells the colored people of the country that it is a humiliation, they will so regard

it, but if you do not tell them so, and regard it rather as a benefit, they will regard it the same. The only harm that will come will be if you cause them to think it is a humiliation.

Mr. Monroe Trotter. It is not in accord with the known facts to claim that the segregation was started because of race friction of white and colored [federal] clerks. The indisputable facts of the situation will not permit of the claim that the segregation is due to the friction. It is untenable, in view of the established facts, to maintain that the segregation is simply to avoid race friction, for the simple reason that for fifty years white and colored clerks have been working together in peace and harmony and friendliness, doing so even through two [President Grover Cleveland] Democratic administrations. Soon after your inauguration began, segregation was drastically introduced in the Treasury and Postal departments by your appointees.

President Woodrow Wilson. If this organization is ever to have another hearing before me it must have another spokesman. Your manner offends me. . . . Your tone, with its background of passion.

Mr. Monroe Trotter. But I have no passion in me, Mr. President, you are entirely mistaken; you misinterpret my earnestness for passion.[4]

Monroe Trotter was known for his firm stance against racial segregation. Then and now, civil rights leaders did not all agree on strategies for gaining equal rights. Notably, Trotter and Booker T. Washington nearly came to blows in the streets of Boston. In 1903 Washington was speaking at the AME Zion Church in Boston. Trotter was in the audience. Trotter questioned Washington's position as an advocate for separation of the races and vocational education. Onlookers had to pull the two men apart.

Their fight was called "The Boston Riot" by the Black press. Trotter was arrested for assault and sentenced to a month in jail. He spent his time there reading W. E. B. DuBois's book *The Souls of Black Folk*.[5] That led him to join DuBois in the Niagara Movement and to establish the National Negro Suffrage League. One must recall the bravery of the men and women of the Niagara Movement. They declared that "[a]ny discrimination based simply on race or color is barbarous, we care not how hallowed it be by custom, expediency or prejudice." Trotter's initiatives would change names several times and, like his newspaper, *The Guardian*, fade from popularity. However, William Monroe Trotter's fearless stance against President Wilson and segregation was historic.[6] DuBois would also find fault with Washington. Trotter, in turn, chose not to join the NAACP. Both Trotter and DuBois agreed that President Wilson did significant harm to the condition of Blacks in America.

THE "RED SUMMER" AND THE ELAINE RIOT

It was during President Wilson's tenure that America witnessed the "Red Summer" of 1919, so named by the NAACP's James Weldon Johnson because that summer American streets ran red with the blood of hundreds of African Americans attacked by White lynch mobs. The barbarity of attacks reached a new low. Men were burned alive, hanged from trees, and castrated, while White families, including children, held picnic lunches beneath the swinging bodies. Seventy-six Black men, women, and children were lynched in 1919. Homes and businesses were destroyed, and Black families were left destitute without any restitution from the government.

In 1919 Moorfield Storey, now a seasoned civil rights leader, was being drawn into yet another case of mob violence. This time it was in Arkansas. He and Walter White, his assistant secretary, were to represent Black farmers in Elaine, Arkansas. This case, *Moore v. Dempsey*,[7] would end with a muted victory in the US Supreme Court. As in the Springfield Race Riot of 1908, which had led to the formation of the NAACP, White-led violence was blamed on the Black victims.

The Elaine Riot was an opportunity for the NAACP to save lives. The clients were Black farmers, victims of mob violence who nevertheless had been convicted and sentenced to die. The NAACP sent undercover investigators to Elaine. They discovered that the farmers had been meeting over the summer of 1919 to discuss selling their crops where they would not be cheated by White middlemen. On September 30, 1919, while the Black farmers met, rumors spread among Whites of an uprising. Thousands of armed Whites surrounded the meeting place and began shooting into the building. The Black men fired back.

A White member of the mob had died. Some of the Black farmers were tried for murder in a hostile courtroom, where even White jurors were intimidated by the mobs lingering outside and Blacks were beaten into false confessions. Storey took the case to the Supreme Court, arguing that the trial judge and jury were afraid, all-White, and biased toward convictions on scant evidence. An angry mob of thousands had surrounded the courthouse, waiting for a guilty verdict, and intimidating even the all White jury. The jurors had understood the tradition that Black defendants had two choices in a case in which a White man was killed or a White woman was allegedly raped: to die by lynching or by state execution, hanging or the electric chair. Even in cases of self-defense, mobs would not allow a jury to acquit. The Elaine Riot defendants had themselves been victims of mob violence.

The Black farmers near Elaine, in Phillips County, Arkansas, had been systematically paid below-market prices for their crops by the White brokers in town. After backbreaking work, these men were told how much their crops were worth and how much they would receive. On the night of September 30, 1919, they and other Black residents of the town of Elaine gathered at their church to discuss joining the Progressive Farmers and Household Union of America. Led by Robert L. Hill, a Black man looking for a quick profit, who may have been unscrupulous and was no civil rights leader, the group retained an attorney to represent them in a lawsuit to obtain settlements for their cotton crops and a statement of their accounts. They believed that membership in a union would allow them to sell their crops without going through the local White brokers, who were cheating them. With the help of a local White attorney named O. S. Bratton, they formed a union.

Their meeting was considered an *insurrection*. Whites, angered at the audacity of the Blacks, circled the church and attacked it. The Blacks defended themselves. A White sheriff was injured, and a White railroad worker was killed. Rumor spread of a Black uprising in Elaine. That last meeting of the Progressive Farmers and Householders' Union of America was held on a hot Tuesday. As word of the shoot-out spread, hundreds of trucks began arriving in the Phillips County towns of Helena and Elaine.[8] By Thursday morning, thousands of armed Whites from other counties and bordering states of Mississippi and Tennessee had converged on the town. Hundreds of White strangers were deputized and given the legal authority to shoot Blacks on sight. Federal troops arrived. Walter White wrote, "A large number of colored people who were killed were put to death by troops who used machine guns to mow down colored people. Citizens' posses, however, murdered a great many more."[9] Perhaps one hundred were murdered in cold blood. Those Blacks who were arrested were placed in holding pens inside a stockade in Helena. Hundreds of Black men, women, and children were charged with first degree murder. Reverend Lee escaped.

Blacks were hunted down and murdered. Clinton Lee, a White man, lost his life. Governor Hillman Brough requested assistance from the US military. The estimated number of Blacks killed ranges from eighty to over two hundred. Blacks were blamed for the riot and were arrested in the hundreds. Within weeks a grand jury was convened, on which no Blacks were allowed to serve. Little more than a month after the riot, Blacks were charged with murder, conspiracy, and participating in an insurrection. Those who testified against other Blacks were freed. The Black prisoners who refused to confess were tortured. Execution awaited convictions.

Moorfield Storey sent Walter White to investigate. In his autobiography, *A Man Called White*, White recalls traveling by train to Elaine in the midst of the furor and posing as a White reporter working for the *Chicago Daily News*. He conducted interviews of locals, including Governor Brough.[10] White was born in Atlanta in 1893 to a middle-class family. He had blond hair and blue eyes. He used his ability to pass for white as a tool to make his way undetected around the South, investigating lynchings and discrimination without being detected. After his death in 1955, the *New York Times* wrote of him: "Mr. White, the nearest approach to a national leader of American Negroes since Booker T. Washington, was a Negro by choice."

After graduating from Atlanta University in 1916, White worked in insurance. His civil rights career began when he organized a protest against the Atlanta Board of Education because he and other Blacks had been informed that the board planned to eliminate seventh grade for Black students in order to finance the building of a new high school for White students. White's organizing skills and courage led him to join and then found the Atlanta branch of the NAACP. In 1918 he moved to New York City as assistant secretary to Moorfield Storey.

Due to his very light complexion, this Black man walked among the White residents of Elaine without being detected. What he learned was horrific. At the height of the massacre, "Negroes were being hunted and 250 shot-down like beasts, in the Arkansas cane breaks, because they had organized to employ a lawyer in an endeavor to obtain settlements and statements of account from the landlord under the sharecropping system."[11] Whites had arrived by car and train for the "nigger hunt."

The self-determination of Blacks and this savagery of White violence were connected. An editorial in a local newspaper, the *Arkansas Gazette*, warned that Blacks would be annihilated "unless Negroes cease to be led by the lure of Liberty and equal political rights."[12] It was necessary for the NAACP to fight to protect Black lives and lobby for federal antilynching laws as an overarching civil rights strategy to gain self-determination. Mob violence had been the impetus for the NAACP. Mob violence intimidated Black voters even after grandfather clauses and White-only primaries had whittled down their numbers from thousands to a few hundred. Mob violence and lynching was the last resort for desperate White supremacists in a war to maintain power. They would rely on their ability to create carnage for decades to come.

Walter White discovered that his secret of posing as a White reporter was out. He barely escaped Arkansas with his life after rumors started to fly about a Black man investigating the Elaine Riot who was passing for White. Someone heard that an imposter was in their midst. White took the next train back to New York City. The NAACP investigator reports that while seated in the "White section" of the train, he overheard the conductor bragging about what they would do to that Black man passing for White if they caught him. That trip from Arkansas to New York City was the longest train ride of White's life.

In October, Governor Brough appointed a committee of seven to investigate and assign guilt. The committee reached a compromise with the White mob circling the courthouse, promising that the men would be executed if the mob abstained from lynching them. The *Helena World* published an article titled "Inward Facts about the Negro Insurrection," which presented the results of the committee's investigation. Local newspapers inflamed White anger.

The article in the *Helena World* reported that the race riot in Phillips County was "a deliberately planned insurrection of the negroes against the whites, directed by . . . Progressive Farmers and Household Union of America, established for the purpose of banding negroes together for the killing of white people."[13] The article was quite lengthy and among other things stated that Robert L. Hill, who had organized the union, told Black people "to arm themselves in preparation of the day when they should be called upon to attack their white oppressors."

By early November Arkansas began criminal trials that lasted one week and resulted in twelve defendants receiving the death penalty; eighty received prison terms of one to twenty-one years. The Black defendants were represented by the renowned attorney Scipio Africanus Jones. Jones was the wealthiest Black man in Arkansas. A Freemason and business owner, he was born in 1863 to a Black teenage mother and a socially prominent White slaveholder. Moving to Arkansas, Jones became a teacher, attended a local law school, and passed the Arkansas bar in 1893.

Jones was a powerhouse within the Republican Party, attending as a convention delegate and challenging discrimination within the party. He built a national reputation in law as the founder the National Negro Bar Association, which became today's National Bar Association. He was wealthy enough to buy $50,000 in Liberty bonds during World War I. The NAACP called on Scipio Jones, who at one point during the trial represented ninety-nine defendants charged with assaulting members of the White mobs that had formed to kill the Blacks of Elaine, Arkansas.

The murders in Elaine were making news across the country. The Black newspapers called it mob violence. The White newspapers reported a Black uprising against Whites requiring military troops to put down. As White reporters descended on the Phillips County courthouse, they too sought to justify the killing of Blacks and thus the death sentences of the defendants and the continued murder of Blacks well after the riots ended:

Two More Negroes Shot by Troops
Over 200 Arrested For Uprising in Arkansas
Helena, Ark. Two negroes who failed to obey a command of a military patrol were shot and killed Friday at Elaine, the center of the race rioting. Another negro was wounded and the fourth member of the party was arrested. With military control well established no new outbreaks have been reported.
The white casualties as a result of clashes stand at five dead and five wounded. With the exception of Ira Proctor, deputy sheriff, who was seriously wounded, all of the injured are reported recovering. So far more than 200 negroes have been taken into custody. The known negro dead is fourteen with other bodies reported in the canebrakes and underbrush.

A large amount of literature tending to show that the outbreak was due to propaganda circulated among negro tenant farmers, making roseate promises if the negroes would band together and arm themselves, has been seized by military and civil authorities.

An announcement made at military headquarters in Elaine said that about 150 rifles had been taken from negroes who had been arrested, or at the homes of negroes searched by troops. (Friday, October 8, 1919).

By November 1919, twelve defendants had been convicted of murder in the first degree and sentenced to death. "The trial lasted about three quarters of an hour and in less than five minutes the jury brought in a verdict of guilty of murder in the first degree."[14] There were several trials and appeals. In 1923, the case came before the US Supreme Court as _Moore v. Dempsey_.[15] Frank Moore, named petitioner for the group of convicted Black men, argued upon a writ of habeas corpus that they had been convicted of murder under pressure of mob violence without any regard for their rights and without due process of law.

The Supreme Court found that "no juryman could have voted for an acquittal and continued to live in Phillips County and if any prisoner by any chance had been acquitted by a jury he could not have escaped the mob." The defendants were finally pardoned by Governor McRae on January 13, 1925. But until Blacks gained their voting rights, elected judges would continue to conspire against them. The elected prosecutors would not bring race mobs to justice. The elected sheriffs would not arrest the true perpetrators of crimes or investigate wrongdoing against Black victims.

THE NAACP FIGHTS BACK

Now the NAACP's three-pronged approach of litigation, legislation, and protest was offering a bright light of hope in the war for voting rights and the battle to overturn _Plessy v. Ferguson_.[16] But on the heels of that Red Summer of 1919, the presidential election of 1920 placed the issue of voting rights and mob violence at the forefront of the NAACP's competing priorities.

There are many reasons that violence against Blacks increased in 1919: the state of the economy, the return of Blacks to the South from fighting for American freedom in World War I, and the upcoming 1920 presidential election. The NAACP expanded its strategy to use political pressure through letters to congressmen and the Department of Justice, protesting the lynchings and segregation enforced with barbarism to keep Blacks from exercising their legal right to vote:

December 7, 1920
  Walter White
  70 5th Ave.
  New York, NY
  Dear Sir:
  We are making vigorous efforts to get some affidavits but the people
are very thoughtful along this line, to the extent that they are asking if any
protection will be given them by the NAAC or the department of justice of
the Federal government. They realize very keenly that they have no protection as far as the local and state laws are concerned, and would like to be
informed about the aftermath of this matter, which, in my mind, should have
the most careful consideration. Kindly advise me along this line so that I may
intelligently advise my people.
  Madam rumor has it that possibly some responsible persons from this
section will be called upon to appear before the Washington investigating
committee, and despite the fact that you have various newspaper articles
published in the state as to how the people were treated, which, as all of us
know is no secret, still there is the thought of what might happen to such
persons after he returns to his home, after giving such testimony before an
investigating board.
  These lists were made up from individual cards, made out by each voter
in his, or her, own writing, and who held registration certificates, and who
presented themselves at the polls to vote, many others have failed to give us
the cards, despite the fact that they were at the polls, while on the other hand,
a great number did not go to the polls because of the many threats which had
been made upon them. You have the clipping from the Times-Union that
contains the statement from Mr. Ironmonger, the registration officer, to the
effect that 16,000 person [*sic*], who had registered in Duval County did not
vote, the greater portion of these 16,000 were colored voters who remained
away by reason of threats, and others were denied the privilege of voting
who were at the polls.
  I regret the delay in this matter very much indeed, but under the circumstances, I have done my best. Please let me have a line from you. With kind
regards and best wishes, I am.
  Very truly yours
  James W. Floyd

Letters from victims spoke of their valiant efforts to live, work, and
vote, and the daily racism that met each mundane task. The threat was
inherent in each act of self-determination. Each letter requesting help that
arrived at the NAACP office, written with dignity and grace, set out the
acts of terror perpetrated against the writers. They protested their condition to lawyers in New York because the local officials were complicit or
refused to protect the rights of the Black community. These letters, combined with efforts by White congressmen of goodwill, led to the drafting
of federal legislation against lynching.

In an effort to end murderous lynch mobs, the NAACP lobbied to pass a federal antilynching law, known as the Dyer Bill. In 1920 the KKK declared that the NAACP was its arch enemy. The NAACP expended more effort than in any previous lobbying campaign on behalf of the Dyer antilynching bill. The bill passed the House of Representatives. Hopeful, the NAACP took out a one-and-a-half page ad in nine newspapers:

THE SHAME OF AMERICA
Do you know that the United States is the Only Land on Earth where human beings are BURNED AT THE STAKE?

In Four Years, 1918–1921, Twenty-Eight People Were Publicly

BURNED BY AMERICAN MOBS

3436 People Lynched 1889 to 1922
Is Rape the "Cause" of Lynching?

83 WOMEN HAVE BEEN LYNCHED
IN THE UNITED STATES
AND THE LYNCHERS GO UNPUNISHED
THE REMEDY
The Dyer Anti-Lynching Bill is Now Before the United States Senate[17]

But the Dyer bill was defeated by a southern filibuster in the US Senate in December 1922. Mob violence would continue to rule. Archibald Grimke rebuked Americans for the constitutional rights denied to Black people in his speech "The Shame of America, or the Negro's Case Against the Republic," delivered in various locations beginning in 1920:

"We the people!" From the standpoint of the Negro, what grim irony; "establish justice"! What exquisitely cruel mockery; "to insure domestic tranquility"! What height and breadth and depth of political duplicity; "to provide for the common defense"! What cunning paltering with words in a double sense; "to promote the general welfare"! What studied ignoring of an ugly fact; "and secure the blessings of liberty to ourselves and posterity"! What masterly abuse of noble words to mask an equivocal meaning, to throw over a great national transgression an air of virtue, so subtle and illusive as to deceive the framers themselves into believing in their own sincerity. You may ransack the libraries of the world, and turn over all the documents of recorded time to match that Preamble of the Constitution as a piece of consummate political dissimulation and mental reservation, as an example of how men juggle deliberately and successfully with their moral sense, how they raise above themselves huge fabrics of falsehood, and go willingly to live and die in a make believe world of lies. The muse of history, dipping her iron pen in the generous blood of the Negro, has written large across the page of that Preamble, and the face of the Declaration of Independence, the words, "sham, hypocrisy."[18]

The enraged seventy-one-year-old Archibald Grimke had graduated from Lincoln University and Harvard Law School, but was born into slavery. He had witnessed the rise and fall of Reconstruction. In the 1880s he was a leader for women's rights and an internationally known public speaker. He served as president of the American Negro Academy, an organization of Black intellectuals, and was at the first meetings of both the Niagara Movement and the NAACP.

WOMEN VOTERS

Women gained the right to vote in 1920. The Nineteenth Amendment to the US Constitution states:

> The right of citizens of the United States to vote shall not be denied or abridged by the United States or by any state on account of sex.
> Congress shall have power to enforce this article by appropriate legislation.[19]

Black women had worked hard for female voting rights. Unfortunately, they faced racism within the suffragette movement. In 1913 a leading White suffragette, Alice Paul, who had founded the Congressional Union, required Black women to march in a segregated unit of her parade protesting the refusal of men to give women the franchise. Sojourner Truth gave her famous "Ain't I a Woman?" speech at a segregated suffragette convention. Her question was asked of the White women who demanded equal treatment from White men and excluded Black women from the convention.

Black women suffragists Harriet Tubman, Margaretta Forten, Mary Church Terrell, Harriet Forten Purvis, and Ida B. Wells-Barnett, as well as writer Mary Ann Shadd Cary, were forced to fight on all fronts: racism from White men and White women, as well as sexism. But these Black women persevered, participating in the American Equal Rights Association, the National Woman Suffrage Association, and the American Woman Suffrage Association.

The 1920 presidential election provoked greater violence because it was the first election in which women, and in particular Black women, had the right to elect a president. Blacks did not have the numbers to elect a president, but they had the political clout to determine the outcome of an election. After eight years with segregationist Democrat Woodrow Wilson, a change was welcome. Warren Harding, a Republican, was the candidate supported by the Black community.

The following letter from the NAACP branch in Jacksonville, Florida, speaks to the serious level of harm and the responding courage displayed in the Black community by men and women around the election of 1920:

December 6, 1920
 Walter White
 70 Fifth Avenue
 New York City
 Dear Sir;

I am writing to inform you of a case of intimidation that happened to me.

I live in River junction and registered in the 9th precinct but was asked to leave before it was time to vote. On Thursday, October 14, Mr. A.L. Wilson and the deputy sheriff came to my house and told me that I was the leader of the colored people in the effort to have colored women register to vote. I am secretary of the Harding and Coolidge club in my home and I was active in all things that tend to the uplift of my people.

On the following Thursday, which was Oct. the 21, Dr. B.F. Bond and the Sheriff of that county Mr. Gregory came to me and further threatened me. On the 28th Mr. Hayman Dolan and Mr. Creamer a mill owner and Mr. Newberry came and told me as there have never been a lynching in that part they thought it well that I should leave at once to be sure of my life.

So to preserve my life I left that very night and am making my home in Jacksonville.

I am putting this information [in] the hands of the secretary of the Jacksonville NAACP hoping that it may be help in the investigation that is to be held under the direction of the Assn.

Very truly yours
 T.L. Sweet

Walter White found the disenfranchisement of four thousand Blacks in Florida so blatantly horrendous that he contacted the US attorney's office and demanded an investigation, and the office responded by alerting the membership, influential friends of the organization, and members of Congress. The following press release was sent out on December 17, 1920, by the NAACP following a dangerous mission by Walter White, who could pass for White, to investigate the brutal assault on Blacks in Florida who had attempted to vote:

PRESS SERVICE FOR THE NATIONAL ASSOCIATION FOR THE AD-VANCEMENT OF COLORED PEOPLE

The National Association for the Advancement of Colored People, 70 Fifth Avenue, New York, today announced the evidence of the killing of more than 30 Negroes in Florida election riots and terrorization of Colored voters in the South would be presented to the Department of Justice on Friday, December 17.

The evidence is to be presented by Walter White, Assistant Secretary of the Advancement Association, who made a personal investigation of the Ocoee, Florida, massacre and offered his findings to the Department of Justice which has accepted his offer.

But it was difficult for the NAACP to stay focused on voting rights with so many other pressing legal issues involving criminal justice and the Black community.

The failure of federal antilynching legislation meant the impunity of White mob violence would continue, mocking each attempt by Blacks to gain full citizenship. As Grimke stated, despite the words of the Constitution, Blacks were murdered. The NAACP had failed to pressure Congress into passing the Dyer antilynching bill, designed to protect Blacks from mob violence. But they seemed to have a friend in the White House, friendlier in contrast than the segregationist Woodrow Wilson.

THE NAACP DEFENDS THE RIGHT OF SELF-DEFENSE

Warren G. Harding was the first president to give a speech in the South about voting rights and lynching. In Birmingham, Alabama, shoring up support for Republicans, President Harding's speech discouraged the aspirations of Blacks as much as it reproached White mob violence. He told the segregated audience of over thirty thousand:

Let the Black man vote when he is fit to vote, prohibit the white man voting when he is unfit to vote. . . . Especially I would appeal to the self-respect of the colored race. I would inculcate in it the wish to improve itself as a distinct race, with a heredity, a set of traditions, an array of aspirations all its own. Out of such racial ambitions and pride will come natural segregations, without narrowing any rights. . . . [A] Black man cannot be a white man, and that he does not need and should not aspire to be much like a white man as possible in order to accomplish the best that is possible for him. He should seek to be, and he should be encouraged to be, the best possible black man, and not the best possible imitation of a white man.[20]

The Whites in the crowd fell silent, while Blacks cheered. Harding had become the first sitting president of the United States to publicly discuss race relations. It was symbolic. But little in terms of racial progress followed his speech.

Fighting for voting was almost a luxury for NAACP lawyers, who had to choose between clients facing joblessness due to racial discrimination and housing segregation and those who could be given the death penalty for shooting a White man in self-defense. Choosing where to send their small staff of attorneys was always difficult. With limited resources and a dire need for attorneys, priorities became life or death. But the organization had to confront mob violence head on.

It was called the racial case of the century. Few could have guessed there would be many other such sensationalized race cases to follow. But the facts of this one grabbed the organization's attention because it was in the North and involved a Black man on trial for defending his home against a mob. With this case, if the NAACP was successful, there could be a precedent for Black self-defense. The quivering Black man with head bowed in subservience had always been more of a White popular dream than reality. The fear of Black self-defense was at the core of lynching. Self-defense was the first right taken with the advent of chattel slavery. To appease Whites' fear of an uprising, Blacks feigned docility. Pretending to be docile was a survival mechanism, not a personality trait of African Americans. When Blacks had fought back, as in Elaine, they were annihilated to send a message that they had no right of self-defense.

Then, in 1925, the NAACP was asked to represent Ossian Sweet, a Black doctor, in Detroit, who had killed a White man in an act of self-defense and lived to hire an attorney. Sweet had been accused of murder in the first degree. In taking the Ossian Sweet case, the NAACP could fight oppression faced by Blacks in searching for housing and facing the criminal justice system. Dr. Ossian Sweet had moved into an all-White neighborhood in Detroit, Michigan. Soon a mob of angry Whites had gathered, determined to drive the Sweet family out of the community.[21] Dr. Sweet was the White supremacist's greatest fear: an educated Black man who was his social, intellectual, and economic superior. Sweet was raised in Barstow, Florida. He had graduated from Wilberforce College in Ohio and Howard University Medical School.

After doing a year of postgraduate work in Vienna and Paris, Sweet returned to Detroit and in 1925 moved with his family into a Detroit neighborhood with covenants restricting home ownership to Whites only.[22] Other Black families had been driven out of Detroit's White neighborhoods prior to the arrival of the Sweets. The White home owner had sold his house to Sweet without alerting the neighbors, in violation of their restrictive covenant, which was no longer enforceable in court because of the decision in *Buchanan v. Warley* (1917).[23] Angry Whites formed the Waterworks Park Improvement Association. The mob would terrorize the Sweet family into leaving the neighborhood.

On September 9, 1925, a mob of Whites gathered around his home at 2905 Garland, a previously all-White community in Detroit. Previously the Fletchers, a Black family, had been chased out of their newly purchased home by a White mob of over four thousand. They began throwing rocks and screaming profanities. Sweet and his brothers got their guns. Shots were fired. Six of the eleven people inside the Sweet home fired weapons. Two people in the mob were struck. Leon Breiner, a White former coal miner who lived half a block from the Sweets, was killed. The police stormed Sweet's house and arrested all eleven Blacks inside, including Gladys Sweet.

Judge Frank Murphy, thirty-five and anxious to prove the justice system was color-blind, tried the case. NAACP lawyer James Weldon Johnson assisted in Sweet's defense. However, Clarence Darrow, the most famous trial attorney in America, known for defending criminal cases and the *Scopes* monkey case, represented the Sweets at trial. The murder trial began on October 30, with an all-White jury, in a packed courthouse. The prosecutor, Lester Moll, made clear in his opening argument that this case was not about racial prejudice, and that the gunfire from the Sweet home was unprovoked. Darrow opened by describing the fear any Black person would feel when faced with a lynch mob. Eleven defendants, including Ossian Sweet, his brother Otis, and Ossian's wife, Gladys, were charged with homicide in Breiner's death. The case drew national attention. Once again, as was the fear in the Springfield Riot of 1908 and the sporadic lynchings of Blacks in Indiana and Minnesota, the race-based mob violence of the South was being carried up North. The first criminal trial lasted seven weeks and ended in a mistrial because the jury could not decide.

The second Sweet trial began in April 1926. At the second trial, only Henry Sweet was charged with the murder of Breiner. Sweet readily admitted to firing into the lynch mob as it approached the house. If he had been a White home owner, self-defense would have been accepted. Darrow argued, defending the rights of Sweet to protect his family and home from a murderous mob, as any White man would have done. The second all-White jury returned a verdict of not guilty by reason of self-defense. Sweet was free. The NAACP, working with Darrow, gained the freedom of Ossian Sweet. It was the NAACP's triumph of the year.

But the lawyers knew this was an anomaly. This was the North, and the state court judge, though elected, chose to follow the law. In the South, elected officials were intent on appeasing the racial prejudices of the voters even if they did not personally have them. The vote was the only option for changing judges, prosecutors, and sheriffs. Yet, Blacks could not vote in most political primaries below the Mason-Dixon Line.

THE NAACP AND WHITE-ONLY PRIMARIES

The strategy of litigation, legislation, and protest was working. But despite the NAACP's victory at the US Supreme Court in 1915 in Guinn v. United States[24] using its three-pronged attack, the Plessy segregation laws and the Constitution still gave the power to the states to decide qualifications to vote. In state courts, judges elected by the very method Black voters were challenging decided if the qualifications were unfair. Black voters were left struggling to have any role in their political fate. Without the vote, they had no control over the election of the deputies who harassed them, the racist "Black Code" criminal laws used to arrest them, or the judges who illegally sentenced them to hard labor in prisons under a convict-lease system. The Whites who denied their voting rights knew the Black vote could change the outcome of an election even if they did not always have enough votes to elect a candidate.

The Plessy ruling segregated all social interaction, but not political participation.[25] White-only primaries meant that African Americans could be excluded from voting as Democrats, and the Democratic Party held the power in the South. Republicans began to turn their allegiance to the Democratic Party after the Civil War.

In the 1920s the NAACP participated in four voting rights cases challenging White-only primaries: the Virginia case of West v. Bliley,[26] Arkansas's Robinson v. Holman;[27] and in Texas Nixon v. Herndon.[28] The Supreme Court Agreed to hear the appeal of Nixon v. Herndon.[29] Although Alabama and Mississippi were notorious for their methods of disenfranchising Blacks, it was Texas that became the focus of voting rights litigation.

Texas had been the battleground of voting rights combat for decades because it was the home of a politically aware Black middle class and entrenched White supremacists. These White and Black Texans bore an independent fighting spirit that collided after World War I, with the return of Black soldiers triggering a rise in the Ku Klux Klan to put those courageous Black men back in their place. Instead of cowering in fear, Blacks in Texas turned to the NAACP. By 1918 NAACP offices had been opened in Houston, Beaumont, El Paso, Fort Worth, and San Antonio, with as many as twenty-five thousand members.[30]

In retaliation, the Texas legislature passed a law excluding Blacks from the Democratic primary: "[I]n no event shall a negro be eligible to participate in a Democratic primary election held in the State of Texas and should a negro vote in a Democratic primary election such ballot shall be void and election officials are herein directed to throw out such ballot and not count the same."[31].

On July 26, 1924, in El Paso, Texas, Dr. Lawrence A. Nixon was turned away by White judges of elections, who refused to allow him to vote in the primary election. Dr. Lane, a Black medical doctor, was a member of the El Paso chapter of the NAACP. After being turned away, he wrote to the New York office. The arrogance of the law stripping voting rights from all Blacks in Texas, and the collaboration between the NAACP membership and New York office, produced a force with the strategy, expertise, financial backing, and esprit de corps needed to attack White-only primaries with enough force to possibly prevail in the Supreme Court.

The NAACP represented Dr. Nixon in his lawsuit, brought under the Fourteenth and Fifteenth Amendments. Attorneys Moorfield Storey, Arthur Spingarn, and Louis Marshall worked with local Texas activists. The federal trial court judge dismissed the suit on grounds that political matters were not within the jurisdiction of the court. This issue of the court's involvement in politics would not be resolved for several decades. Avoiding political matters was the stance of the Supreme Court. However, the issue regarding White-only primaries and the explicit exclusion of Black voters was accepted for review by the US Supreme Court. The NAACP's case was solid, but heavy reliance on the Supreme Court's interpretation of justice in voting rights cases was not realistic.

Black communities around the country awaited the court's decision, handed down in 1927, with guarded optimism. Any optimism about the court's likely actions was exceptional, given its past supremacist-led decisions. But in *Nixon v. Herndon* Justice Oliver Wendell Holmes wrote: "States may do a good deal of classifying that it is difficult to believe rational, but there are limits, and it is too clear for extended argument that color cannot be made the basis of a statutory classification." It was a victory for all Black voters.

Yet each victorious step had its price. The Klan and other terrorists lynched seventeen Blacks in 1925. Twenty-three Blacks were lynched in 1926. Bertha, Demon, and Clarence Lowman were lynched in 1926 by a mob that included law enforcement officers. That was the year the Senate once again refused to pass the Dyer antilynching bill, which had been reintroduced. Sixteen more Blacks were lynched in 1927, the year of the Supreme Court victory in the *Nixon v. Herndon* case. With each step forward toward Black self-determination, White supremacists met the encroachment on their power with unspeakable violence and unethical manipulations of the legal system.

Despite the ruling that a law denying Blacks the right to vote in the Democratic primary was unconstitutional, Texas remained determined to exclude Blacks from the political process. Less than five years later, in the face of threats to his life and business, Dr. Nixon sued Texas again. In *Nixon v. Condon*, in 1932, the Supreme Court had to rule in another Texas voting case.[32] This time the Texas legislature had enacted article 3107, passed in an attempt to get around the court's ruling in *Nixon v. Herndon*.[33]

This law gave every political party in the state, through its state executive committee, the power to prescribe the qualifications of its own members. Since the Democratic Party was the only party with power to elect a candidate, this meant the party could decide that Blacks were not qualified to be members. When the executive committee adopted a resolution that only White Democrats could participate in the primary elections, Dr. Nixon sued the Texas Democratic primary election judges.

Dr. Nixon lost at his federal court trial as well as at the court of appeals level. Those courts held that Nixon had never tried to register and dismissed his case. But Nixon did not give up. He appealed to the US Supreme Court, which agreed to review the case and found that the Texas legislature controlled the executive committees, which constituted the state involvement needed to trigger the Fourteenth Amendment. Justice Benjamin Cardozo wrote that "[d]elegates of the State's power have discharged their official functions in such a way as to discriminate invidiously between white citizens and black."[34] The court ruled that Dr. Nixon's voting rights had been violated.

In 1929 the NAACP's three primary goals were to achieve voting rights, desegregation, and Black employment. After the death of longtime NAACP advocate Louis Marshall, a wealthy White attorney who had worked at the side of Moorfield Storey in five Supreme Court cases, Herbert Lehman, former lieutenant governor of New York, joined the NAACP board of directors. Felix Frankfurter joined the NAACP legal committee. Frankfurter, an immigrant from Austria, grew up impoverished on Manhattan's Lower East Side but became a Harvard Law School professor, and in 1938 he would become a justice of the US Supreme Court.

With each loss in court, the White supremacists in the Texas legislature would create a new law to disenfranchise Blacks. Texas refused to allow Blacks to vote in Democratic primaries. Since Democrats were the majority party and defeated Republicans in the general election, exclusion from the Democratic Party meant exclusion from any real political participation. In 1935 Albert Townsend, the White clerk of Harris County, Texas, refused to give R. R. Grovey, a Black man, a ballot for a Democratic Party primary election. The Democratic leadership had passed a resolution on May 24, 1932, restricting eligibility for membership in the Democratic Party in Texas to White citizens. Grovey sued. The NAACP thought the past cases would lead to another victory in court.

The Supreme Court, led by Justice Owen Roberts, voted unanimously against Grovey in *Grovey v. Townsend*.[35] The court ruled that the Democratic Party had not violated his Fourteenth and Fifteenth Amendment rights when they excluded him, and all other Black voters, from the polls to vote on the Democratic ticket. Justice Roberts reasoned that voting as a Democrat in a political primary was not covered under the Fifteenth

Amendment or considered state action under the Fourteenth Amendment. The court said neither *Nixon v. Herndon* nor *Nixon v. Condon* applied to voting in a primary election.[36] Whites could legally restrict Blacks from voting in Democratic primaries.

General elections were under the authority of the government. However, Democratic primaries were considered private and beyond the reach of congressional control. But without access to the primary, Black voters could not control the candidates in the general election. Once again, they were vulnerable to anti-Black/pro-White supremacy politicians.

THE NAACP AND SUPREME COURT NOMINEES

In 1930 the NAACP was faced with the nomination of a known White supremacist to the US Supreme Court. John J. Parker, a North Carolina judge, was nominated by President Herbert Hoover. Parker opposed voting rights for Blacks and supported amending the North Carolina constitution to add a poll tax and literacy tests, as well as reinstating the grandfather clause, which had been struck down by the Supreme Court in *Guinn*.

On March 21, 1930, President Herbert Hoover nominated Judge Parker. The NAACP rallied its entire arsenal to oppose his confirmation. The organization had learned from the antilynching campaign how to oppose passage of discriminatory laws as vigorously as fighting for legislative protections. The NAACP's Washington Bureau investigated Parker, finding that he was a vocal segregationist, and decided to block his ascent to the highest court.

They found that in 1920 Parker had delivered a speech on the "Negro question" to his alma mater in which he had said, "The participation of the Negro in the political life of the South is harmful to him and to the community, and is the fruitful source of the racial prejudice which works to his injury. As a class he has learned this lesson. He no longer desires to participate in politics."[37] Judge Parker had gone on to say "the participation of the Negro in politics is a source of evil and danger to both races and is not desired by the wise men in either race or by the Republican party of North Carolina."[38]

President Hoover refused to withdraw Parker's nomination. However, Walter White presented the past speeches of Parker as proof of his animosity toward Black Americans and delineated Parker's unsuitability to members of the Senate Judiciary Committee. The NAACP brought to bear the full onslaught of political pressure on President Hoover and Congress with letters, visits, and calls while supporting a steady field of NAACP protesters with signs; they finally moved the Senate to defeat Parker's confirmation 41–39. Critics have called this political victory a clumsy success. However, it was a remarkable accomplishment for any organization to be successful in both the Supreme Court and Congress. This strategy, inspired by NAACP president Joel Spingarn, would become a trademark of the NAACP.

THE NEXT STEPS: BEING PROACTIVE

Taking on cases and issues in a reactive manner was no longer acceptable to the NAACP. It needed a proactive legal plan to overturn *Plessy* and meet its goal of unencumbered access to the polls for all eligible African Americans. Many great lawyers had worked with the NAACP. However, a legal defense fund was needed to raise money to employ the first full-time NAACP legal counsel.

As long as the *Plessy v. Ferguson*[39] decision allowed "separate but equal" to be the law of the land, the rights of Black citizens would be ignored. Racial segregation had given most Whites a badge of superiority. With that badge came a reckless disregard for the rights of African Americans and even a license to brutalize those Blacks who stood up for their constitutional and human rights.

In 1935, when the Supreme Court ruled against Grovey, more than eighteen Black men, women, and children became victims of heinous murder by lynch mobs: burned to death, hanged, castrated, shot multiple times, gutted, and dragged to their deaths. Despite the danger, Blacks sought out NAACP attorneys to represent them in a fight to vote in which, given the decision in *Grovey*, there was little certainty of victory. In 1935 the NAACP decided to plan its litigation. The board of directors voted to chart out the major issues facing African Americans.

To combat any political progress Blacks may have gained, Oklahoma passed laws to strip Blacks of their right to vote. The state enacted a law requiring an application for voter registration to be submitted only between the dates April 30, 1916, and May 11, 1916. If an eligible voter failed to register during this period, he or she would be precluded from ever voting. (In case of illness or absence from the state, an eligible voter could register between May 10, 1916, and June 30, 1916, but once again, if the voter missed the deadline, he or she could not ever vote in Oklahoma.)

In 1934 a Black man named I. W. Lane tried to register to vote in Wagoner County, Oklahoma. He was within the time period. But the election officials threatened his life and refused to allow him to register. The county registrar, on the orders of his superiors, refused to "register any colored person." Lane brought a legal action for $5,000 in damages in federal court under section 1979 of the Civil Rights Act of 1871, which states:

Every person who, under color of any statute . . . of any State or Territory, subject, or causes to be subjected, any citizen of the United States . . . within the jurisdiction thereof to the deprivation of any rights, privileges, or immunities secured by the Constitution and laws, shall be liable to the party injured in an action at law.

Section 1979, as enacted by Congress, was designed to facilitate enforcement of the Fifteenth Amendment.

At trial, Lane's NAACP attorney, James Nabrit, argued that a conspiracy existed among the county, precinct registrars, and the county election boards to prevent "the registration of negro voters solely on account of their race, color and previous condition of servitude."

The state argued that there was no discrimination since the law did not just prohibit Blacks from voting; it prohibited anyone who had neither voted in 1914 nor registered in 1916. Of course, the law had been created in response to the Supreme Court's ruling striking down Oklahoma's grandfather clause in *Guinn and Beal v. United States*.[40]

James Nabrit was a Black attorney practicing in Houston. He would later move to Washington, D.C., to teach law at Howard University Law School and become president of the college. Nabrit was a graduate of Morehouse College in Atlanta and Northwestern Law School in Chicago. To expand their reach, the New York office of the NAACP teamed up with local attorneys such as Nabrit. When Dr. Lane's case went to trial, the judge found that Lane could not substantiate that he had ever attempted to register. It was his word against that of the election officials who had refused to allow him to register. The court of appeals supported the decision of the trial court.

Finally, in 1939, the US Supreme Court ruled against Oklahoma in *Lane v. Wilson*.[41] Justice Felix Frankfurter, who had resigned from the legal committee of the NAACP to ascend to the Supreme Court, chastised Oklahoma's obvious racial bias: "The [Fifteenth] Amendment nullifies sophisticated as well as simple-minded modes of discrimination."[42]

Yet the law was a symbol of freedom that did not exist in reality for most Black voters, especially in the South. In 1940 Elbert Williams was murdered in Brownsville, Tennessee, because he was "caught" motivating Blacks to register to vote. Elbert Williams was a founding member of the Brownsville branch of the NAACP. On June 20, he was arrested for planning an NAACP meeting. His body, with two bullet wounds, was dragged from the river three days later. No one was charged with the crime.

Blacks were kept away from the polls by intimidation or by law, and usually both. Southern states, especially Texas, fought to maintain White-only political primaries. Under law, if political parties were considered private clubs, then they could not be racially restricted under *Plessy v. Ferguson.*

Tired of always playing defense, the NAACP decided it was time to take an "offensive approach." Attorney Charles Hamilton Houston gained a US Supreme Court victory in *Baltimore City*.[43] Donald Gaines Murray was admitted into the segregated University of Maryland Law School. It was a sweet victory for young NAACP attorney Thurgood Marshall, who was working under the tutelage of Houston. In 1930 Marshall had been denied admission to Maryland's Law School because of his race and had attended Howard Law School instead.

It was time for the NAACP to take back lost ground. Self-determination meant being free to travel. Interstate transportation fell under the power of Congress, based on the commerce clause of the US Constitution (article 1, section 8). Back in the 1880s, the Supreme Court had determined that states could not segregate passengers when they were traveling between states. (The *Plessy* segregation law stemmed from intrastate train transportation and had been devised by a Louisiana legislature that knew it was limited to transportation within its borders.) However, the supremacists' tradition of segregation had crept back into interstate transportation.

The NAACP began to take cases challenging the segregation of Black passengers on interstate transportation to defend the rights of Black voters and the Blacks who traveled to the South to assist them. Trains and buses were racially segregated. A bus traveling from the North to the South would pull over at the Mason-Dixon Line and demand that all people of color move to the rear. Blacks and Whites could not occupy the same seats.

Even African American US representative Arthur W. Mitchell was not immune to "Jim Crow" segregation. In *Mitchell v. United States*,[44] decided in 1941, the NAACP was once again arguing before the Supreme Court. This case involved racial segregation on interstate trains, an issue that had been fought and won previously but was back again.

The Interstate Commerce Act of 1887 had prohibited such discrimination despite the custom of states that required Blacks to move to the back as trains arrived at the Mason-Dixon Line en route to southern destinations. Representative Mitchell, a resident of Chicago and the first Black Democrat elected to the US House of Representatives, brought legal action after being forced into a segregated interstate rail car. On April 20, 1937, Mitchell left Chicago on the Illinois Central Railroad. He requested a sleeping car, but none was available. Shortly after leaving Memphis and crossing the Mississippi River into Arkansas, the car became filled to capacity with White passengers.

The conductor, in accordance with custom, forced Mitchell, under threat of arrest, to move into the car reserved for Blacks. "This was in purported compliance with an Arkansas statute requiring segregation of colored from white persons by the use of cars or partitioned sections providing 'equal, but separate and sufficient accommodations' for both races." The car for Whites was air-conditioned and had hot and cold running water and separate flushable toilets for men and women. Mitchell said the car for Blacks was filthy and foul smelling, was not air-conditioned, and only the toilet in the women's section was equipped for flushing; there were no wash basins, soap, towels, or running water. Mitchell filed a legal complaint charging that the segregated cars violated federal law, but it was dismissed.

Mitchell appealed to the US Supreme Court. Chief Justice Charles Evans Hughes not only stated that Mitchell could bring such an action, he also wrote:

> We have repeatedly said that it is apparent from the legislative history of the [Interstate Commerce] Act that not only was the evil of discrimination the principal thing aimed at, but that there is no basis for the contention that Congress intended to exempt any discriminatory action or practice of interstate carriers affecting interstate commerce which it had authority to reach.

This ruling also meant that trains could not outfit cars with a partition separating the White and Black passengers, which had been attempted on trains traveling from North to South. Without political power, people of color could not repeal such laws or enact others.

Discrimination against Asian, Latino, and Native Americans was also rampant. Since the thought of racial equality was unfathomable for some Whites in the South and the North, the NAACP could expect little cooperation from Congress.

With an eye toward appearing before the Supreme Court in 1942, the NAACP changed its legal strategy on voting rights, seeking out cases that could lead to the end of the White-only primary, poll taxes, and general obstacles to voting such as literacy tests. Like proposed antilynching laws, the Geyer anti-poll tax bill passed the House of Representatives but was defeated by filibuster in the Senate, in 1942. States in the South used poll taxes to restrict Black voters. Poll taxes had to be paid before a registered voter could vote at the polls. This was a financial burden on poor people of all races, but these taxes were usually excused for poor Whites and were only used to prevent poor Blacks from voting. Those Black farmers, sharecroppers, mechanics, or domestics who could afford to pay their poll taxes planned to exercise their right to vote. That meant trouble, from losing employment to harassment or even death by lynching. Although poll tax laws did not indicate a specific race, the rolls were divided by race, allowing government officials to keep record of the Black voters or "troublemakers."

It took nearly ten years for the Supreme Court to return to the voting rights issue. The NAACP was once again triumphant in 1944, in *Smith v. Allwright*,[45] which originated in Harris County, Texas.[46] Charles Hamilton Houston, the first official legal counsel of the NAACP, led his team from New York City. In Texas, NAACP attorney Thurgood Marshall, a Howard Law School graduate, studied under and was mentored by Charles Houston. William Henry Hastie, who was also a student under Houston, would later become the first Black federal judge.

As dean of Howard Law School, Charles Houston taught students in every aspect of constitutional law. As chair of the NAACP Legal Committee, he trained his civil rights attorneys to remain calm under pressure, ignore the racism inside and outside of the courtroom, and establish the trial record for an appeal to the US Supreme Court. Thurgood Marshall and William Hastie had learned their lessons well.

Marshall and Hastie represented Lonnie Smith, a Black dentist who had been denied a ballot to vote in the Democratic Party primary by the judge of election, S. E. Allwright. He sued. As in prior cases, the trial court and appeals court sided against Smith. The NAACP attorneys had now gained the skills to win before the nation's highest court. In 1944 *Smith v. Allwright* was decided in favor of Lonnie Smith.[47] The Supreme Court ruled that any Democratic primaries that were restricted to only White citizens violated the Fourteenth and Fifteenth Amendments of Black voters. The Supreme Court overturned its ruling in *Grovey*. Blacks could vote in the Democratic Party primary and the general election.

In *Smith v. Allwright* the NAACP helped the court to understand the connection between voting access in a primary election and voting in a general election. Refusing Blacks a Democratic primary ballot meant a voter had next to no say in selecting the candidates presented in the general election. At that time, Democratic candidates in the general election were guaranteed a victory over Republican candidates because the Democrats far outnumbered Republicans. With the NAACP victory in *Smith*, the primary and general elections became subject to congressional authority.

Justice Owen Roberts dissented. Roberts had stood up for the Japanese interned during World War II. But he could not see the intent or the effect of the exclusion of Blacks from the Democratic Party and its primaries. With the changing composition of the Supreme Court, the NAACP hoped the acceptance of total White supremacy was changing as well. Franklin D. Roosevelt was now president. More Republicans and Democrats became Dixiecrats in response to Roosevelt's New Deal economic reforms and his stance as a moderate on race. Eleanor Roosevelt joined the NAACP board.

The NAACP took cases involving discrimination in courts martial involving Black soldiers during World War II. Every American was expected to focus on the war effort and place individual rights aside, including African Americans. But after the war A. Philip Randolph and other civil rights leaders met with President Harry Truman about segregation in the armed forces, which led to a desegregated military on July 26, 1948, by Executive Order. The Supreme Court would not address voting rights again for the next ten years. But Blacks could not wait for the court, as their expectation of equality was quickly diminished and lynching met every step of progress.

The primary was invented to disenfranchise Black voters.[48] Despite the court's ruling in *Smith v. Allwright*, Blacks were prevented from voting in Alabama, Georgia, Florida, Mississippi, and South Carolina. The tactic employed by South Carolina's legislature was to repeal all election laws and call the Democratic Party a private club as opposed to a state-run entity. South Carolina's Democratic Convention had first met to disenfranchise Blacks in 1895. It had passed laws creating primaries and then limited access to those primaries to White voters only.

Now, although *Smith v. Allwright* made it illegal for any government to exclude Blacks from voting, South Carolina excluded Blacks from the primary elections by stating that primaries were private meetings. Under *Plessy*, a private meeting or social setting could be segregated by race.

The NAACP brought a case in South Carolina that would successfully challenge the all-White Democratic primary. Decided in 1947, *Elmore v. Rice* centered on George A. Elmore, the professional photographer turned civil rights activist.[49] In South Carolina, Democrats controlled every office in the local, state, and federal governments. As a self-styled private club, the Democratic Party still chose all federal, state and other officers.

On August 13, 1946, Elmore was turned away from the Democratic primary in Richland County, South Carolina. He was qualified to vote, but he was not allowed to vote despite the ruling in the *Grovey* case. Born in Holly Hill, South Carolina, in 1905, George Elmore put his life on the line by challenging the exclusion of Blacks from the Democratic Party primary election. Despite threats from the Ku Klux Klan, he filed a lawsuit in federal court. Excluded from the Democratic Party, South Carolina African American leaders formed their own Progressive Democratic Party and challenged the state's White-only primary.[50]

The local NAACP wanted to enforce the *Smith v. Allwright* decision, which had struck down the White-only primary. The national NAACP legal team, led by Thurgood Marshall, with the young maverick Robert L. Carter and Harold R. Boulware, local chief counsel for the South Carolina branch of the NAACP, at his side, argued that exclusion from the primary meant exclusion from the general election.

The court agreed that excluding voters in the general election was unconstitutional. In *Elmore v. Rice* the court reviewed the eighty-year-long path to this case,[51] one covered with obstacles, violence, and death and based on a fear of placing political power in the hands of the formerly enslaved. District Judge J. Waties Waring's ruling opened the primary to all South Carolinians. The state ignored the ruling, and in 1948 Judge Waring issued an injunction mandating that the state Democratic Party open its membership rolls and allow all parties, without regard to "race, color, creed, or condition," to participate in the August primary.

The state's Democratic Party Executive Committee required voters to take an oath to support the social, religious, and educational separation of the races. Judge Waring's court rejected the oath, and his decision was affirmed by the US Court of Appeals for the Fourth Circuit. The US Supreme Court refused to review the case. On July 23, 1948, Democratic Party chair W. P. Baskin advised county chairs to enroll all constitutionally qualified electors. This case did not go the Supreme Court because the trial court and the court of appeals agreed with the NAACP.

In his ruling on the case, Judge Waring wrote:

> The constitutional amendments following the bloody conflict of the 1860s came upon and to a people totally unprepared for the change in the status and relationship of the white and black races. The potential voters in the former slave holding states were about doubled by the new federal laws and every effort was made to prevent a deluge of untrained, unlettered, and unprepared citizens from taking over control of the state government. That these efforts and the methods adopted were both born of necessity may be argued with show of reason. But many years and several generations have passed since the time such necessity arose and existed.[52]

Judge Waring ruled that the Democratic Party of South Carolina could no longer exclude Black voters: "It's time for South Carolina to join the Union. It is time to fall in step with the other states and to adopt the American way of conducting elections."[53] The judge immediately experienced violent repercussions. He required twenty-four-hour security, crosses were burned in his yard, and rocks were thrown through his windows. But in 1948 more than thirty thousand elated Blacks in South Carolina registered to vote in the Democratic primary.[54]

With the *Elmore* decision, another decisive victory for Black voters in hand, the NAACP turned to defending those rights won on paper. With every voting victory, segregationists enacted elaborate voting laws to take the place of the laws that had been defeated. Such laws did not refer to the race of the voter, but their discriminatory effect and intent remained the same. Election officials were given the power to decide who met the eligibility requirements. Poll taxes and literacy tests were used to protect White political supremacy.

Race riots continued to torment Black communities. No one was safe. There was mob violence in Detroit in 1942. In 1943 White mobs attacked Blacks in Harlem, New York; Mobile, Alabama; Columbia, Tennessee; St. Louis, Missouri; Beaumont, Texas; Philadelphia, Pennsylvania; Indianapolis, Indiana; Baltimore, Maryland; and Washington, D.C. In 1946, the year of the *Elmore* success in the trial court and again after the victory in the appeal the next year, White mobs returned to attack Blacks in Detroit, Michigan, Philadelphia, and Columbia, as well as Athens, Alabama.

As World War II was waged overseas, African Americans had been at war in their homeland. Most Blacks in the South still could not vote for any of the elected officials who would send them into battle. With victories against the White-only primary under its belt, the NAACP turned its sights on poll taxes.

In July 1905, W. E. B. DuBois and William Monroe Trotter convened a conference of Black leaders to renounce Booker T. Washington's accommodationism. They met at Niagara Falls in Ontario, Canada, because hotels on the American side of the falls barred Blacks. Photograph shows a group of founding members: (l. to r.) front row, Henry L. Baily, Clement G. Morgan, W. H. H. Hart, and B. S. Smith; middle row, Frederick L. McGhee, Norris Bumstead Herndon, J. Max Barber, W. E. B. DuBois, and Robert Bonner; back row, H. A. Thompson, Alonzo F. Herndon, John Hope, and an unidentified man, possibly James R. L. Diggs. *Source:* W.E.B. DuBois Library, Special Collections & University Archives, UMass Amherst.

W. E. B. DuBois (1868–1963), an eminent scholar-activist, cofounded the Niagara Movement and the NAACP and emerged as a leader in the Pan-African Movement. DuBois left academia in 1910 to become the NAACP's director of publicity and research, its only black officer at that time. Photo by Cornelius Marion Battey. *Source:* Library of Congress, Prints & Photographs Division, Visual Materials from the NAACP Records [LC-DIG-ppmsca-38818].

Mary White Ovington (1865–1951), a social worker and freelance writer, was a principal NAACP founder and officer for almost forty years. Photo by Charles James Damph. *Source:* Library of Congress, Prints & Photographs Division, Visual Materials from the NAACP Records [LC-DIG-ppmsca-23826].

Moorfield Storey (1845–1929), a prominent constitutional lawyer and past president of the American Bar Association, became the NAACP's first president (1910–1929). Storey prosecuted the NAACP's early Supreme Court victories. *Source:* Library of Congress, Prints & Photographs Division, Visual Materials from the NAACP Records [LC-DIG-ppmsca-23830].

James Weldon Johnson (1871–1938) began his association with the NAACP in 1916. As field secretary, Johnson organized new NAACP branches across the South. His hiring as secretary in 1920 signaled the rise of Black leadership in the NAACP. *Source:* Library of Congress, Prints & Photographs Division, Visual Materials from the NAACP Records [LC-USZ62-42992].

On July 1, 1917, two White policemen were killed in East St. Louis, Illinois, in an altercation caused when marauders attacked Black homes. The incident sparked a race riot on July 2, which ended with forty-eight killed, hundreds injured, and thousands of Blacks fleeing the city when their homes were burned. On July 28, the NAACP protested with a silent march of 10,000 Black men, women, and children down New York's Fifth Avenue. *Source:* Photo by Underwood & Underwood. Library of Congress, Prints & Photographs Division, Visual Materials from the NAACP Records [LC-DIG-ds-00894].

William English Walling (1877–
1936), a prominent socialist and
journalist, was descended from
wealthy Kentucky slaveholders. He
was a founder of the Intercollegiate
Socialist Society, the Women's
Trade Union League, the Social
Democratic League, and the NAACP.
Source: Library of Congress, Prints
& Photographs Division, Visual
Materials from the NAACP Records
[LC-DIG-ppmsca-23824].

Henry Moskowitz (1879–1936), a
Romanian Jewish émigré, attended
the University Settlement's boys'
club as a youth. There he met fellow
socialist William English Walling,
with whom he traveled to Eastern
Europe in 1905 to study social and
economic conditions. Moskowitz's
involvement in the NAACP was
indicative of early Jewish support.
Source: Library of Congress, Prints
& Photographs Division, Visual
Materials from the NAACP Records
[LC-DIG-ppmsca-23827].

Charles Hamilton Houston (1895–1950) was the chief strategist of the NAACP's legal campaign that culminated in the *Brown v. Board of Education* decision. In 1935 the NAACP hired Houston as its first salaried Special Counsel and created the Legal Department under his supervision. *Source:* Library of Congress, Prints & Photographs Division, Visual Materials from the NAACP Records [LC-USZ62-131020].

A sign on the side of a school bus that reads "NAACP Voter Registration Drive." *Source:* Library of Congress, Prints & Photographs Division, Visual Materials from the NAACP Records [LC-USZ62-126801].

NAACP officials inspect a "tent city" of African Americans who were driven from their homes after registering to vote in Fayette County, Tennessee (circa 1960). *Source:* Library of Congress, Prints & Photographs Division, Visual Materials from the NAACP Records [LC-USZ62-131066].

NAACP supporters marching with "Vote for Freedom" signs in Selma, Alabama (circa 1965). *Source:* Library of Congress, Prints & Photographs Division, Visual Materials from the NAACP Records [LC-USZ62-123478].

5

~

Poll Taxes and Literacy Tests

We have come over a way that with tears has been watered,
We have come, treading our path through the blood of the slaughtered.

—James Weldon Johnson, "Lift Every Voice and Sing" (1899)

Civil rights was deadly work. On the night of December 25, 1951, NAACP leaders Harry and Harriette Moore became martyrs for the cause. Attacked while asleep in their beds, the couple soon died of their wounds, suffered from a handmade bomb placed beneath their house by White segregationists who sought to silence them. The true number of lives lost in the struggle to gain equal rights for Black Americans in the twentieth century may never be known.

But the price these martyrs paid would benefit Americans. In the 1950s the number of those being lynched decreased. However, the murder of civil rights activists never stopped. Those Whites who desperately clung to political supremacy killed the young, the elderly, women and men, Black and White. Yet Blacks voted, defiantly.

AFTER WORLD WAR II

After the victory in *Smith v. Allwright* in 1944, activists were called to duty across the South.[1] Their mission was the registration of Black citizens to vote. The law meant nothing if the right to vote was still only available to Whites and the Democratic Party was still seen as an exclusive private club for Whites only. The NAACP was determined to use the victory in

Elmore v. Rice (1947) in South Carolina as a battering ram for an incursion into the Deep South: Alabama, Mississippi, Louisiana, Florida, and Texas. The decade leading up to the passage of more federal laws to protect the rights of African Americans was tumultuous and violent. Black men and women returned from World War II with a renewed pride. Rural Black farmers had traveled to Europe in the military. Black women moved from small southern towns where they worked as domestics to northern cities and attended college. The sight of Black Americans in military uniforms ignited the kind of mob violence last seen during the Red Summer of 1919, after World War I.[2]

The NAACP announced that the southern Black vote had doubled between 1948 and 1952. An increase in lynching and mob violence met the Black community's new sense of pride and civic expectation. As the last great migration of Blacks from the South filled major cities, NAACP membership rose to over 300,000. The plan to use litigation, legislation, and protest to fight segregation was working. But the segregationists' deep-seated need to maintain a system of servile Blacks and racial privilege remained. When they challenged the system too often, activists paid with their lives.

On February 28, 1951, the NAACP filed a desegregation case representing Oliver Brown and his daughter Linda. *Brown v. The Board of Education of Topeka* was consolidated with public school cases in Delaware, South Carolina, Washington, D.C., and Virginia.[3] It was expected that the NAACP attorneys would masterfully juggle a docket of cases covering criminal justice, education, military service, public accommodations, housing, and voting rights. Blacks in Alabama stood up courageously against *Plessy*-type tactics, such as when the all-White Alabama legislature passed an amendment to its constitution, proposed by state senator E. C. "Bud" Boswell, to disenfranchise more than 100,000 Black voters, leaving fewer than 3,700 eligible to vote; most of them were threatened with death if they attempted to do so.

When the Boswell amendment became law, activist E. D. Nixon, of Montgomery, Alabama, organized a voter registration drive to challenge it. The NAACP's Birmingham and Mobile branches began "Operation Suffrage" to challenge the law. In Mobile, the Voters and Veterans' League was led by George N. Leighton, a Chicago attorney. Leighton had graduated from Howard University in 1936 magna cum laude and from Harvard Law School in 1946. He filed a federal lawsuit challenging the Boswell amendment. In 1949 the Supreme Court held with the NAACP in *Davis v. Schnell*, overturning the Boswell amendment as a violation of the Fifteenth Amendment.[4]

Undeterred, in 1951 White supremacists in Alabama passed a law requiring voters to be able to read and write any section of the state constitution, as well as to be of good character and to swear that they were not part of any group or agency devoted to overthrowing the government. They were able to get around the decision in *Davis v. Schnell* by adding a provision that required a uniform voter questionnaire, allegedly making the interview process equal for all potential voters, so there was no obvious racial discrimination.

As noted in the *Columbia Law Review* in 1947: "Every device of disenfranchisement which the judiciary has destroyed, with few exceptions, has been replaced by a new scheme designed by the southern states to perpetuate the myth of 'white supremacy.'"[5] A similar sentiment could be expressed about every era of America's history since the Fifteenth Amendment was ratified. In some instances, the judiciary has assisted in the destruction of Black voting rights and the perpetration of White supremacy.

The NAACP national office brought cases to court and assisted chapters in their voting rights lawsuits across the country. Oklahoma lawmakers again attempted to undermine the voting rights of Blacks, resulting in *Hodge v. Tulsa County Election Board* (1948).[6] Local Oklahoma NAACP attorney Amos T. Hall's challenge was dismissed based on a case going back to the 1895 Supreme Court decision in *Mills v. Green*, in which the South Carolina legislature was allowed to change registration requirements to a date in the past.[7]

The NAACP knew it needed its cases to reach the US Supreme Court. Protests and lobbying for protection of constitutional rights were part of the three-prong approach, but Thurgood Marshall knew a victory in the high court meant national relief. Case-by-case litigation before state court judges elected by and representing the old Whites-only Democratic Party was a losing strategy, costing time, money, and vital effort that the organization could not afford. War is a battle of attrition. The side with the most resources usually wins. Too often the adversary was a state government with taxpayer-funded legal departments. Ironically, Black would-be voters were paying taxes to the government denying them the right to vote.

Local NAACP attorneys W. J. Durham and U. Simpson Tate brought a lawsuit in Dallas, Texas, in 1949, challenging the denial of the right to vote in two primary elections. In Harrison County, the White-only Democratic Party had changed its name to the Citizens Party of Harrison County, Texas. The Citizens Party was originally created in 1878 as part of the White-only primary takeover when federal troops were removed at the end of Reconstruction. That's how long Blacks had suffered this political oppression. Under its rules, although the county was majority Black, the Citizens Party excluded Black members, and therefore Blacks could not vote in any primary elections. At trial the Citizens Party, the only political party in the county, admitted having refused plaintiffs the right to vote in its primary elections because of their race and color, but denied that in so doing its members had acted as administrative officers of the state of Texas, because they considered themselves part of a private club. The trial court judge dismissed the lawsuit, ruling in favor of the Citizens Party, stating that Blacks could vote in the general election. The loss in *Hodge v. Tulsa* was rectified three years later. In 1951, in *Perry v. Cyphers*, a Texas appellate court found it unconstitutional when testimony revealed that only White voters could vote in elections, and Negroes are systematically excluded from voting because of their race and color.[8] A portion of the testimony of appellee, J. W. Cyphers, appears as follows:

> Q. Mr. Cyphers, I believe that you said you held the primary elections pursuant to Article 3163. A. Yes.
>
> Q. That is, of the Revised Civil Statutes of 1935 and the subsequent amendments. A. It was.
>
> Q. Now, do you have a membership roll? A. We do not.
>
> Q. Do not. I believe the only way you determine the qualification of a voter or an elector to vote in the Citizens primary is that he presents a poll tax receipt showing that he had paid his poll tax? A. It is.
>
> Q. And that he resides in the proper precinct? A. It is.
>
> Q. Is that right? A. That is right.
>
> Q. And any person, white person, who has such poll tax receipt, if presented during the proper hours, is permitted to vote? A. He is.
>
> Q. And the only qualifications to vote in the Citizens primary is that the voter is white and he holds a poll tax receipt? A. That is in accordance with a resolution passed by the mass meeting.
>
> Q. There is a mass meeting passed resolution that only white electors can vote? A. That is right.
>
> Q. And upon that resolution and the fact that he has a poll tax receipt and he is white, he is permitted to vote? A. And residence qualifications.
>
> Q. And residence qualifications. I mean all the other qualifications, pardon me. And if a Negro citizen is qualified; that is, he has all the qualifications prescribed and required by the constitution and the statutes, and he has a poll tax receipt and he presents himself in the proper precinct and he is not permitted to vote, because he is a Negro? A. He is not. No other race except the white.
>
> Q. No other race. Thank you. I believe the Executive Committee of which you are a member, you appoint or select the election judges? A. We do.
>
> Q. — to hold the primary elections? A. We do.

Q. And you prepare the ballots and distribute the ballots to the election judges? A. I do.

Q. The election judges take the same statutory oath to hold the election that the Democratic primary election officials take? A. They do.[9]

The Texas appellate court found that the Supreme Court's decision in *Smith v. Allwright* protected the right of Black voters to have a voice in primary elections. Lawyers for the Citizens Party claimed that there were not connected to the Democratic Party and therefore the *Allwright* decision did not apply to them.

The appellate court made its disagreement with this position clear:

This is uncontradicted testimony by one of the appellees, J. W. Cyphers, to the effect that he was Chairman of the Citizens Party, which was organized in 1876, and that he had voted as a lifelong Democrat in such party since 1908; that the Citizens Party has held primary elections in Harrison County, Texas, since 1908, and he had no recollection of any other political party having held a primary election for county or precinct officers during that period; that the Democratic Party held primary elections in Harrison County for the candidates who ran for district, state, and federal offices, and the County Chairman, while the Citizens Party held its primary elections for the various county and precinct offices; and that the Democratic Party nominees, along with the nominees of the Citizens Party, all appeared on the Democratic ballot at the general election held in November of every even year. He further testified that the primary elections of the Citizens Party were held in accordance with Article 3163 of the Revised Civil Statutes of Texas, Vernon's Ann. Civ. St. Art. 3163, that the Citizens Party determined the qualifications of persons entitled to vote in its primaries, and that the only qualifications for membership and voting in such party were that the prospective voter be a white person, have certain residence qualifications, and be the holder of a poll tax receipt; that the requirement that a person be white in order to vote in a Citizens Party primaries was made effective by virtue of a resolution passed at a mass meeting of the Citizens Party held each even year.

The exasperation of the appellate court is palpable:

Ours is not the province to step down into the forum and debate with open minds the issues here presented. This is a Government of laws and not of men. We are sworn to uphold and defend the Constitution of the Republic, and our oath embraces the duty and obligation to adhere to the mandates of our Courts of Last Resort as to the proper construction and interpretation to be placed upon it.[10]

Yet even such positive legal decisions by judges of goodwill and respect for the law only applied to that particular county.

NAACP ACTIVISTS

The opposing army of segregationists controlled the country. A troop of dedicated NAACP activists fought one small battle at a time. In a war, such a battle strategy does not bode well for success. Tens of thousands of counties were discriminating against the rights of Black voters. Piecemeal litigation, sporadic protests, and lukewarm legislation served few and greatly benefited the opposition.

From its inception, the NAACP created a public voice to break the silence surrounding thousands of lynchings of Black men, women, and children. The country would be told the plight of Black citizens in a democracy that went to war on behalf of the world's safety yet allowed African Americans to be slaughtered for attempting to vote. Assistance with the mission of informing the public about discrimination was the primary role of *The Crisis* magazine, the voice of the NAACP.

However, journalists like Ted Posten, Carl T. Rowan, William Huie, Zora Neale Hurston, and Hodding Carter joined the work of newspapers like the *AFRO-American*, *Philadelphia Tribune*, and *Chicago Defender* to record the growing movement in civil rights and the violence of segregationists. Even in the face of journalists recording their sinful deeds, the brutality of White racists against fellow Americans never ceased.

In Groveland, Florida, Harry Moore, the executive director of the Florida branches of the NAACP, lived in constant mortal danger. Thurgood Marshall was defending four Black men falsely accused and later convicted of raping a White woman in 1949: Charles Greenlee, Sam Shepard, Walter Irvin, and Ernest Thomas. Thomas was gunned down by a posse of one thousand when he tried to leave the state. Sixteen-year-old Greenlee was given a life sentence. Irvin and Shepard were sentenced to die in the electric chair. Despite racial tensions and threats against his life, Marshall was able to get them a second trial.

After witnessing Marshall in court, Sheriff Willis McCall had little intention of risking a possible release of the two defendants. McCall was transporting the handcuffed prisoners when, he later claimed, they tried to escape. He shot both of them and thought he had killed them. However, Irvin played dead and listened while Sheriff McCall lied about the supposed escape attempt. Later, safely in the hospital, Irvin told prosecutors that Sheriff McCall had shot them both in cold blood. However, the prosecutor refused to bring McCall to trial. Harry Moore conducted his own investigation and called for the arrest of McCall.

Harry Moore and Harriette, his wife, had established the Florida branches of the NAACP. Registering Black voters resulted in the loss of their teaching jobs. When the Groveland defendants were beaten in jail, Moore leveled charges of police brutality. He placed his life on the altar for racial justice. On Christmas night in 1951, while Harry and Harriette Moore were asleep, a bomb exploded under their Brevard County, Florida, home. Many believed the bomb was placed by McCall; others pointed at members of the KKK. It would take nearly sixty years to achieve some form of justice, when in 2006 Florida attorney general Charlie Crist revealed the identities of four men he believed had conspired to kill Harry and Harriette Moore: known segregationists Earl Brooklyn, Tilman Belvins, Joseph Cox, and Ed Spivey. All were already deceased.

The Old Guard at the NAACP was disappearing. In 1934, W. E. B. Dubois had been dismissed from the organization he had helped to create. Walter White passed away in 1955, after twenty-five years of service. Morefield Storey had died in 1929. James Weldon Johnson, the first Black leader of the NAACP, had died in a car accident in 1938. The first legal counsel, Charles Hamilton Houston, died in 1950. It is thought that Houston literally worked himself to death, expending every part of his being to overturn *Plessy v. Ferguson*'s "separate but equal" doctrine. Houston was the legal architect of the civil rights strategy. Before his death, the NAACP had embarked on his ten-year strategy to end America's segregated education by building precedents in Supreme Court cases.

In Louisiana, the home of *Plessy*, the NAACP's victory in *Smith v. Allwright* led to an increase in Black voter registration, to 130,000. The NAACP won an interstate commerce case, resulting in segregation on interstate trains, buses, and airports being banned. The NAACP filed suit against Levitt and Sons Development Corporation for failing to allow Blacks to buy homes in Levittown, New York, and Pennsylvania. Perhaps it was its achievements in voting rights and the NAACP victory in *Brown v Board of Education*, which led to the desegregation of public schools, that resulted in an all-out assault on Black communities.

Reverend George Lee was murdered on May 7, 1955. Rev. Lee was president of his NAACP chapter in Mississippi and used his church as a meeting place, where he urged parishioners to register to vote.[11] While visiting relatives in Money, Mississippi, Emmett Till, a fourteen-year-old boy from Chicago, was dragged from his grandfather's home and tortured for getting out of his place with a White woman, Carolyn Bryant, the wife of a store owner. Only after national attention was given to Till's case by the NAACP and other organizations did an investigation reveal the horrific torment the boy suffered before his body was thrown into the Tallahatchie River. Roy Bryant and his half brother J. W. Milam were acquitted of the murder by an all-White jury after less than an hour of deliberation.

It was in this era of unabated terrorism that on December 1, 1955, only months after the lynching of Emmett Till, a seamstress and local NAACP branch secretary, Rosa Parks, refused to give up her seat on a public bus. It was the law in Montgomery, Alabama, for Blacks to relinquish their seats on any form of public transportation if no seats were available in the designated White section of the bus. Blacks paid in the front, then exited and reentered at the rear of the bus. Even if they were seated in the segregated "Negro Only" section of the bus, any White person, of any age or gender, could rightfully take their seats.

Blacks had to show respect for White authority. As the portable sign separating the White front section from the Black back rear section was moved further down the row of seats, Blacks had to relinquish their seats until every White passenger was safely seated. It did not matter how long the Black passenger had been in the seat or if every Black person who had been seated was now cramped and standing in the rear. No White could stand while a Black person remained seated.

The Montgomery City Council had no Black members in 1955 when local NAACP secretary Rosa Parks refused to follow the order of bus driver James F. Blake to give up her seat. This was not the first encounter between Parks and Blake. Initially, Rosa Parks was going to take a different bus because of the horrible treatment she had received the last time she had ridden with Blake. But it had been a long day working at a Montgomery department store when she took a seat on that Cleveland Avenue bus, and what happened to her triggered the boycott of all buses in Alabama's capital city. Parks was arrested for refusing to give up her seat, and when word of her arrest reached NAACP members, it unleashed a deep resentment against decades of mistreatment and humiliation on city buses. A civil rights movement began in 1955 in response to the arrest of Rosa Parks.

While the bus boycott was taking place, a legal challenge brought by the NAACP was making its way to the Supreme Court. It began with a girl named Claudette Colvin. The NAACP had thousands of young members. At age fifteen, Claudette Colvin was a member of the NAACP Youth Council. Rosa Parks was the adviser to the local Youth Council. Because of the many classes and programs provided by the NAACP, even at her young age, Colvin knew she was being treated unfairly. On March 2, 1955, Claudette Colvin was riding the Capital Heights bus home from school when White passengers filled up the seats in their cordoned-off section.

The bus driver ordered her to move. Colvin refused to give her seat to a White passenger as instructed by the White bus driver. Whites glared. Other students averted their eyes or watched the vicious scene in fear. Claudette sat in silence, refusing to move, and the police were called. Then, after warning her again, the bus driver and Montgomery police grabbed Claudette. As they dragged her from the bus she screamed: "I have constitutional rights."

Claudette Colvin was convicted of disturbing the peace and violating Montgomery's segregation law.[12] *Browder v. Gayle* (1956) was an appeal of her criminal conviction and those of activist Aurelia Browder, the elder stateswoman Susie McDonald, and initially Mary Louis Smith. The women were represented by local NAACP attorney Fred Gray, who would represent other members of the civil rights movement in Alabama, including Martin Luther King Jr. and other NAACP members jailed throughout Alabama.

The trial court supported Montgomery's right to enforce its segregation laws. The federal government had ruled that interstate transportation could not be segregated by law. However, city buses were within state boundaries, or intrastate transportation. However, on May 11, 1956, a three-judge federal court found in favor of Browder, McDonald, Colvin, and Smith. On November 13, 1956, the Supreme Court affirmed the three-judge court ruling that segregation on the city buses was unconstitutional. The bus boycott was brought to a victorious end on December 21, 1956, when the US Supreme Court refused Mayor Gayle's petition for a rehearing.

THE NAACP UNDER ATTACK

But *Plessy v. Ferguson* was still law. Although the decision in *Brown v. Topeka Board of Education* had ordered the desegregation of public schools, there had been little movement to end segregation. The NAACP faced a backlash of attacks intended to crush the organization by draining it of funds and members. Attacks against the organization reached a peak when some states began demanding NAACP membership lists. In Louisiana, Alabama, and Arkansas, subpoenas ordered that the names and addresses of NAACP members be given up, which the group contested in 1958 in *NAACP v. Patty*.[13]

The White Citizens' Council of America was formed after the Montgomery bus boycott and *Brown v. Topeka Board of Education*. The Council was an association of groups with a mission to maintain the "Southern Way of Life." Its primary strategy was to stop the NAACP. The White Citizens Council used political power and violence in equal measure in its efforts to maintain White supremacy. In 1956 Martin Luther King Jr. asserted, "They must be held responsible for all of the terror, the mob rule, and brutal murders that have encompassed the South over the last several years." Yet the Eisenhower administration remained silent as the White Citizens Council grew in strength as a counterweight to the NAACP in the South and the progress that the Black community had made.

In 1955 NAACP membership reached a record high of 309,000. First the attorney general of Louisiana demanded the organization's membership list. When the NAACP refused, it was barred from doing business in the state. Then the attorney general of Alabama, without a hearing or trial, barred the NAACP from doing business in Alabama. The Alabama attorney general required the NAACP to provide its membership lists even though the Alabama chapter had been granted a corporate charter to do business in the state in 1918.

The NAACP was conducting boycotts of businesses that refused to serve Blacks, were segregated, or would not hire Black employees. With lawsuits in Alabama and Louisiana over the membership lists draining time and funds, and members afraid their names would be revealed, the organization was in a fight for its life. Membership was the lifeblood of the NAACP, but it was draining away. The membership lists had to be protected at all costs. Black teachers were being asked to reveal their membership in the NAACP or risk termination. If the White Citizens Council gained access to those names, reprisals could rein down on Blacks like the terror of the Red Summer.

The NAACP refused to provide the membership lists. The civil rights organization argued that Alabama's request violated the First and Fourteenth Amendment rights of its membership. The group was threatened with contempt. The trial court ordered the group to provide its membership list or pay a fine of $10,000. The leadership still refused. The fine was increased to $100,000 if the NAACP did not comply within five days of the court's order. The NAACP argued that its members had the right to associate freely and advance their beliefs and ideas without intimidation.

During the trial, the organization presented incontrovertible evidence that members who revealed their identity were exposed to economic reprisals, loss of employment, threats of physical harm, and public hostility. Alabama refused to protect NAACP members threatened with harm, stating that it was not responsible for the actions of its private (White) citizens. The Supreme Court had ruled during the era of Reconstruction that private discrimination was beyond the scope of civil rights laws.

Alabama politicians demanded the NAACP's membership lists. The state argued that the list of names and addresses would reveal whether the NAACP was a communist organization or conducting business activities in violation of Alabama law. Alabama's attorney general argued that the NAACP must give up the membership list because the Supreme Court had forced the Ku Klux Klan to provide its membership list in 1928 in *Bryant v. Zimmerman*.[14] In that case, the state of New York sought the membership list of the Buffalo chapter of the Knights of the Ku Klux Klan.

The KKK had refused, arguing that it was similar to the Elks and Masons and therefore exempt from such a demand. The Klan lost because the Supreme Court found a real and substantial distinction between the Masons and a Klan group that conducted a "crusade against Catholics, Jews and Negroes." The Alabama attorney general argued that membership in the NAACP was similar to membership in the KKK. The Alabama courts agreed.

The NAACP appealed to the US Supreme Court. Writing on behalf of the court, Justice John M. Harlan, grandson of the Justice Harlan who had filed the famous dissent in *Plessy v. Ferguson*, reversed the state court. The court held that providing the membership lists was not a requirement within the statute, especially given that Alabama's attorney general had not requested lists of any other organizations.

The "chilling effect" or fear of reprisals against members of the NAACP outweighed the curiosity of the attorney general's office. In deciding in favor of the NAACP, the Supreme Court also considered the character of the organization. In *Bryant* the KKK had refused to furnish any of the requested information. In this case the NAACP had furnished all requested information except for the membership list.

Alabama defied the Supreme Court's ruling. The NAACP remained in contempt. *NAACP v. Alabama* was appealed to the Supreme Court on three separate occasions. This case illustrates the bitterness between state courts and the more progressive federal courts during the modern civil rights era. State courts and state legislatures in the South adamantly refused to recognize the rights of Blacks. In turn, they refused to respect the primacy of the Supreme Court when it ruled against segregation and race discrimination.

In 1956, the successful 381-day Montgomery bus boycott, led by Rev. Dr. Martin Luther King Jr., was a turning point in the civil rights struggle. White supremacists fought back against the NAACP with lawsuits and communist witch hunts. Louisiana had more than 161,000 registered Black voters. The supremacists countered with the Southern Manifesto, signed by almost all White southern members of the US Congress.

When Congress passed the Civil Rights Act of 1957, giving the US attorney the power to sue on behalf of citizens and creating the US Commission on Civil Rights, more southern states engaged in the tactic of filing lawsuits seeking NAACP membership lists or threatening to remove its charter to do business, ostensibly because of communist influences within the organization. In response, the NAACP Legal Defense Fund, Inc., became completely independent from the NAACP. Other groups created formal organizations to protect themselves from personal liability. Martin Luther King Jr., Ella Baker, and others founded the Southern Christian Leadership Conference (SCLC) in Georgia. In 1958 arsonists set fire to the home of George Raymond, president of the Pennsylvania branches of the NAACP.

This was a test of wills the NAACP could not afford to lose. The Supreme Court ruled in 1958 that the NAACP was not required to submit the names and addresses of its members to the state of Alabama. The Alabama state court, in defiance, scheduled a trial on the issue of whether the NAACP had complied with the membership disclosure requirement. The trial court ruled against the NAACP and permanently forbade the organization from doing business in the state. The Alabama Supreme Court refused to hear the appeal of the NAACP because of an alleged error in the format of the group's court briefs. The NAACP appealed again to the US Supreme Court.

Alabama argued that the activities of the NAACP undermined the people's right to racially segregate. The complaint against the organization stated in part that the NAACP:

> 1) furnished legal counsel to represent Autherine Lucy in proceedings to obtain admission to the university [of Alabama]; . . .
>
> 3) engaged in organizing, supporting, and financing an illegal boycott to compel a bus line in Montgomery, Alabama, not to segregate passengers according to race; . . .
>
> 9) encouraged, aided, and abetted the unlawful breach of the peace in many cities in Alabama for the purpose of gaining national notoriety and attention to enable it to raise funds under a false claim that it was for the protection of alleged constitutional rights; . . .
>
> 10) encouraged, aided, and abetted a course of conduct within the state of Alabama, seeking to deny to the citizens of Alabama the constitutional right to voluntarily segregate.

The US Supreme Court stood its ground.

Once again, the Supreme Court found that the Alabama regulation did not support the ouster of the NAACP. The court made it clear that an organization could not be prohibited from doing business in the state based only on its advocacy for racial justice; precluding the NAACP from maintaining a chapter in Alabama was a mechanism to restrict the freedom to associate for the collective advocacy of ideas. The court stated that "freedoms such as [these] are protected not only against heavy-handed frontal attack, but also from being stifled by more subtle government interference."

While the court was addressing the issue of membership in *NAACP v. Alabama*, a similar case arose in Arkansas. In *Bates v. Little Rock*, decided in 1960, Daisy Bates and Birdie Williams were convicted of failing to disclose the names of the members of the Little Rock branch of the NAACP.[15] In 1957 Little Rock had amended its Arkansas occupation license tax ordinance to require an organization operating within the municipality to supply information about its membership, officers' salaries, dues, contributors, and net income. In addition, the records of the NAACP chapter were required to be open to the public.

Bates was president of the NAACP of Little Rock, and Williams was president of the North Little Rock NAACP. Both women acted as custodians of the records and provided all information except the names and addresses of members. They were both arrested and held in contempt. Bates and Williams based their refusal to provide the names on the anti-NAACP climate in Arkansas. Public disclosure of the names could lead to harassment, economic reprisals, and even bodily harm.

The City of Little Rock countered that it had enacted the ordinance to reach certain organizations that were abusing their nonprofit status. The ordinance sought organizations in Little Rock, Arkansas, that claimed immunity from the payment of occupation licenses. Arkansas claimed it needed the names to ensure that the NAACP was not engaged in commercial business. The Arkansas Supreme Court upheld the contempt convictions of Bates and Williams. On appeal to the US Supreme Court, the convictions were overturned. Justice Potter Stewart wrote the opinion on behalf of the court.

In its decision, the court questioned the relationship between the stated purpose of the ordinance and the effect of the law on the First Amendment rights of the NAACP's members. The court ruled that disclosure of the NAACP's membership lists would significantly interfere with the freedom of association of its members. In addition, the court found that the NAACP had not requested nonprofit organization status. Therefore, it did not fall within the scope of the ordinance. Joseph McCarthy, the infamous senator from Wisconsin who had been the anti-Communist leader of the House Un-American Activities Committee, died in 1957.

However, in 1961 Louisiana sued the NAACP under a statute requiring an out-of-state organization to file an affidavit stating that none of its officers was a member of a Communist, Communist-front, or subversive organization, on the grounds that organizations with connections to the Communist Party were prohibited from doing business in Louisiana. Another state law required disclosure of the names and addresses of members and officers. The law, allegedly passed in 1924 to restrict the Ku Klux Klan, was only enforced against the NAACP. Using the guise of investigating Communists and subversives was yet another mechanism for preventing Blacks from fighting against racial oppression. To demonstrate their patriotism, Blacks complied. However, members of the NAACP chapters who complied with the order were immediately fired from their jobs.

The case was moved from state to federal court. Relying on the decisions in *Bates v. Little Rock* and *NAACP v. Alabama*, the federal district court entered an injunction prohibiting Louisiana from enforcing the anti-Communism statute. The state of Louisiana appealed. The US Supreme Court upheld the injunction, finding that the disclosure of the membership list was not required if it resulted in hostility against the members on the list. In addition, statutes that infringed on First Amendment rights had to be more narrowly drafted to achieve their stated purpose of detecting Communists. The states retaliated against the success of the NAACP and other civil rights advocates in these cases.

NAACP v. Button was decided by the Supreme Court in 1963. Virginia had enacted legislation to prohibit any organization from retaining a lawyer from outside the state. The law required that an out-of-state attorney hired by a resident of the state must have no pecuniary or financial interest in the case. The NAACP was headquartered in New York. The organization's attorneys represented clients in civil rights cases around the country. This law was meant to stop the NAACP from receiving any money if it was the victor in those cases.

The NAACP sued to stop the enforcement of this law as a violation of its members' Fourteenth Amendment rights. The Virginia courts ruled against the NAACP. On appeal, the US Supreme Court reversed the Virginia Supreme Court.[16] The Supreme Court ruled in Button that litigation was a form of speech protected by the First Amendment. Freedom of speech is protected against state action by the Fourteenth Amendment, and advocating for civil rights is a mode of expression and association. Virginia could not prohibit the civil rights advocacy of the NAACP, its affiliates, or its legal staff.

It was NAACP attorney Robert Carter, an African American, who devised the successful strategy based on freedom of association that ended the treacherous demands for the organization's membership lists. Carter had graduated from high school at age sixteen and was only twenty-one when he wrote a thesis on freedom of association for his master's degree in law (LLM) at Columbia University. But the price of progress in the war over the vote was often bitter.

While these attacks on the NAACP drained resources, attacks on Black farmers in the rural South cost them their homes, livelihoods, and even their lives. The term "tent city" was applied to the communities of Black sharecroppers who were evicted for voting and forced to live in tents set up in open fields. Tents in open fields housed Black families, especially sharecroppers who had registered to vote or attempting to register to vote. They were then were thrown out of their homes by landowners. There was no running water, electricity, or toilets or protection from the heat, cold, or insects.

The local Black communities kept these homeless families fed and clothed. Black farmers gave up parts of their fields for the tents. Tent cities sprang up across the South following the push for voting rights. The tent city in Lowndes County, Alabama, outside of Selma, was one of the largest. In Lowndes County, deep political activism was born from decades of deprivation. The Black Panther Party was founded there. The black panther was chosen as a symbol for those who could not read and as a sign of power. Later, Stokely Carmichael, a voting activist in Alabama, carried the Black Panther symbol and Black Power philosophy to Oakland, California, where it made history.

LITERACY TESTS

The NAACP brought women into the fold. Black women in Montgomery were crucial to the success of the Montgomery bus boycott. They worked in all aspects of the movement for racial justice. They were attacked, were jailed, and assisted in creating the strategies. Constance Baker prepared legal briefs in *Brown v. Topeka Board of Education* and had worked beside the NAACP secretary in Arkansas, Daisy Bates, to desegregate Central High School in Little Rock, Arkansas. She started as a law clerk for Thurgood Marshall and became the first female lawyer hired by the NAACP.

Baker's mother founded the New Haven, Connecticut, branch of the NAACP. Constance Baker was the ninth of twelve children of parents from the small Caribbean Island of Nevis. As a chef at Yale University, her father sheltered her from segregation. However, at age fifteen she discovered that segregation existed in the North as well as the South when she was excluded from a public beach in Connecticut. That's when she decided to be a civil rights attorney.

With no money for college tuition, like so many other intelligent Black women, Constance was forced to work as a domestic, cleaning the homes of White women. But after Baker gave a speech on Black history, her prospects changed. Clarence W. Blakeslee, a White businessman, heard Baker and decided to give her a scholarship to attend Fisk University in Tennessee. However, Baker had never lived in the South, and in segregated Nashville she came face to face with the depth of Jim Crow racism. She returned to the North, vowing to do something about America's racism.

After completing college at New York University in 1943, Baker became one of only two female students to enter Columbia Law School. She was hired by the NAACP to work on housing segregation and voting rights cases. In 1957 Baker stood beside local NAACP attorney Jess Brown of Vicksburg, Mississippi, and New York NAACP attorney Robert L. Carter as they joined the renowned leader the of NAACP, Thurgood Marshall, in arguing the voting rights case *Darby v. Daniel*.[17]

James Daniel was the circuit clerk of Jefferson Davis County, Mississippi. NAACP members H. D. Darby and other Black Mississippians attempted to pass the oral and written literacy test. But each time they were told by Daniel that they had failed. The test required potential voters to read and discuss a provision of the US Constitution, determined by the registrar, Daniel. All of the applicants failed every test, several times.

H. D. Darby brought a suit in federal court against James Daniel and Joe T. Patterson, the attorney general of Mississippi. Marshall and his team thought they had finally developed strong enough precedents based on the victories in *Guinn v. United States, Lane v. Wilson, Smith v. Allwright,* and *Davis v. Schnell* to defeat the cornerstone of White political supremacy: the Mississippi Plan of 1890.

They were wrong. The three-judge federal court ruled against them. Judge Ben Cameron wrote:

> The essence of the action before us, therefore, is discrimination on the part of the defendant Daniel, discrimination against plaintiffs, Negroes, and in favor of white persons. After listening to the oral testimony and examining the documents carefully we are unable to find any tangible or credible proof of discrimination. There is no proof that any white person was ever treated in any manner more favorably than plaintiffs or any other Negroes. The mere showing that of 3,000 qualified voters in Jefferson Davis County, only forty to fifty are Negroes is not sufficient. Plaintiffs carry the burden of showing that plaintiffs have been denied the right to register because they are Negroes, and that white people similarly situated have been permitted to register. This record contains no such proof. The disparity between numbers of registrants, as has been so often pointed out, results doubtless from the fact that one race had a start of several centuries over the other in the slow and laborious struggle toward literacy. This record does not, in our opinion, show that defendant has practiced discrimination. From our observation of his demeanor during the trial and while on the witness stand and of the evidence generally we are convinced that he has shown himself to be a conscientious, patient and fair public official, exerting every effort to do a hard job in an honorable way.[18]

While they were still reeling from this loss, on March 24, 1959, an appellate court, with Judge Cameron in tow, ruled against Black potential voters like Albert J. Tullier in another case challenging discriminatorily administered literacy tests. This time the case was brought against Frank Giordano, the registrar of voters for the Parish of Plaquemines in Louisiana. After the Supreme Court's ruling in *Plessy v. Ferguson,* the Louisiana legislature had amended its constitution to exclude Black voters. In 1898, when approximately 44 percent of all the registered voters in the state were Black, a policy was put in place denying them the right to vote based on race. The Black vote never reached more than 1 percent. From the grandfather clause to literacy tests to White-only primaries, for eighty years Louisiana schemed to exclude Black voters.

OTHER CHALLENGES

Constance Baker married Joel Motley Jr. She continued to work as a civil rights attorney, traveling into the deep South to visit clients, investigate race-based assaults, and try desegregation cases. Baker-Motley found herself representing James Meredith in his bid to desegregate the University of Mississippi. After a successful legal challenge by the NAACP Legal Defense Fund, led by Baker, Meredith was allowed to attend Ole Miss in 1962. However, the backlash leveled against Meredith resulted in riots, death threats, and the need for military protection.

Young people challenged racial divides and desegregation rulings. The Freedom Riders risked their lives to enforce Supreme Court decisions against segregated interstate transportation. From 1961 to 1963, Black and White Freedom Riders sat together on buses traveling from the North into Alabama, Mississippi, and South Carolina, testing the laws banning segregation. Baker-Motley was called back to New York after she witnessed White mobs viciously attacking the Freedom Riders who were integrating Trailways and Greyhound buses during the summer of 1961. The integrated group of activists was beaten with rocks, bottles, and metal pipes. Their bus was set ablaze while shouting, crazed mobs yelled "burn them alive." Twenty-one-year-old John Lewis, who would later become a US congressman, was one of the first to volunteer to ride the bus to South Carolina, where he was beaten but then dragged away to safety before the crowd could take his life.

Lewis was a fearless member of the NAACP and the Student Non-Violent Coordinating Committee (SNCC) and wanted to be part of an effort to change America by challenging state laws that were being enforced despite the Supreme Court's rulings about desegregating public transportation. A few years later, in 1965, Lewis would walk across the Edmund Pettus Bridge next to Martin Luther King Jr., protesting for voting rights in Alabama, only days after being beaten unconscious by Alabama state troopers led by segregationists intent of keeping Blacks second-class citizens in their own country.

Lewis realized that the laws were only as good as the prosecutors and judges who enforced them, none of whom were elected by Blacks. Nor could they ever be removed by Blacks, unless African Americans obtained the right to vote. Perhaps heeding the call of President John F. Kennedy—"ask not what your country can do for you, ask what you can do for your country"—college students like John Lewis entered the war for voting rights. They converged on the South, intent on breaking the chains of White political supremacy and giving all Americans access to the ballot box. These young volunteers suffered the same harassment, beatings, and murder as previous activists.

The NAACP took on gerrymandering in 1957. Blacks in urban areas and rural communities found that after finally securing the right to vote, it had little effect on the election because of gerrymandering. Voting districts were being intentionally drawn to create districts that would keep Blacks as minorities so that their votes would not change the outcome of elections. Local NAACP attorney Fred Gray and NAACP Legal Defense Fund attorney Robert Carter represented C. G. Gomillion and the class of Blacks who challenged the changed boundaries in *Gomillion v. Lightfoot*.[19]

At trial, the district court dismissed the NAACP's lawsuit, stating that the court had no right to intervene in state political matters without clear evidence of racial discrimination. This was based on the *Colegrove v. Green* decision from 1946.[20] Back then the Supreme Court had given the state and local governments latitude, especially in political matters. But times had changed. Blacks in Tuskegee sued Phil Lightfoot, their mayor, when they found their voting districts had been formed in a manner that prevented them from electing any Black politicians or even White ones who represented their interests.

In *Gomillion v. Lightfoot*, the NAACP discovered that White legislators in Alabama had redrawn the boundaries of Tuskegee, Alabama, into an irregular, twenty-eight-sided figure.[21] Prior to redistricting, the city of Tuskegee was square shaped. After the city passed Act 140 in 1957, the redefined boundaries resulted in discriminatorily depriving Black voters of the right to vote in municipal elections. When asked why the town had redrawn the districts to exclude Black residents, Mayor Lightfoot could not provide one governmental reason for it. The motive was squarely racial. Such manipulation of voting districts was now being challenged by the NAACP.

After *Gomillion*, the Supreme Court entered a modern era of voting rights. It chose to place *Colegrove* in its time period of overt oppression. The Court had already ruled in *Baker v. Carr* that it could decide political issues, whereas in *Colegrove* the Court had not wanted to get involved in the political thicket.[22] The Court ruled that the redistricting plan that took away the voting rights of Black farmers was meant "to despoil colored citizens, and only colored citizens, of their theretofore enjoyed voting rights."

In 1964 Alabama tried again to undermine Black political power. In *Reynolds v. Sims* the Supreme Court ruled in favor of the Black community, deciding that voting districts must be equal. Alabama's voting districts were based on the population in 1901. Since that time, thousands of Blacks had moved to the cities of Mobile, Montgomery, and Birmingham. "Yet, Bullock County, with a population of only 13,462, and Henry County, with a population of only 15,286, each were allocated two seats in the Alabama House, whereas Mobile County, with a population of

314,301, was given only three seats, and Jefferson County, with 634,864 people, had only seven representatives."[23]

In *Reynolds v. Sims*, the court ruled that the right to vote was a fundamental right. Alabama had violated the equal protection clause. Districts must provide "no less than substantially equal state legislative representation for all citizens." States were required to make "honest and good faith" efforts to construct districts as nearly of equal population as practicable. One person one vote. Although this was not a case brought by the NAACP, the result was a victory for voting rights. Allies of the NAACP and other groups willing to do battle to enforce the constitutional rights and protections long denied Black communities joined the battle, including the SNCC and CORE.

THE TEST AND THE TAX

The poll tax burdened every Black citizen who considered voting. Each resident was required to pay a yearly tax to the local jurisdiction. The tax may have helped the local schools, parks, or road maintenance. However, failure to pay the tax prohibited a citizen from voting. Although the amount was relatively nominal, for poor farmers, sharecroppers, and anyone living in poverty, the tax was a financial burden that could not be overcome. If a year was missed, then one year of taxes in addition to the current voting year was required in order to register to vote.

Literacy test registrars rejected most Blacks who attempted to register. Poll tax laws and literacy tests had bested all attempts by the great legal minds of the NAACP in New York and strategies by the greatest protest organizers in the NAACP branches. The fight for voting rights in the courtroom, and the resulting loss of life in communities nationwide, led the NAACP to work with progressive congressmen to seek legislation. However, Rep. Emanuel Celler (D-NY) chose to pursue passage of an amendment to the Constitution that would end poll taxes in all federal elections.

But even if an amendment on poll taxes passed, states would still have the power to enact poll tax legislation that would affect state elections. Whether an amendment or federal law should be the strategy was debated. A federal law could be ruled unconstitutional by the US Supreme Court, which had already upheld poll taxes, arguing that when the tax was applied equally, with no specific race mentioned in the law, there was no discrimination. However, election officials had a great deal of flexibility in deciding when to waive the tax.

As so crudely predicted by Gov. Vardaman, the Mississippi Plan of 1890, which combined the poll tax with a literacy test, was a successful weapon for political exclusion across the country for many generations. This was especially true in the South because of the poor public school systems and poverty. The diabolical nature of combining the two qualifications meant that even those Black potential voters who could afford to pay the poll tax still faced the literacy test. The US Constitution gave states the power to decide the qualifications for voters, as long as those qualifications did not discriminate based on race.

However, local election officials devised literacy tests expressly intended for the applicant to fail. The following excerpt is taken from an actual literacy test used in Mississippi. The applicant must reveal if he or she has ever been arrested. Then the applicant must copy a section of the state constitution, designated by the election registrar. Then the applicant must:

19. Write in the space below a reasonable interpretation (the meaning) of the section of the Constitution of Mississippi which you have just copied:
20. Write in the space below a statement setting forth your understanding of the duties and obligations of citizenship under a constitutional form of government.

An election official could give a literacy test on any topic.

The literacy test was an obstacle for Black voters that pushed back against every effort by the NAACP to enroll Black voters. In Louise Lassiter's hometown of Northampton County, North Carolina, a citizen had to read or write a section of the North Carolina Constitution or the US Constitution in order to register to vote. Lassiter, who was forty-one years old, wanted to vote in the special election scheduled for July 13, 1957. But she refused to take a test to qualify to vote. On June 22, 1957, Louise Lassiter challenged the literacy tests. She would not submit to an educational test required by North Carolina General Statute 163-28 as amended.

The North Carolina registrars were responsible for judging whether the reading or writing of a section of the North Carolina Constitution or the Constitution of the United States was done "in a proficient manner." Average citizens, in rural areas, were attempting to register to vote. In this county the register of elections, Helen H. Taylor, held court in the general store. Most Blacks, too intimidated to attempt the test, would not dare to ask to take the test. They knew trouble would follow. Others learned early in life that there was no use causing trouble about a test that could never be passed by anyone Black.

CHALLENGING THE TEST

Louise Lassiter, a Black resident, had had enough of Taylor's intimidation tactics. In a state where half of the farmers' children, White and Black, did not graduate from high school, she knew North Carolina was not concerned about literacy among its voters. This literacy test was meant to undermine Black political power. It prevented Blacks from voting people like Taylor out of office. Despite the hard looks of contempt that followed her around the store, Lassiter filled out the forms to register to vote. Then she refused to take the test.

Lassiter accepted the risk of losing her job and possibly being killed by a lynch mob. After Lassiter had completed all parts of the registration form, Taylor placed a literacy test in front of her. Lassiter told the register of elections and all of the other Whites watching her that their test was a violation of her constitutional rights. Because she refused to take the test, they denied her a ballot. She appealed Taylor's decision. In 1957 her case was heard first by a board of elections, which ruled against her. In 1958 she appealed and lost again. This time the North Carolina Supreme Court cited *Guinn v. United States*, which had been a victory for the NAACP because it outlawed the grandfather clause, but it had also upheld the use of literacy tests if they were given without racial bias.

Lassiter was represented by local attorneys Taylor Mitchell and James R. Walker, who belonged to a local civil rights group. Walker was a grassroots civil rights organizer as well as a trained litigator, known as the "Mr. Civil Rights" of North Carolina.[24] Once funds from their legal committee were depleted, Walker contacted the NAACP office in New York City for help. John Wertheimer recounts that the NAACP met Walker's request for funds "coolly." With competing priorities, the national office had gained a reputation for rebuffing those local attorneys who acted as "lone wolves" outside its national strategy for dealing with civil rights cases.

The NAACP had reason to be concerned about cases that could create a bad precedent or result in troubling legal decisions that would cause more harm than good. Like Homer Plessy's challenge of the Separate Car Act in Louisiana, which resulted in national segregation, good intentions could result in an even worse racial situation. Walker believed he had the right strategy and took his voting rights case to the US Supreme Court. All of the prior cases had challenged the discriminatory way in which the literacy test was administered or the electors' failure to give the test to Black potential voters. Louise Lassiter's case was the first to claim that she had a right to vote without taking any test to prove her literacy.

On June 8, 1959, the Supreme Court ruled against her and unanimously in favor of North Carolina's right to give literacy tests. Justice William O. Douglass cited the use of literacy tests in Alabama as well as Oregon and Massachusetts.[25] Then the court reaffirmed *Williams v. Mississippi*.[26] Once again, the Mississippi Plan stood. As the NAACP had feared, the outcome of *Lassiter v. Northampton County Board of Elections* case meant that the states could continue to administer literacy laws as long as they were not discriminatory on their face. The court stated that North Carolina's law did not apply to any particular race, creed, color, or sex. North Carolina wanted literate voters, and the Supreme Court found a connection between the state's requirement to have the ability to read and write sections from its constitution and the right to vote.[27]

Literacy laws became even more elaborate and diabolical. Potential voters were required to count the number of jelly beans in a large jar just by looking at it. Walker's next case in North Carolina involved a literacy test that required the applicant for registration to take dictation and pronounce certain words on a list. Following are examples of Louisiana literacy test requirements that were upheld by the courts.

Applicant must correctly answer any four of the following six questions so as to evidence an elemental knowledge of the Constitution and Government, an attachment thereto, and a simple understanding of the obligations of citizenship under a republican form of government.

1. The church that we attend is chosen
   a. by the National Government.
   b. by ourselves.
   c. by the Congress.
2. The President must be at least
   a. twenty-five years old.
   b. thirty years old.
   c. thirty-five years old.
3. It is important for every voter
   a. to vote as others tell him to vote.
   b. to vote for the most popular candidates.
   c. to vote for the best qualified candidates.
4. The name of our first President was
   a. John Adams.
   b. George Washington.
   c. Alexander Hamilton.
5. The Constitution of the United States places the final authority in our Nation in the hands of
   a. the national courts.
   b. the States.
   c. the people.
6. The President of the Senate gets his office
   a. by election by the people.
   b. by election by the Senate.
   c. by appointment by the President.

Applicant's answers must be provided on Form No. 11 furnished by the Registrar for permanent records.

This card must be returned to the Registrar
DO NOT WRITE ON THIS CARD Form No. 2
Applicant must correctly answer any four of the following six questions so as to evidence an elemental knowledge of the Constitution and Government, an attachment thereto, and a simple understanding of the obligations of citizenship under a republican form of government.

1. The Congress cannot regulate commerce
   a. between States.
   b. with other countries.
   c. within a state.
2. The general plan of a State government is given
   a. in the Constitution of the United States.
   b. in the laws of the Congress.
   c. in its own State constitution.
3. The name of our first President was
   a. John Adams.
   b. George Washington.
   c. Alexander Hamilton.
4. The President gets his authority to carry out laws
   a. from the Declaration of Independence.
   b. from the Constitution.
   c. from the Congress.
5. Our towns and cities have delegated authority which they get from the
   a. State.
   b. Congress.
   c. President.
6. A citizen who desires to vote on election day must, before that date, go before the election officers and
   a. register.
   b. pay all of his bills.
   c. have his picture taken.

Applicant's answers must be provided on Form No. 11 furnished by the Registrar for permanent records.

These tests were rarely graded in plain sight or in front of the applicant attempting to register. The answer sheet was not shared with the applicant. Civil rights groups began conducting voter education classes on the constitution. Freedom schools were developed in which local teachers taught classes on the state and federal constitutions to members of the community in the evenings and on weekends. But without knowing what questions would be asked or how the test would be graded, even the most educated Black person could be given failing marks by Whites with less education and of lower social status.

As with literacy tests, attorneys attacked the poll tax with legal and legislative strategies. Unlike the literacy tests, poll taxes were based on residency requirements and property ownership, which stemmed from English law in colonial America. During the colonial era only property owners could vote or run for public office. Owning property was evidence of a vested interest in the community. In the twentieth century, the argument could be made that the requirement to pay a tax had very little to do with voting. That weaker connection was a vulnerable place for the NAACP to strike. In addition, because most states maintained poll tax information in racially segregated lists, election officials could treat White and Black citizens differently. Only the all-White board of elections knew who had paid the tax and was thus eligible to vote.

CHALLENGING THE TAX

Civil rights advocates began striking out against poll taxes. In 1963 NAACP member Evelyn Butts challenged poll taxes in Virginia. Butts was a resident of Norfolk, Virginia, the mother of three daughters, the wife of a disabled war veteran, and president of the Oakwood Civic League. She had led desegregation efforts in Norfolk before setting her sights on voting rights. In 1964 Annie E. Harper challenged the Virginia poll tax, which required a payment of $1.50 for each of the three preceding years for which an elector was assessable. Harper argued that she could not afford the tax and was being denied the right to vote based on her poverty. The trial court judge in Virginia dismissed both the Butts and Harper cases, basing its decision on a more than twenty-year-old Supreme Court decision in *Breedlove v. Suttles*,[28] in which poll taxes were upheld as legal as long as they were not racially biased. But a great deal had changed since the days of lynching and the Great Depression, and poll taxes would fall.

The NAACP began lobbying Congress intensely to put an end to the poll tax by federal law, not through a constitutional amendment. The NAACP's man in Washington was Clarence Mitchell. Known as the Lion in the Lobby, Mitchell had opened the Washington office as part of the organization's strategy to prevent harmful legislation from being enacted and encourage laws beneficial to the Black community. The NAACP still felt the sting of its antilynching loss. To protect the community, it needed eyes and ears in civil rights on Capitol Hill.

A former director of the St. Paul Urban League in Minnesota, Clarence Mitchell was a general with an innate ability to forecast trouble and then counter it. As the NAACP's right hand since 1950, Mitchell knew well the intricacies of Congress's parliamentary procedure and the congressmen who plied it. Referred to as the 101st Senator, Mitchell was widely respected on The Hill. His efforts spanned the administrations of eight presidents. He had a hand in guiding all of the civil rights laws passed in Washington during his tenure. He was a witness at the congressional hearing on whether to abolish poll taxes.

Representative Emanuel Celler, his Brooklyn, New York, accent in full effect, chaired the 1961 hearing on abolition of the poll tax in federal elections. Celler, the powerful, longtime chairman of the House Judiciary Committee, had an extensive record of civil rights advocacy. A Democrat from New York City, he knew members of his party were violating the rights of Black voters. Celler wanted to end poll taxes and was willing to amend the US Constitution to do it. The bespectacled and stooped-shouldered Celler, born in 1881 and known for his dry wit, withering judgments, and bulldog tenacity, called for a congressional hearing on the matter.[29]

On March 12, 1962, a hearing of the House Judiciary Committee was held on poll taxes. Celler presided. One witness, William Higgs, an attorney from Mississippi, testified about the difficulty created by having to pay the poll tax. The tax was not only a financial burden, it was a statement of self-determination that placed anyone paying it on the list of troublemakers. Paying the tax signaled a plan to exercise one's right to vote. The tax had to be paid at the local sheriff's office or city hall. Faced with a refusal to accept payment of the tax, Black voters could do little more than contact their local NAACP office. Few arguments against the tax had mentioned the inherent violence and intimidation involved in merely attempting to pay the poll tax.

Statement of William L. Higgs, Jackson, Miss.

The Chairman: What is the amount of the poll tax in Mississippi?

Mr. Higgs: The poll tax is at least $2, and many counties as much as $3.

The Chairman: Is it cumulative?

Mr. Higgs: No, it is not. If it is not paid during the month of January primarily each year, then one may not vote for the next two years. One who did not pay his poll tax in January of this year cannot vote in any election up until the year 1964 in Mississippi.

***

Mr. Higgs: . . . So many counties have the $3 assessment, $2 of which is mandatory. Please forgive me for being precise with these words.

Then to make the point I was about to make. The 1960 census for Mississippi, the general social and economic characteristics, shows that the median income for a Negro family in Mississippi is about $1,440. Many families in

Mississippi—as much as a third of them—have median incomes of $1,000 or less for the whole family.

If you take the average Negro family of, say, five and divide it into this, you will see that the whole family has somewhat of $3 a day upon which to live. The poll tax for man and wife is $4—at least $4. This means 1 day's subsistence for the entire family in Mississippi would go just to pay the poll tax.

Though many people seem to think that the amount of the poll tax is not great and not a deterrent to voting, we in Mississippi have found that it has been a great deterrent. You compare this with the median income of the white families, which is more than $4,200 per year, which is three times as much, then, indeed, it would not be a great deterrent to whites. But, of course, it has been and is the Negro population in the State of Mississippi.

The Chairman: Are there any difficulties surrounding the payment of the poll tax—that it must be paid in certain hours and certain places in Mississippi?

Mr. Higgs: Yes. I am very glad you asked that question. There is great difficulty. In several counties in Mississippi, or in many counties in Mississippi, the sheriffs will not accept payment of poll tax. In many counties, the citizenry are so afraid to attempt to pay the poll tax that it [n]ever gets paid.[30]

Governor Ross Barnett, a known segregationist, countered the hearings and any attempt to repeal poll taxes with a telegram to Rep. Celler, reminding him that under article 1, section 2 of the US Constitution, the states have the sole power to determine the qualifications for voters electing representatives and senators. In attempting to pass a constitutional amendment abolishing poll taxes, the Congress was preempting the states' power to decide who is qualified to vote.

A *Congressional Quarterly* (*CQ*) issue of 1962 reveals a behind-the-scenes look into the passage of this amendment. On March 16, 1962, Senator J. W. Fulbright (D-AR) "pointed out that the Civil Rights Commission in its 1959 report said that while the poll tax might have a 'deterrent effect,' it did not appear generally to be discriminatory upon the basis of race or color." The Commission stated that "Negroes now appear to encounter no significant racially motivated impediments to voting in 4 of the 12 Southern states: Arkansas, Oklahoma, Texas and Virginia." (The Commission had avoided the poll tax subject in its 1961 report.)

The *CQ* report adds: "Sen. John Stennis (D Miss.) argued that 'voting is a privilege; it is not a right.'" The poll tax, said Stennis, "is a very reasonable and a very effective regulation. It requires that a person manifesting an interest in an election shall pay a small amount for the privilege of participating in the election."[31] During this time, using its three-prong strategy of litigation, legislation, and protest, the NAACP began a directed lobbying effort against poll taxes as the legal challenges in cases like *Breedlove v. Suttles* made their way up to the US Supreme Court.[32] In Congress, testimony was taken on banning the tax.

Unlike the history of defeat of antilynching legislation in the Senate, this time the Senate moved forward first, before the House, to eliminate the poll tax. Bills to ban the poll tax by federal law, rather than by constitutional amendment, had been approved five times between 1942 and 1949 by the House but died each time in the Senate, with filibusters in 1942, 1944, and 1946. The Senate passed legislation banning the poll tax by a vote of 77–16 on March 27, 1962. At that time, five states still required a poll tax for voting: Alabama, Arkansas, Mississippi, Virginia, and Texas. All but Texas legislators voted against the amendment. Senator Spessard Holland, a Florida Democrat, and most of his supporters argued that banning the poll tax must be done by amending the Constitution; if not, the states would be left with the option of enacting federal legislation and reviving the poll tax at a later date.

On August 27, 1962, the House passed legislation banning the poll tax by a vote of 295–86. President John F. Kennedy said, "Today's action by the House of Representatives in approving the poll tax amendment culminates a legislative effort of many, many years to bring about the end of this artificial bar to the right to vote in some of our states. This is a significant action which I am confident will be approved quickly by the required 38 state legislatures."

However, behind closed doors, as a *CQ* report indicates, the NAACP, along with other civil rights groups, feared an amendment strategy to end poll taxes. They lobbied against ending poll taxes through passage of an amendment to the Constitution:

> In a related development, seven civil rights groups March 21 issued a statement urging defeat of any constitutional amendment to abolish the poll tax, saying a vote for the Holland amendment would be a "vote against civil rights." They said the amendment "would provide an immutable precedent for shunting all further civil rights legislation to the amendment procedure."
>
> [The groups opposed to the Amendment] were the American Jewish Congress, American Veterans Committee, Americans for Democratic Action, Anti-Defamation League of B'Nai B'rith, International Union of Electrical Workers (AFL-CIO), National Assn. for the Advancement of Colored People, and United Automobile Workers (AFL-CIO).[33]

NAACP Washington Bureau Chief Clarence Mitchell was in California for a speaking engagement during Rep. Celler's subcommittee hearings on the abolition of the poll tax, but he submitted a statement placing the organization's opposition on the record, which reads in part:

> Statement of Clarence Mitchell, Director of the Washington Bureau of the National Association for the Advancement of Colored People

I wish to thank the committee on behalf of the National Association for the Advancement of Colored People for this opportunity to testify. . . . The National Association for the Advancement of Colored People has consistently advocated the elimination of the poll tax and other artificial restrictions on the right of citizens to choose the persons who will enact the laws under which they are governed.

Just as consistently, the association has supported the position that the elimination of the poll tax should be accomplished by simple congressional legislation, rather than by constitutional amendment.

It has been the position of the association, simply supported by legal analysis, that the poll tax can be eliminated by congressional action without an amendment. To accept the amendment method of elimination would appear to be conceding that a law passed by Congress would be unconstitutional. This would be a bad precedent, inasmuch as the constitutional issue is raised whenever a piece of civil rights legislation is considered. Once this concession is made, we might look to a pattern of trying to dispose of all civil rights questions by proposing constitutional amendments.

Such a course would give lukewarm supporters of civil rights a chance to avoid making a strong battle, and would give opponents an opportunity to block amendments in the States. . . .

The administration has adopted the sixth grade voting provision and is supporting the bill introduced by the chairman of this committee to accomplish that objective (H.R. 10034).

This presents an opportunity for congressional Members of both parties to support their party platforms by combining the voting literacy and poll tax provisions in one bill. To this end we respectfully urge that an anti-poll tax amendment to H.R. 10034 be adopted by the Judiciary Committee.

Unless this approach is utilized, it is our fear that the use of the constitutional amendment method of eliminating the poll tax will lead to an unnecessary and long delay in the disposition of this problem, with no compensating assurance of eventual success. (March 12, 1962)[34]

Fortunately Mitchell's fears were unrealized. For the first time in the history of the NAACP, such caution was not necessary.

On January 23, 1964, the US Constitution was amended. The Twenty-fourth Amendment states:

Section 1. The right of citizens of the United States to vote in any primary or other election for President or Vice-President, for electors for President or Vice-President, or for Senate or Representative in Congress, shall not be denied or abridged by the United States or any State by reason of failure to pay any poll tax or other tax.

However, success was not enough. The grandfather clause, White-only primaries, and now the poll tax had been defeated. These were victories. But there was still a need to protect the right to vote from the many-headed snake of racism. The NAACP leadership knew that without pro-active legislation, there would be yet another legal scheme to undermine the political power of African Americans and other people of color. The ban on the poll tax was one of two civil rights legislative proposals made by the Kennedy administration in 1962; the other was yet another attempt to ban literacy tests. Again the proposal to bar the arbitrary use of literacy tests was defeated. It died in a Senate filibuster.

Given the inherent difficulty in amending the Constitution, Clarence Mitchell had reason to be concerned. An amendment requires the approval of two-thirds of Congress and three-quarters of state legislatures, and the NAACP and other groups believed that any future developments in civil rights would have been nearly impossible to achieve using this method. But President Johnson feared that a law passed by Congress or an Executive Order could be overturned by the Supreme Court. The first civil rights legislation since the 1957 Civil Rights Act, creating the Equal Employment Opportunity Commission and the Civil Rights Division of the Justice Department, had to be a constitutional amendment.

Overshadowed by the federal Civil Rights Act of 1964 that would swiftly follow, the abolition of poll taxes remains a remarkable achievement. The difficulty in changing the US Constitution is evident in the limited number of amendments that have ever been successful. But the murders of and assaults on civil rights workers and the hundreds of jailed foot soldiers throughout the South were now regular stories on television news and in the newspaper. More action was needed.

There was not enough time and too few resources to continue to take a piecemeal approach toward the voting rights war. The Twenty-fourth Amendment dealt a blow to the enemy, but the NAACP had its sights set on making a much greater impact. Federal legislation was needed to reach private discrimination. Nearly a hundred years before the Supreme Court had refused to protect Blacks from individuals who privately discriminated against them. For the first time, the NAACP had a president in the White House and the willing friends in Congress necessary to attack racism.

Although developments of 1964 dealt a near death blow to poll taxes, the year was filled with loss of life in retaliation. Civil rights activists, even in death, influenced the law and politics of this nation. It still took the loss of many lives for Congress to pass the Civil Rights Act of 1964 and the Voting Rights Act of 1965.

6

~

The Voting Rights Act

Stony the road we trod, Bitter the chastening rod,
Felt in the days when hope unborn had died.

—James Weldon Johnson, "Lift Every Voice and Sing" (1899)

There was a sacred price paid to achieve the Voting Rights Act of 1965.
"Few events in American political life have had as profound or as far-reaching consequences as has passage of the Voting Rights Act of 1965."[1]
The NAACP and the Justice Department of the United States would bring
about sweeping changes only because of the passage of the Voting Rights
Act. In 1962 the NAACP LDF had twenty-nine cases before the Supreme
Court, more than any other law firm in the country except the Solicitor
General's Office of the federal government.[2]

The NAACP LDF assisted local NAACP attorneys C. B. King and D.
L. Hollowell in their suit against the White elected officials of Albany,
Georgia, who had maintained segregated voting locations, in *Anderson
v. Courson*.[3] Race was a factor in every aspect of voting. In *Anderson v.
Martin* (1964), the NAACP brought a lawsuit successfully challenging a
Louisiana law that required ballots to specify the race of the candidates
running for office. Louisiana defended its measure as necessary information for the electorate; moreover, "the labeling applie[d] equally to Negro
and white." However, the history of racism in America would undermine
the chances for Black, as opposed to White, candidates.

The NAACP LDF persuaded a unanimous court in *Anderson v. Martin*
that it was a violation of the Fourteenth Amendment rights of Dupuy H.
Anderson to require a candidate's race to be on the campaign ballot.[4] Jack

121

Greenberg, LDF director, argued that the only reason to include race on a ballot was for discriminatory purposes, "so that people can react to it."[5] The Supreme Court struck down Louisiana's statute as a violation of the equal protection clause.

In Virginia, voting records and property tax assessments were segregated by race. E. Leslie Hamm sued. In *Hamm v. Virginia State Board of Elections* (1964), the Supreme Court affirmed the trial court's decision to desegregate this basic information. The court said, "Separation of white and colored on the poll tax, residence-certificate and registration lists as well as on the assessment rolls renders these provisions invalid under the equal protection clause of the Fourteenth amendment." Jack Greenberg argued the case for the plaintiffs.

However, the tactic of states' demanding membership lists and accusing the NAACP of hiding communist activity had taken a toll on the organization. Membership in the NAACP was down. Finally, in 1964, the Supreme Court ruled in favor of the NAACP in its fourth appeal in the 1956 case *NAACP v. Alabama*. The organization did not have to reveal its membership list, and it could continue doing business in the South without fear of White elected officials intent on reprisal against either the organization or its membership.[6]

As Black politicians rose to power, buoyed by the Voting Rights Act of 1965, the NAACP and NAACP LDF began their next fifty years of fighting to enforce legislation gained by tireless advocacy and the blood of the slaughtered.

Only two years earlier, Rev. Dr. Martin Luther King Jr. had stood before the largest gathering of protesters in American history. On August 28, 1963, the March on Washington for Jobs and Freedom brought together more than 200,000 Americans, protesting for racial justice, voting rights, and fairness in front of the Lincoln Memorial in Washington, D.C.[7] The NAACP, along with the SCLC, SNCC, National Urban League, National Negro Congress, National Association of Colored Women, and many other national civil rights organizations, played a role in this historic march.

The NAACP and the NAACP LDF were now separate organizations with a common mission: to advance the rights of African Americans. The Supreme Court of Chief Justice Earl Warren, who had presided over the renowned *Brown v. Board of Education* case, was the target of unprecedented attacks by brazen White supremacists still hanging on to tyrannous authority across most of America. But it was in the South that the voting rights war was most evident.

From 1963 to 1965 a force grew that was capable of breaking the century-long grip of White supremacy known as Jim Crow on voting rights. Those two years saw human tragedy and legal triumph. On June

12, 1963, Medgar Evers, voting rights leader, was assassinated in front of his family in Jackson, Mississippi. On that sweltering August day in 1963, Dr. Martin Luther King Jr. told the world about his dream at the March on Washington, inspiring millions to push their government to do more for civil rights.

Then, on September 15, 1963, four Black girls were killed in the bombing of the Sixteenth Street Baptist Church in Birmingham, Alabama, by Klansmen retaliating against the nonviolent civil rights protests that had made national news there. Cynthia Wesley, Carole Robertson, and Addie Mae Collins, all fourteen years old, and Denise McNair, age eleven, were buried under stone and rubble in a shockingly depraved act of cowardice that brought even conservative Whites in Congress and across the nation to the side of Dr. King's nonviolent movement for social change.

In 1964, the passage of the Twenty-fourth Amendment, which abolished payment of poll taxes to vote in federal elections, was ratified. But the carnage continued as Blacks in the South were threatened with lynching, beaten, and run out of their homes for paying the tax or attempting to register to vote, by the Ku Klux Klan and members of the White Citizens Council. Literacy tests remained an obstacle, with registrars asking Blacks seeking to register to vote such test questions as the number of bubbles in a bar of soap or to recite the preamble of the Constitution from memory. Mississippi required Blacks to complete a twenty-one-page form and give their interpretation of one of 285 sections of the state's constitution.

On the night of June 21, 1964, three members of CORE who had come to Mississippi to register Blacks to vote went missing. College students James Chaney, Andrew Goodman, and Michael Schwerner were kidnapped and murdered in Mississippi by Klansmen. The FBI's search for their bodies took weeks and captured national attention. National outrage followed the discovery of the decomposed bodies of these voting rights martyrs. Goodman and Schwerner had been shot at point blank range, while Chaney had been beaten mercilessly and shot three times.

That Freedom Summer of 1964, directed by the Council of Federated Organizations, attracted thousands of students, Blacks and Whites, from the North to the South.[8] They and local NAACP members registered Black voters, set up freedom schools to assist in passing literacy tests, and organized Black communities to fight for their constitutional rights. The NAACP LDF set up an office in Jackson, Mississippi, representing hundreds of Freedom Summer workers who were arrested for protesting segregation, registering Black voters, engaging in civil disobedience through sit-ins, and resisting harassment by local sheriffs intent on maintaining White supremacy.[9]

Events of the Freedom Summer revealed the lethal violence that accompanied the exercise of the rights won by the NAACP in the Supreme

Court. Interracial groups of CORE members traveling by bus were brutally attacked in Montgomery, Alabama. More than a thousand activists were arrested, eighty Freedom Summer workers were beaten, and thirty-seven churches were bombed or burned, along with thirty homes and businesses.[10] Yet instead of being intimidated, hundreds more volunteers arrived in the Deep South to demand change that could not be brought about by litigation alone.

THE CIVIL RIGHTS ACT

The Civil Rights Act of 1964 was a product of political negotiation by the NAACP and pressure from the SCLC and representatives of many civil rights organizations, who met with the Johnson administration. Any change to the oppressive political conditions under which Black Americans lived must be national. Piecemeal litigation, thousands engaged in protests, and local legislative changes were not enough. The writer and civil rights advocate James Baldwin, accompanied by a delegation of artists and activists, had met with Attorney General Robert Kennedy in May 1963 during the Kennedy administration. After President Kennedy's assassination, Martin Luther King Jr. met with President Lyndon Johnson.

Decades earlier, the NAACP had faced bitter disappointment twice over its failure to pass antilynching legislation. This time, so close to passage of the 1964 Civil Rights Act, the NAACP left nothing to chance, relying on its Washington bureau chief, Clarence Mitchell Jr., known as the 101st Senator and a strategic genius at lobbying Congress in the interest of Black communities. Historian Denton Watson provides an insider's perspective on Mitchell in *Lion in the Lobby*. Although both presidents at the time these bills were proposed were southerners, the NAACP's success with the civil rights legislation in the 1960s was probably a product of President Johnson's poverty in contrast with Wilson's elitism, and the skills learned from anti-lynching efforts decades earlier.

The NAACP could do little to reach private discrimination in public accommodations prior to passage of the Civil Rights Act of 1964. In the Civil Rights Cases of 1883, the Supreme Court had struck down federal protections under the Civil Rights Act of 1875, ruling that Congress could not protect Black people against private discrimination. That Supreme Court decision allowed prejudice, racial hatred, and segregation to be practiced in housing, public accommodations, and private businesses for nearly a century. As the NAACP LDF and the NAACP worked on legal cases together, Clarence Mitchell, always a gentleman with an intensity of purpose, undertook a major lobbying effort regarding both the Civil Rights Act and the proposed federal voting rights legislation.

Litigation, legislation, and protest had been the strategy of the NAACP under its first president, Moorfield Storey. Its effectiveness was proven again by the most sweeping civil rights legislation passed since the Civil War era. But it did not come without bloodshed. Once again, violence played a role in spurring on Congress to address the abuse of rights taking place in the South. Headlines kept civil rights in the news despite the looming conflict in Vietnam.

If Black Americans had had civil rights, there would have been no need for Chaney, Goodman, Schwerner and thousands of young Freedom Summer volunteers to go to Mississippi.

THE DETROIT NEWS
**FBI Jails Sheriff, 15 in 3 Rights Killings
Mississippi Refuses to Help in Arrests.**[11]

The murders of Chaney, Goodman, and Schwerner on June 21, 1964, prompted even foot-dragging legislators to pass the Civil Rights Act of 1964.[12] The act was signed into law on July 2, 1964. President Lyndon B. Johnson said of the Civil Rights Act:

We believe that all men are entitled to the blessings of liberty. Yet millions are being deprived of those blessings—not because of their own failures, but because of the color of their skin.

The reasons are deeply imbedded in history and tradition and the nature of man. We can understand—without rancor or hatred—how this all happened.

But it cannot continue. Our Constitution, the foundation of our Republic, forbids it. The principles of our freedom forbid it. Morality forbids it. And the law I will sign tonight forbids it.

That law is the product of months of the most careful debate and discussion. It was proposed more than one year ago by our late and beloved President John F. Kennedy. It received the bipartisan support of more than two-thirds of the Members of both the House and the Senate. An overwhelming majority of Republicans as well as Democrats voted for it.

It has received the thoughtful support of tens of thousands of civic and religious leaders in all parts of this Nation. And it is supported by the great majority of the American people.[13]

It was the most sweeping civil rights legislation since Reconstruction. Finally, the federal government had established a legal right to bring a lawsuit against private acts of discrimination. The NAACP now had the weapon it needed to attack White supremacy practiced by individuals in places large and small.

In December 1964, Rev. Dr. Martin Luther King Jr. traveled to Oslo, Norway. The world watched as he received the Nobel Peace Prize. Dr. King said:

> Your Majesty, Your Royal Highness, Mr. President, Excellencies, Ladies and Gentlemen:
> I accept the Nobel Prize for Peace at a moment when 22 million Negroes of the United States of America are engaged in a creative battle to end the long night of racial injustice. I accept this award on behalf of a civil rights movement which is moving with determination and a majestic scorn for risk and danger to establish a reign of freedom and a rule of justice. I am mindful that only yesterday in Birmingham, Alabama, our children, crying out for brotherhood, were answered with fire hoses, snarling dogs and even death. I am mindful that only yesterday in Philadelphia, Mississippi, young people seeking to secure the right to vote were brutalized and murdered.[14]

But none of this alone was enough to pass a voting rights act.

"BLOODY SUNDAY"

Across the South, Blacks could not vote against the sheriff who beat them or the local judge who would not fairly adjudicate their cases or the school boards that still segregated their children a decade after the *Brown v. Board of Education* decision ruled that segregation in public schools was inherently unequal and a violation of the Fourteenth Amendment. Martin Luther King Jr. met with President Johnson about the proposed Selma to Montgomery march and the need for voting rights legislation.[15] President Johnson needed Dr. King to show Congress why voting rights legislation was necessary. The showdown on voting rights would take place in the little farming town of Selma, Alabama, located in Dallas County, fifty miles outside Montgomery on the banks of the Alabama River.

It was dangerous. Nearby Lowndes County was known as "Bloody Lowndes" because of the brutal tactics of White supremacists there and its bloodstained jail cells. Yet Black farmers and business owners had risen up against exclusion by the White-only Democratic Party to create their own political party, the Black Panther Party.[16] On the evening of February 26, 1965, twenty-six-year-old Jimmie Lee Jackson became a martyr, shot dead by an Alabama state trooper who tracked him down after Alabama troopers descended on a peaceful SNCC-led protest march in Selma and attacked the protesters.[17]

In March 1965, the SCLC, NAACP members, and the SNCC planned to lead a peaceful march protesting the denial of their right to protest for voting rights. Governor George Wallace vowed to stop any such march, citing safety factors. The marchers assembled at Brown Chapel African

Methodist Episcopal Church, a short walk from the Edmund Pettus Bridge, on the morning of March 7. Brown Church was the meeting place for SCLC members. This was in defiance of an antimeeting injunction meant to stop civil rights groups from assembling. However, just as the enslaved used religious services to plan uprisings and escapes, Sunday services at Brown Chapel allowed the demonstrators to meet without defying the injunction.

Then, after services, the group of six hundred walked four blocks over to the Edmund Pettus Bridge. They were en route to the state's capital, Montgomery. The afternoon was overcast. At the foot of the opposing side of the bridge awaited a phalanx of troopers wearing gas masks. On the other side of the bridge was Dallas County, known for its ferocious racism and troopers led by County Sheriff Jim Clark and Commanding Officer John Cloud. Clark was notorious in Dallas County for incidents such as the time a peaceful group of Black men attempted to register to vote at the Selma courthouse. Dr. King's close friend, Rev. Cordy Tindall "C.T." Vivian, led the men. Sheriff Clark blocked the courthouse door, pushing the men away and hitting Rev. Vivian so hard Clark broke his own hand. Vivian would later write in his book *Black Power and the American Myth*, "Blacks often found they had won the privilege of voting at the expense of their right to live."[18]

On March 7, Clark had hurriedly deputized nearly one hundred local White males, arming them with nightsticks and tear gas to use against unarmed Black elders, women, and men who only desired to vote. Because it was a Sunday, there was very little traffic. Reverend Hosea Williams of SCLC and student activist John Lewis of the SNCC were on the front lines of what became a one-sided bloodbath. America watched in horror as Lewis and other peaceful marchers, women like Amelia Boynton, and the elderly were beaten unconscious by troopers encouraged by segregationist governor Wallace. Newspaper headlines and television cameras captured the unprovoked attack on unarmed Black protesters, wearing their blood-soaked church clothes. The assault galvanized a nation.

The brutal attack became known as "Bloody Sunday." Reporters and a television camera captured Alabama's all-White state troopers, some on horseback, wildly attacking Black men, women, and children with nightsticks and tear gas on the bridge, named for Edmund Pettus, a Democratic segregationist, Grand Dragon of the Ku Klux Klan, and confederate soldier; it was a fitting voting rights battleground.

The Washington Post
Tear Gas, Clubs, Halt 600 in Selma March

State Troopers Beat
and Injure Many Negroes
Monday, March 8, 1965[19]

President Lyndon Johnson had watched on television in horror as armed men attacked the unarmed demonstrators while they ran or lay helpless on the ground. Johnson issued a statement promising to demand legislation protecting the voting rights of African Americans.

Due to a scheduling miscommunication, Rev. Martin Luther King Jr. was absent that day. But King led the protesters on a second attempt to cross the bridge and march to Montgomery on Tuesday, March 9. Supporters arrived from around the country. This time thousands of demonstrators of all backgrounds, led by Dr. King, approached the top of the bridge. They faced even more Alabama state troopers. But King stopped, knelt to pray, and then turned around, leading the stunned protesters away.

Meanwhile, the NAACP LDF was representing the group in federal court. Judge Frank Johnson, in Montgomery, had ordered a hearing on the events in Selma. Jack Greenberg of the NAACP LDF and local NAACP cooperating attorney Fred Gray, of Tuskegee, advised Dr. King not to lead a protest march across the bridge until Judge Johnson allowed it. To do otherwise would violate his court order. So King turned around without crossing the bridge. That day became known as "Turnaround Tuesday."

King's followers were confused, and members of the SNCC felt betrayed by this abbreviated march. However, at the federal hearing Greenberg and Gray presented a solid case before Judge Johnson that resulted in an order allowing the march to Montgomery.

On March 9, White supremacists fatally beat Rev. James Reeb, a White Unitarian minister from Boston who had participated in the second march. "His murder underscored the willingness of ordinary whites to maintain the established order."[20] Local Black demonstrators could not help feeling bitter when national news covered the beating death of Rev. Reeb but was silent when young Jimmy Jackson was gunned down by troopers inside a restaurant following a peaceful march.

Dr. King led a third march on March 21, 1965, arriving in Montgomery on March 25, this time with over twenty-five thousand marchers having joined the demonstration for voting rights. This third march was protected by the National Guard and a federal court order barring any interference by state troopers. This simple request to vote in a country that called itself a "beacon of democracy" for the world to emulate would be denied again. After thousands marched to Montgomery, Viola Liuzzo, a White volunteer from Detroit, was murdered by Klansmen while driving a Black voting rights volunteer to the airport in Montgomery, Alabama.

A hundred years after President Abraham Lincoln signed the Emancipation Proclamation, much had improved since Ovington and Villard made that "Lincoln Day Call" that would result in the founding of the

National Association for the Advancement of Colored People. However, progress was still counted in terms of traumatic events needed to spur legislators into action. Deadly reprisals followed each step. After "Bloody Sunday," America was nearly ready for a voting rights act.

The legacy of the Supreme Court's decisions in *Dred Scott* and *Plessy* had met its match in *Smith v. Allwright* and *Brown v. Board of Education.* Protesters testing their constitutional rights stood up to segregationists, who would not accept that Blacks had rights that they need respect. But passage of the extensive piece of federal legislation contemplated by President Johnson would require an extraordinary confluence of horrific events, liberal White Democrats and Republicans, shamed Dixiecrats, student protests, presidential pressure, and watchful lobbying by the NAACP.[21]

When Rev. Dr. Martin Luther King Jr. arrived in Selma, Alabama, he knew he was entering a war zone. Blacks were primed for activism, from the tent cities, to the Black Panther Party, to Black candidates who ran for office even when they knew there was little chance of winning because most Blacks were not allowed to vote. But it was the violent attacks by state troopers on the Edmund Pettus Bridge that galvanized a nation, giving President Lyndon B. Johnson the political might to pass a voting rights act.

JOHNSON AND THE VOTING RIGHTS ACT

On March 15, before the third attempt to march in Selma, President Johnson presented his demands for a voting rights law to both houses of Congress. The man from Texas who had stalled civil rights legislation as a senator was ready to confront his southern past and his racist peers.

Historian Robert A. Caro, the renowned expert on Lyndon Johnson, described the man's career, from his rise in the Senate, to a decline in power as vice president, to the assassination of John Kennedy, which handed him the White House.[22] There is little evidence in this progression to support the idea that this man would become the key figure in the making of civil rights law. In particular, there is no inkling that this southern politician would become responsible for the most extensive voting rights legislation since Congress passed the Fifteenth Amendment.

As a US senator, Johnson had stalled the civil rights legislation of 1957 and stripped away its protections. Now he endeavored to go down in history as a champion of racial justice and became responsible for the passage of the greatest civil rights legislation of the twentieth century. He used his knowledge of the Senate rules to keep the Civil Rights Act from defeat in 1964 when a southern Democrat added "sex" to the language of the 1964 act, which outlawed discrimination based on race, color, religion, or national origin.[23] Gender equality was as controversial as, or even more so than, racial equality. Despite Howard W. Smith's (D-VA) change, the Civil Rights Act was signed into law with the added protection against sex discrimination.

Civil rights legislation was passed faster than perhaps even the NAACP thought possible. Johnson had been renowned for his ability to shepherd through or completely halt any bill. President Johnson was the last Speaker of the House to rise to the office of president. He wanted a place in history, and civil rights could get it for him. Johnson chose to place all of his political capital behind passage of legislation created to assist the poor and marginalized.

When his administration began, Johnson had declared a war on poverty. On January 8, 1964, in his State of the Union Address, President Johnson warned a nation still grieving over the assassination of John Kennedy in November 1963 that he planned to take bold steps toward social reform. He declared an unconditional "War on Poverty." Johnson also told millions of listeners in the North and South that segregation must come to an end.

Johnson was born poor in 1908, during rigid segregation, and struggled through the Great Depression. He picked cotton under a blazing sun by day as a child. He knew that at night Blacks and Mexicans were lynched. He witnessed firsthand the misery of poverty and racism. Johnson was an expert on disenfranchisement of Blacks. He rose through the political ranks in Texas in the all-White Democratic primary system and the private club created to prevent Blacks from voting when Texas's all-White primary was struck down.

Yet, Johnson asked Congress for better schools, health care, homes, training, and job opportunities to "help more Americans, especially young Americans, to escape from squalor."[24] He sought programs to assist the elderly and the rural poor. Congress responded with the Economic Opportunity Act (EOA) of 1964 and the Civil Rights Act of 1964. The EOA created programs to improve housing, education, job training, and Social Security. President Johnson's War on Poverty continued in the footsteps of President Franklin Roosevelt's New Deal of the 1930s. Many southerners hated him for it. Like Roosevelt, he was viewed as a traitor to his kind.

President Johnson asked to increase the minimum wage and unemployment insurance. He knew there were similarities between the poverty of Whites and Blacks. Both experienced miserable lives in destitution, bereft of opportunity. His War on Poverty began in Appalachia, an area of 205,000 square miles stretching from Mississippi to upstate New York, in which millions of poverty-stricken White Americans lived in rural communities. One in three persons (mostly White) in Appalachia lived in poverty.

AN AMERICAN PROBLEM

On August 6, 1965, President Johnson signed the Voting Rights Act into law. That night Johnson spoke to the American people:

Mr. Speaker, Mr. President, Members of the Congress:
I speak tonight for the dignity of man and the destiny of democracy.
I urge every member of both parties, Americans of all religions and of all colors, from every section of this country, to join me in that cause.

At times history and fate meet at a single time in a single place to shape a turning point in man's unending search for freedom. So it was at Lexington and Concord. So it was a century ago at Appomattox. So it was last week in Selma, Alabama.

There, long-suffering men and women peacefully protested the denial of their rights as Americans. Many were brutally assaulted. One good man, a man of God, was killed.

There is no cause for pride in what has happened in Selma. There is no cause for self-satisfaction in the long denial of equal rights of millions of Americans. But there is cause for hope and for faith in our democracy in what is happening here tonight.

For the cries of pain and the hymns and protests of oppressed people have summoned into convocation all the majesty of this great Government—the Government of the greatest Nation on earth.

Our mission is at once the oldest and the most basic of this country: to right wrong, to do justice, to serve man.

In our time we have come to live with moments of great crisis. Our lives have been marked with debate about great issues; issues of war and peace, issues of prosperity and depression. But rarely in any time does an issue lay bare the secret heart of America itself. Rarely are we met with a challenge, not to our growth or abundance, our welfare or our security, but rather to the values and the purposes and the meaning of our beloved Nation.

The issue of equal rights for American Negroes is such an issue. And should we defeat every enemy, should we double our wealth and conquer the stars, and still be unequal to this issue, then we will have failed as a people and as a nation.

For with a country as with a person, "What is a man profited, if he shall gain the whole world, and lose his own soul?"

There is no Negro problem. There is no Southern problem. There is no Northern problem. There is only an American problem. And we are met here tonight as Americans—not as Democrats or Republicans—we are met here as Americans to solve that problem.[25]

The effect of the new law was immediate. Prior to the Voting Rights Act,

despite the earnest efforts of the Justice Department and of many federal judges, these new laws have done little to cure the problem of voting discrimination. According to estimates by the Attorney General during hearings on the Act, registration of voting-age Negroes in Alabama rose only from 14.2% to 19.4% between 1958 and 1964; in Louisiana it barely inched ahead from 31.7% to 31.8% between 1956 and 1965; and in Mississippi it increased only from 4.4% to 6.4% between 1954 and 1964. In each instance, registration of voting-age whites ran roughly 50 percentage points or more ahead of Negro registration.[26]

The Justice Department of the United States defined the protective mechanisms within the Voting Rights of 1965. Section 2 of the act, which closely followed the language of the Fifteenth Amendment, applied to literacy tests a nationwide prohibition against the denial or abridgment of the right to vote.[27] Section 2 states:

No voting qualification or pre-requisite to voting, or standard, practice, or procedure shall be imposed or applied by any State or political subdivision to deny or abridge the right of any citizen of the United States to vote on account of race or color.

Among its other provisions, the act contained special enforcement provisions targeted at those areas of the country where Congress believed the potential for discrimination was the greatest.[28]

Section 5 of the act requires preclearance of districting plans affecting racial minorities. The act covered specific states and counties that had a history of discriminating against African Americans. Both Alabama and Texas were required to seek federal government approval prior to enacting laws that could affect Black voter participation. This requirement was later expanded to include all people of color and several other jurisdictions.

Under section 5, jurisdictions covered by these special provisions could not implement any change affecting voting until the attorney general or the US District Court for the District of Columbia determined that the change did not have a discriminatory purpose and would not have a discriminatory effect.[29] In addition, the attorney general could designate a county covered by these special provisions for the appointment of a federal examiner to review the qualifications of persons who wanted to register to vote. Furthermore, in those counties where a federal examiner was serving, the attorney general could request that federal observers monitor activities within the county's polling places.[30]

MORE BATTLES

The Voting Rights Act had not included a provision prohibiting poll taxes, but had directed the attorney general to challenge their use.[31] The Voting Rights Act was challenged in 1966 by South Carolina (and joined in the case by Mississippi, Alabama, Virginia, Georgia, and Louisiana). But the Supreme Court stated in *South Carolina v. Katzenbach*:

> Congress had found that case-by-case litigation was inadequate to combat wide-spread and persistent discrimination in voting, because of the inordinate amount of time and energy required to overcome the obstructionist tactics invariably encountered in these lawsuits. After enduring nearly a century of systematic resistance to the Fifteenth Amendment, Congress might well decide to shift the advantage of time and inertia from the perpetrators of the evil to its victims.[32]

The Voting Rights Act removed the states' authority to use literacy tests and poll taxes in local elections. South Carolina argued that Congress had overreached its constitutional authority when it passed the Voting Rights Act, in violation of states' rights. But the Supreme Court found:

> The South Carolina Constitutional Convention of 1895 was a leader in the widespread movement to disenfranchise Negroes. Key, Southern Politics, 537-539. Senator Ben Tillman frankly explained to the state delegates the aim of the new literacy test: "The only thing we can do as patriots and as statesmen is to take from [the 'ignorant blacks'] every ballot that we can under the laws of our national government." He was equally candid about the exemption from the literacy test for persons who could "understand" and "explain" a section of the state constitution: "There is no particle of fraud or illegality in it. It is just simply showing partiality, perhaps, [laughter,] or discriminating."[33]

The Supreme Court upheld the Voting Rights Act.

In *Katzenbach v. Morgan*, also in 1966, New York State challenged a section of the Voting Rights Act that allowed Puerto Ricans to register to vote without taking the state's literacy test, which was in English, if they had at least a sixth-grade education.[34] Norman Redlich of the NAACP LDF argued the case at the Supreme Court. The court ruled in favor of the Voting Rights Act and found that section 4(e) did not exceed the powers of Congress. The act was intended to allow more people to vote.

Poll taxes had been outlawed in federal elections by the Twenty-fourth Amendment. But they remained in effect in state elections. States could force voters to pay poll taxes in order to vote in local elections for offices such as commissioner, judge, school board, sheriff, and mayor. These were the elected offices that had for a century exercised direct control over the quality of life of Black Americans. Voting in these local elections was essential to Black self-determination.

In 1966 the NAACP LDF represented NAACP member Annie E. Harper in her lawsuit challenging poll taxes required in Virginia local elections. In Norfolk, Virginia, Evelyn Butts brought a similar poll tax case, represented by attorney Joseph Jordan, forty-one, a Black veteran wounded in World War II. Thurgood Marshall argued the case for the government as solicitor general. *Harper v. Virginia Board of Elections* challenged Virginia's poll tax law, which required a payment of $1.20, as a violation of the equal protection clause of the Fourteenth Amendment.[35]

The Supreme Court agreed. Justice William O. Douglas wrote: "We conclude that a state violated the equal protection clause of the 14th Amendment whenever it makes the affluence of the voter or payment of any fee an electoral standard."[36] White supremacists had created poll taxes in the 1800s to disenfranchise the Black vote. In 1966 the court ruled that local elections, like federal elections, were to be free of poll taxes. With this decision, the Supreme Court finally overturned *Breedlove v. Suttles*, the 1937 case that had upheld state poll taxes.

Finally, cases could be brought that struck at the heart of the Mississippi Plans of 1890 and 1901. In *Louisiana v. United States*, the NAACP, working with the US attorney general's office, brought a lawsuit against the states of Mississippi and Louisiana challenging their use of literacy tests and other discriminatory conduct.

The Supreme Court found that the Louisiana legislature had created a "Segregation Committee." The court stated:

> That committee cooperated with Citizens Councils to instruct registrars to promote white political control and to begin wholesale purges of Negroes from the voting rolls. At least 21 parishes in the mid-1950's began applying the interpretation test, to which was added in 1960 a comprehension requirement, applicable to all persons, which the State Registration Board ordered rigidly enforced. The District Court, in view of the virtually unlimited discretion given voting registrars by the Louisiana laws and because the 21 parish registrars had used the interpretation test to keep Negroes from voting, held that test, on its face and as applied, invalid under the Fourteenth and Fifteenth Amendments and 42 U.S.C. § 1971(a), and enjoined its future use in the State.[37]

In Mississippi, the court's decision revealed the core of segregationist policy that had denied Black Americans their constitutionally sacred right to vote for generations. The court found that the US attorney general's office had the right to sue a state for denying the vote to Black citizens from 1890, when Mississippi changed its constitution to purposely deprive Blacks of their rights.

Justice Hugo Black, a former member of the Ku Klux Klan turned racial progressive, wrote the opinion against Louisiana:

> Charging that appellees, the State of Mississippi, the Election Commissioners, and six voting registrars of that State were destroying the right of Mississippi Negroes to vote, the United States brought this action for relief under 42 U.S.C. §1971(d) and other provisions. The complaint alleged a longstanding, carefully executed plan to keep Negroes in Mississippi from voting. It stated that, in 1890, in order to restrict the Negro franchise, a new constitution was adopted, § 244 of which established as a voting prerequisite reading, understanding, or giving a reasonable interpretation of a section of the state constitution; that this provision, when coupled with Negro ineligibility until about 1952 to vote in the decisive Democratic primary election, within nine years reduced the percentage of qualified voters who were Negroes from over 50% to about 9%, and, by 1954, only about 5% of Negroes of voting age were registered; that, in 1954, § 244 was amended to make all of its previously alternative requirements apply and to make an applicant additionally demonstrate "a reasonable understanding of the duties and obligations of citizenship," a requirement which registrars allegedly have applied in a racially discriminatory manner; that, in 1960, two discriminatory voting statutes were adopted, one imposing a "good moral character" qualification, and the other (contrary to federal law) permitting destruction of some voting records; and that, in 1962, a "package" of legislation was enacted further to impede Negro voting registration. The District Court dismissed the complaint for failure to state a claim upon which relief could be granted, held that the Election Commissioners were not proper parties, that the registrars could not be sued jointly, and that venue was improper as to some.[38]

Dr. Martin Luther King Jr. had said that "the arc of the moral universe is long, but it bends towards justice."[39]

INTERNAL BATTLES

Finally, the Mississippi Plan had fallen. America was changing. The NAACP was changing also. So, too, was the Supreme Court. After that Freedom Summer of violence, NAACP LDF attorney Constance Baker-Motley returned to New York City and entered politics. President Johnson nominated her to be the first Black female federal judge. Thurgood Marshall was destined to ascend to the Supreme Court bench. The role of the NAACP was changing. The voting rights struggle became a cold war, with state legislators creating elaborate schemes to dilute Black voting strength through redistricting ploys and election machinations.

All wars have inner conflicts and disputes between allies. Tensions and distrust mounted between the NAACP and NAACP LDF director

Jack Greenberg. Thurgood Marshall wanted a judgeship on the Supreme Court. President Johnson had started Marshall on that path, beginning with a position on the Second Circuit Court of Appeals and the position of solicitor general, arguing on behalf of the federal government he had sued so frequently in the past. Decades of the unstable life of a civil rights litigator would be rewarded with the stability of a government position that offered security for his family, rest, and eventually retirement.

True to the promise he had made in 1961, President Johnson nominated Marshall to the Second Circuit Court of Appeals and as solicitor general. Robert Carter, a veteran of World War II and many civil rights battles, and Jack Greenberg are both in that iconic photo, standing next to Thurgood Marshall on the steps of the US Supreme Court after the *Brown* decision. Carter had been passed over as director of the NAACP in favor of Jack Greenberg.

Greenberg was a legal strategist who argued before the Supreme Court forty times. Also a veteran of World War II, he took on civil rights cases like a soldier in battle. He even referred to it as "trench warfare." Carter was soft spoken but analytical and could be described as a disciplined activist. Both Carter and Greenberg worked beside Marshall from the early days of *Brown v. Board*, Greenberg leading the office while Marshall went down South to litigate cases. But Carter was second in charge under Marshall.

Greenberg knew the director's job was his. Marshall informed Carter of his selection of Greenberg in a letter that Carter was instructed to open only after reaching his vacation destination in Italy. Carter was devastated. He had assumed he would become director-counsel. But a falling out between Marshall and Carter may have caused Marshall to select Greenberg. Both men were brilliant, hard working, and dedicated to civil rights. There is a long history of collaboration between African Americans and Jewish Americans on civil rights issues. Later, Kivie Kaplan would become president of the NAACP from 1966–1975.

The NAACP had originally been founded by White progressives. But now for many members, having a White leader of a Black civil rights organization ran counter to the twentieth-century philosophy of self-determination that was being expressed by women, people of color, and other formerly marginalized groups. With the loss of a common foe, divisions widened between civil rights organizations that had once worked together closely.

Thurgood Marshall, the first Black Supreme Court justice, was a symbol of great pride for the NAACP and the Black community. Over time, Marshall, the original Mr. NAACP, found himself an icon unable to make a difference. He had grown used to having an impact as a civil rights attorney in charge of the most recognized organization for social justice in America. As one of nine justices, his vote rarely changed the outcome of a ruling. As conservative presidents Richard Nixon, Gerald Ford, and Ronald Reagan nominated conservative justices, Marshall found himself in the minority, or alone, writing fiery dissents even in civil rights cases.

SICK AND TIRED

By the late 1960s the Black community was bitterly divided. Many no longer embraced nonviolence. Blacks were impatient for the change that should have come with voting rights. Too many lives had been lost in the struggle over the ballot. Blacks had the vote. Blacks were elected to Congress. It had all been promised in the Constitution of 1789. But there was little to show for decades of debilitating sacrifice and loss.

Reverend Dr. Martin Luther King Jr. was assassinated on April 4, 1968. Back in Montgomery, at the end of his journey from Selma Dr. King had asked the tired crowd of thousands: "How long? Not Long was the response." But the Black community was divided about how long change was taking. Many no longer chose to embrace the nonviolent course of action proscribed by the late Dr. King. Young Blacks, especially, were impatient for the promised change that would come with voting rights. So many lives had been lost in the struggle over the ballot: leaders, foot soldiers, and civilians alike.

Perhaps the anticipation of change and its late arrival caused the tremendous release of grief-filled anger and rioting that followed the murder of Reverend King. To many Blacks, there was too little to show for decades of debilitating sacrifice and his loss to an assassin's bullet. The riots began. Decades of rage erupted into the streets.

Yet in 1968, the war over those rights begged the question of just how long the struggle would continue. Political progress was made in the wake of Dr. King's assassination. Before the passage of the Voting Rights Act, Fannie Lou Hamer had helped create the alternative Mississippi Freedom Democratic Party (MFDP). In 1964 she, along with members of the MFDP, had attended the Democratic National Convention in Atlantic City. At the convention, Hamer spoke of the beating she received in retaliation for registering to vote. She gave a nationally televised speech critical of a country that would allow the convention's Mississippi delegation to exclude Blacks and a political party that would not seat the MFDP.

The Democratic Party's Executive Committee offered two at-large seats. Hamer turned them down as mere tokens. Hamer resented the NAACP for attempting to control voting rights for rural Mississippi from New York City. Although the NAACP attorneys traveled to Mississippi as often as they could afford to, Hamer had lived there all of her life and knew the players. Hamer had been beaten, threatened, and fired upon while working as an advocate for voting rights. When asked why she persisted, Hamer responded, "All my life I've been sick and tired. Now I'm sick and tired of being sick and tired."[40] She gave voice to the feelings of millions of African Americans.

In 1968 Hamer attended the Democratic Convention in Chicago as the first Black delegate from the South to be seated at a national political convention since Reconstruction. The unrest surrounding that convention overshadowed that vindication of her years of hard work. Unfortunately, Hamer never achieved the political positions she sought in Mississippi, nor did the MFDP gain the traction needed to make the changes Blacks needed there.

Wharlest Jackson, Mississippi NAACP treasurer, was martyred in 1967 when a bomb exploded in his car. He was probably killed because he had accepted a job promotion to a position only held by White men, at Armstrong Tire & Rubber Plant in Natchez, Mississippi. Once again, a Black man was forgetting his place, and White supremacists needed to reestablish their self-esteem. No one was arrested for this cowardly act. In 1965 local NAACP president George Metcalfe had taken a promotion at Armstrong Tire & Rubber. When he turned on the ignition of his car, it blew up. Metcalfe barely survived. But no one was arrested. Klansmen were suspected. These are among many civil rights–era cold cases.

Times were changing within the civil rights community. The "Young Turks" of the NAACP demanded Black Power programs more focused on urban Black political, economic, and educational issues. The NAACP LDF successfully represented the Black, powerful, and irreverent Harlem congressman and leader of the historic Abyssinian Church, Adam Clayton Powell Jr., in defense of his seat in the House of Representatives, in *Powell v. McCormack* in 1969.[41] In this case, a special House committee had investigated Powell for alleged misuse of travel funds as chair of the Committee on Education and Labor.

He had been held in contempt of Congress, yet won reelection despite the cloud of controversy. However, the House had expelled him in 1966, and when Powell returned to the Capitol, Speaker of the House John Mc-Cormack refused to administer the oath of office. Representative Powell challenged his expulsion as discriminatory, because White members abused funds and weren't punished, and he requested his back pay. When the case came to the Supreme Court, it ruled in favor of Powell.[42] However, the Powell political dynasty was damaged.

NAACP political wizard Clarence Mitchell led the organization's Washington lobbying effort. The ability to lobby for progressive legislation and oppose the ascent of racially biased judges while litigating civil rights cases was the hallmark of the NAACP. This strategy began with its successful opposition to Judge Parker, a racist from North Carolina, who was nominated to the Supreme Court in 1930. In 1969 the NAACP successfully defeated the Supreme Court nomination of Clement F. Haynsworth.

As expected, the totalitarian enemy of any democracy, represented by White supremacists, struck back. In *Allen v. Board of Electors*, the states of Virginia and Mississippi argued that the voting law was unconstitutional and that Congress had exceeded its authority in passing the Voting Rights Act.[43] The Supreme Court ruled in favor of the act and reaffirmed that states listed under section 5 for preclearance must first submit any changes to their voting laws to the federal government for approval before enacting them. The court also ruled that private parties can bring a lawsuit under the Voting Rights Act.[44]

In Brooklyn, New York, the case of *Cooper v. Power* challenged the gerrymandering of voting districts that kept millions of Black voters from electing their choices for Congress.[45] Despite the large Black population there, not one Black person had been elected to Congress from Brooklyn. Andrew Cooper led a legal challenge, later joined by the NAACP, to change the voting districts. The successful conclusion of the *Cooper* redistricting case would pivot Shirley Chisholm, a Black Brooklyn public schoolteacher, into the House of Representatives. Chisholm entered Congress in 1969 as the first Black female US representative, only three years after passage of the Voting Rights Act.

The Voting Rights Act had turned the tide in the voting rights war. In Louisiana, birthplace of the *Plessy* doctrine of "separate but equal," more than 350,000 Black residents registered to vote in 1969. "Few events in American political life have had as profound or as far-reaching consequences as has passage of the Voting Rights Act."[46] The NAACP and NAACP LDF would make sweeping changes because of the passage of the Voting Rights Act and the sacrifices it required. But the voting rights war was far from over. States would continue to attack the protections provided by this extraordinary legislation. The organization was embattled from outside and within.

7

~

Vote Dilution, Photo Identification Laws, and Civil Death

Yet with a steady beat, Have not our weary feet,
Come to the place for which our fathers sighed?

—James Weldon Johnson, "Lift Every Voice and Sing" (1899)

More black elected leaders symbolized an oppressed community's rising political power and the power of Black voters and of the Voting Rights Act. As Black politicians took their places in federal, state, and local offices, the entrenched opposition rallied. The voting rights war had not ended. When tactics changed, the NAACP and NAACP LDF remained diligent. Blatant racial intimidation decreased, but did not end. Even with the end of poll taxes, property ownership requirements, and literacy tests, states still had the constitutional authority to decide voting qualifications and create voting districts.

Voting rights cases were now fought over those voting districts, the intent of legislators when redistricting, and qualifications needed to vote. Times were changing. Conservative justices of the Supreme Court began to replace the Warren court that had presided over *Brown v. Board of Education* and most of the NAACP's civil rights–era voting cases. Those qualifications could not be discriminatory or race based on their face. Nor could they be enacted with an intent to harm a particular racial or ethnic group. The Voting Rights Act contained a preclearance provision, which required a state with a racial history of discrimination against voters to submit their proposed voting laws to the federal government for review. Only with federal government approval could these states enact or change their voting rights laws. The Voting Rights Act, Civil Rights Act, and Fair Housing Act ushered in a period known as the New Reconstruction.

However, the Voting Rights Act was set to expire in 1970. When signed into law, it was only meant to last five years. But with skillful lobbying of the White House by Clarence Mitchell Jr. of the NAACP's Washington bureau, the Voting Rights Act was extended by President Richard Nixon. Then Mitchell helped to defeat Nixon's US Supreme Court nominee to replace departing US Supreme Court Justice Abe Fortas with an appellate judge from Georgia, G. Harrold Carswell, a segregationist who once said in a speech that he had tried to "out-nigger" his opponent in a race for the Georgia legislature.[1] Unfortunately, Mitchell would not be able to prevent the ultraconservative William Rehnquist from ascending to the court in 1972.[2]

Literacy tests were dying, but it was a lingering death. In 1970 some states held on to these unfair tests despite the Voting Rights Act. Congress lowered the voting age to eighteen in 1971 with the Twenty-sixth Amendment. A case from the Northwest combined both issues when Oregon sued to keep its literacy test. The Oregon legislature opposed efforts to lower the voting age by constitutional amendment.[3] The US Supreme Court ruled against Oregon's literacy test in *Oregon v. Mitchell* in 1970. In 1971, the newly ratified Twenty-sixth Amendment reduced the voting age from twenty-one to eighteen years old. As with the ratification of the Twentieth Amendment, which gave women the vote, the political power of African Americans increased with the expansion of the franchise, this time to include younger voters. The impact was nearly immediate.

It was in 1971 that the Congressional Black Caucus was founded by thirteen US representatives—John Conyers (MI), Gus Hawkins (CA), Parren Mitchell (MD), Charles Diggs (MI), Louis Stokes (OH), Bill Clay (MO), Robert Nix Sr. (PA), Ron Dellums (CA), Charles Rangel (NY), George Collins (IL), Ralph Metcalfe (IL), Walter Fauntroy (DC), and Shirley Chisholm (NY)—making history a hundred years after the Fifteenth Amendment was ratified. At their first Washington event, actor and activist Ossie Davis, the keynote speaker, reminded this prestigious group that it was about "the plan—not the man."

Voting-related murders had declined, but they had not ended. Terrorism as a tool of suppressing the vote remained a threat. White supremacists fearing diminished political power have retaliated against Black political and economic progress for a hundred years. It was in 1870, more than a hundred years before passage of the Voting Rights Act, that Hiram Revels first rose to the US Senate; he had faced greater threats than any member of the CBC. In 1971, the year the Congressional Black Caucus was conceived, firebombs destroyed the home of NAACP Tennessee branch president James Mapp, who had led the desegregation of the Hamilton

School District and the local voter registration project. However, NAACP branches continued their relentless push forward, despite the danger. African Americans, and now people of color outside the Black community, could rise to political leadership on the municipal, state, and federal levels due to the sacrifices of NAACP activists like James Mapp.

In 1972, Representative Shirley Chisholm was the first African American from a major political party to run for president. That same year, former NAACP director Robert L. Carter became a federal judge, an appointee of President Richard M. Nixon, a Republican. Carter was born into *Plessy's* Jim Crow segregation. It was his legal strategy that had saved the NAACP from the attempts of White segregationists to acquire its membership lists. Nixon's appointee Attorney General Ed Meese used the civil rights division to deconstruct civil rights, nearly reversing decades of the hard-fought freedoms NAACP members had died to acquire.

Ironically, in this era of tremendous political progress by African Americans, the NAACP and the NAACP LDF were besieged by internal and external conflicts. The success of the NAACP came with a price. There was a *Bakke*-like political backlash in the country. The war in Vietnam and the riots that surrounded it took their toll. At one point there was a question as to whether the country would survive. Within the Black community there was also change. The protracted fight for even basic civil rights had cost the lives of the community's dearest heroes. Yet the fight had not been completely won. With passage of the Civil Rights Act of 1964, Voting Rights Act of 1965, and Fair Housing Act of 1968, the community thought the worst of the war was over and the time had come to enjoy the spoils of victory: freedom.

The United States and the Soviet Union had been engaged in the Cold War since the Korean War. The Soviet Union, which was an ally during World War II, was now the enemy. The civil rights movement was in a similar cold war in the 1970s as territoriality took the place of unity and shared goals. With the murder of Dr. Martin Luther King Jr. and conservatives taking greater control of the Supreme Court, civil rights organizations could ill afford a continuing decline in membership and financial contributions. There was simmering animosity over the rise in Black political power; but overt intimidation, murder, and casualties had decreased drastically. The battles returned to the courts.

Funding for Black civil rights organizations generally, and the NAACP in particular, decreased as integration and opportunities increased. This led to dependence on private donations from non-Black, wealthy grantors and foundations, which in turn influenced the civil rights agenda. With its decision in 1978 in the *Bakke* reverse discrimination case, the Supreme Court removed a weapon from the civil rights arsenal.[4] There was no longer an assumed race-based harm. Each plaintiff would have to make the case on an individualized basis. History meant little except in voting rights cases, all due to the Voting Rights Act.

In 1975 Republican President Gerald Ford signed a reauthorization of the Voting Rights Act, with a provision eliminating all literacy tests and adding language protections for Latinos and other non-English-speaking voters. Retaliation for exercising and enjoying constitutional rights led to heavy reprisals. Opposing forces used the courts to stop Blacks from protesting against businesses that discriminated against them. For example, in March 1966 African Americans in Port Gibson, Mississippi, and other areas of Claiborne County had picketed White businesses that were accused of racial discrimination in hiring and their treatment of Black customers. The local branch of the NAACP had called a meeting at the First Baptist Church, at which hundreds voted to boycott certain White merchants.

The merchants had retaliated with a lawsuit against the NAACP for losses caused by the boycott. The *Claiborne Hardware* case resulted in years of litigation and a court order to pay $1.25 million. However, like the retaliatory cases brought against the NAACP in the 1950s by states attempting to acquire the organization's membership lists, victory was achieved at last. On appeal, in 1982 the Supreme Court ruled in favor of the NAACP.[5] It had been a long, costly, and hard-fought battle. The NAACP won. Boycotts had been proven to be an effective means of protest by the NAACP and other groups. The world-renowned Montgomery bus boycott, retail store boycotts in Harlem, New York, and Woolworth counter boycotts were a galvanizing mechanism for the community, cost little, drew media attention to discrimination, and created change. However, despite the victory, after the *Claiborne* case a fear of protracted litigation virtually ended the boycott as a form of protest. The NAACP had lost a formidable weapon.

However, the NAACP LDF had continued the charge ahead to the next voting battle. It was close to home, in New York City. In 1977 Jews in Brooklyn, New York, challenged the voting districts that had been changed after decades of discrimination. The NAACP LDF was an amicus or friend of the court, defending the redistricting of Brooklyn, in *United Jewish Organizations v. Carey*.[6] The case was appealed to the US Supreme Court. Jack Greenberg argued the case for the NAACP LDF. Because of a history of discrimination, Brooklyn was under the preclearance provision of the Voting Rights Act. The Hasidic community complained about the redistricting plan, alleging that it violated their Fourteenth and Fifteenth Amendment rights and that New York State had gone too far to create Black districts. The Supreme Court disagreed, ruling for the state and upholding the districts. The Court ruled that Hasidic Jews had no right "to a separate community recognition . . . and racial considerations were permissible to correct past discrimination."[7]

In his *Bakke* dissent, Justice Marshall recounted how states created "various techniques, including poll taxes, deliberately complicated balloting processes, property and literacy qualifications, and finally, the white primary."[8]

Marshall's dissent in *Bakke* not only recounted America's history of slavery, Jim Crow segregation and lynching, he reminded his colleagues that only one year before it decided race could be used to right the wrongs of discrimination. Their Brooklyn voting rights case of 1977 was a distant memory. In 1978, Justice Lewis Powell, who was discovered secretly advising conservative leaders with his "Powell Memorandum," wrote an opinion stripping affirmative action of its power. Universities could no longer address systemic historical racism. Affirmative action policies were now restricted to current specific discriminatory practices; and race could only be one of several factors in the policy. The *Bakke* decision sent the civil rights community into an era of self-doubt, fearful of losing ground. Instead of moving forward, the NAACP and the LDF were trying to fend off attacks. Conservatives smelled blood. Their new weapon was "reverse discrimination." They were on the offensive. Defending against these attacks would require money.

The NAACP was operating at a fiscal deficit. Funders were selecting the offspring legal organization, the NAACP LDF, over its much larger, needier parent, the NAACP. Black communities were confused by the overlapping missions and name. Both organizations received donations, both were nonprofits, and both worked on cases. However, the NAACP LDF was known for Thurgood Marshall and took credit for the famous *Brown v. Board of Education* victory. The internal bickering between the NAACP and the NAACP LDF continued to smolder. A truce was called in the name of social justice. There was little time for recriminations. But this truce would prove temporary. A turf war was being mounted between these two organizations.

THE *BAKKE* CASE: "REVERSE DISCRIMINATION"

In 1978 the court was reviewing a case that challenged affirmative action based on "reverse discrimination." The court had been leaning toward the conservative side since the addition of Justice William Rehnquist. In 1952, Rehnquist had been a law clerk at the Supreme Court during *Brown v. Board of Education,* and it was widely known that he had suggested the country was not yet ready for desegregated schools in 1954, disagreeing with the court's ruling in *Brown.* He wanted the *Plessy* segregation to remain the law of the land. Now he shared the bench with the mastermind behind the *Brown* case, Thurgood Marshall. As an attorney in Arizona, Rehnquist sought to eliminate Black and Latino voters from the rolls through literacy tests and was a vocal opponent of the Voting Rights Act. Rehnquist had been appointed by President Richard Nixon in 1971, with a controversial confirmation vote of 65–33, taking his seat in 1972. Later he would be elevated to the post of chief justice by Ronald Reagan. The Supreme Court was returning to its conservative roots. As with *Brown*, the issue of race and education would set the stage for this civil rights era.

In 1978 the civil rights community was on edge. Affirmative action was now in the crosshairs of the Supreme Court in *Regents of the University of California v. Bakke.*[9] To many Blacks, the election of President Ronald Reagan, the former governor of California, was a return of White conservatism in race relations. The *Bakke* case was a symbol of that return and a strike back at Black political progress made under the Voting Rights Act and affirmative action.

In California a thirty-five-year-old White applicant, Allen Bakke, was denied admission to the medical school of the University of California at Davis because of his race. Although his age was also a probable reason for the rejection of his application, an age discrimination lawsuit was not filed. Bakke claimed he was denied admission based on "reverse discrimination," in violation of the equal protection clause of the Fourteenth Amendment, and he sued the University of California.[10]

Under a special admissions program, Black, Asian, Native American, and female applicants were given an allotted sixteen out of a total of hundreds of spaces in the medical school. The school had reasoned that Black doctors were needed and most likely to practice medicine in medically underserved areas. In its decision, the Supreme Court held that the program developed by the University of California Medical School, intended to remedy the present effects of their past discrimination, was unconstitutional because it prevented Whites from competing. The program to alleviate the harm to students of color violated Title VI of the Civil Rights Act of 1964.

Thurgood Marshall dissented. He begins with a pointed history lesson from slavery to Jim Crow discrimination. Then, Marshall reminds the Court that "[o]nly last Term, in *United Jewish Organizations v. Carey*, 430 U.S. 144 (1977), we upheld a New York reapportionment plan that was deliberately drawn on the basis of race to enhance the electoral power of Negroes and Puerto Ricans; the plan had the effect of diluting the electoral strength of the Hasidic Jewish community. We were willing in UJO to sanction the remedial use of racial classification even though it disadvantaged otherwise 'innocent' individuals."[11] There was no demand for specific evidence of race discrimination in that case and individualized harm. Legal remedies for past harm had ended. Similar to the political expediency that ended Reconstruction, African Americans were left to fend for themselves.

Justice Lewis Powell voted to approve the use of race in school admissions only if there was a proven compelling government interest and evidence of the medical school's own discrimination. Only then could a remedy be given to Black applicants. Three hundred years of institutionalized racial oppression meant nothing. Bakke's Fourteenth Amendment rights had been violated.

The amendment created for the freed slaves, which had lain dormant for a century due to the Supreme Court's decisions in the 1880s, became a new weapon to regain supremacy. Justice Powell stated:

> Nothing in the Constitution supports the notion that individuals may be asked to suffer otherwise impermissible burdens in order to enhance the societal standing of their ethnic groups. Second, preferential programs may only reinforce common stereotypes holding that certain groups are unable to achieve success without special protection based on a factor having no relationship to individual worth.

Slavery, racial segregation, terrorism, lynching, and discrimination were nearly forgotten by the Supreme Court. *Bakke* was the turning point.

Nominated by President Richard Nixon, Warren Burger, the chief justice from 1969 to 1986, was a conservative and elitist. But as a northerner born in Minnesota, his social philosophy was more class-based than race-based segregationism. He would disappoint Nixon's planned demise for all liberal decisions. There was a strong enough progressive voice on the court remaining from the Warren era to support busing to integrate public schools (*Swann v. Charlotte-Mecklenberg Board of Education*, 1971), legalize abortion (*Roe v. Wade*, 1973), lower the voting age (*Oregon v. Mitchell*, 1970), defend freedom of the press in the Pentagon papers case (*New York Times v. U.S.*), and question the death penalty (*Furman v. Georgia*, 1972). But under the Burger Court, police authority was greatly expanded and protest rights narrowed.[12]

For the NAACP, the Burger Court was a difficult transition from the more progressive Warren Court. With each generation came new legal challenges to voting rights. America was already forgetting why policies like affirmative action and federal legislation to protect rights were ever necessary. The NAACP would have to learn to play a defensive role in the war for voting rights.

DILUTED VOTES/DILUTED POWER

Then, President Jimmy Carter was defeated in his reelection bid in 1980. A conservative Republican governor of California, Ronald Reagan, ushered in a wave of conservative policies in the 1980s. In 1982, a brilliant young conservative attorney in the Civil Rights Division, by the name of John Roberts, was devising a method to gut the Voting Rights Act of its preclearance provision. The NAACP and NAACP LDF lost their ally in the federal government. Instead, Roberts and a Harvard attorney, Ted Cruz, worked to dismantle the core elements of civil rights legislation, while retaining its public veneer. Racial progressives on the Supreme Court retired and were replaced with conservatives. The Warren court of *Brown v. Board of Education* fame was nearly gone. The William Rehnquist court was forming.

By 1980 the NAACP had lost members. Although far from perfect, civil rights laws protected opportunities, and the decline in lynching and overt individualized racial oppression prompted Black would-be NAACP members to turn away from the nation's oldest civil rights organization. However, articles in *The Crisis* reminded the community to remain vigilant, because the Klan and White supremacist organizations were moving North. The fight for voting rights had not ended; strategies had changed.

Vote dilution was the new weapon for maintaining White supremacy. Blacks could vote, but their votes would not elect candidates or change the outcome of an election in a district with a majority White population. The NAACP LDF brought cases opposing vote dilution. In *Mobile v. Bolden*, an at-large voting system was used to restrict the Black vote in Mobile, Alabama.[13] Despite their high numbers, Blacks could not elect the candidates of their choice for mayor or city council due to the manner in which the voting structure was created.

Black populations in cities with an at-large voting system found their votes consistently diluted by the majority of White voters. NAACP member Wiley E. Bolden brought a class action challenging the at-large electoral system as a violation of the Fourteenth and Fifteenth Amendments. Bolden sought an electoral system with single-member districts. A minority group could be a majority in a single-member district. The trial and appellate courts ruled in favor of the Black plaintiffs. However, the US Supreme Court reversed, refusing to strike down the at-large electoral system.[14]

The court's ruling in favor of the City of Mobile demanded that the Black plaintiffs provide evidence of intentional racial discrimination. A disproportionate effect on Black voters was insufficient to prove discrimination. The Supreme Court's ruling against Black voters in *Mobile v. Bolden* changed the requirement for proof of discrimination to intent.

Proving intent in this new stealth battle was nearly impossible. This attack on the Voting Rights Act could negate its power altogether. However, due to the lobbying efforts of the NAACP, the Voting Rights Act was reauthorized by Congress, with a provision eliminating the *Mobile v. Bolden* intent requirement and signed into law by President Ronald Reagan.

But, a turf war erupted between the NAACP and the NAACP LDF. Disputes over funding, organizational mission, and leadership led to accusations fueled by smoldering resentments that can be traced back to the departure of Thurgood Marshall. In 1985 the NAACP brought a lawsuit against the NAACP Legal Defense and Educational Fund, Inc., demanding the return of its signature name (*NAACP v. NAACP LDF*).[15] A federal trial court ruled in favor of the NAACP, but on appeal, the court ruled for the Legal Defense Fund. The LDF had started out as a legal committee of the NAACP but had begun to overshadow its parent. The LDF was better known because of Thurgood Marshall's role in *Brown v. Board* and other Supreme Court cases. It could raise funds based on its reputation as a giant in legal history. While the NAACP bore the administrative costs and obligations of a membership organization, the LDF could be free to operate as a nonprofit elite law firm that answered only to a board of directors.

Animosity deepened after the federal appellate court ruled in favor of the LDF's retaining the famous name. While hard feelings between the organizations simmered, the Voting Rights Act needed to be reauthorized again. Its sunset provision meant that it would expire if the Senate did not vote to continue it. Through coordinated, but icy, deliberations, the NAACP and the NAACP LDF worked together to lobby for reauthorization. The two organizations accepted that the war for voting rights should not be affected by their internal conflicts. Divide and conquer had been used as an effective weapon against oppressed people of color for centuries.

Ultraconservative jurist William Rehnquist ascended to the chief justice position on the Supreme Court in 1986. If the Burger Court had required defensive strategies to maintain the progress made during the liberal Warren Court era, then it was under the ultraconservative Rehnquist Court that civil rights leaders braced for a full head-on assault. The court had shifted to the right. In the early 1970s President Nixon had appointed Associate Justices Harry Blackmun, Lewis Powell, and William Rehnquist, as the liberal wing faded. In 1986 President Ronald Reagan nominated conservative Antonin Scalia to the court. These appointments were part of a long-term tactic to turn the court down a conservative path. It worked. Thurgood Marshall and fellow progressive William Brennan soon held little influence outside of writing searing dissents.

It was in 1986 that the Voting Rights Act was put to the test again, in a case involving discriminatory effect without proof of intent to discriminate. It was bound for the Supreme Court. In North Carolina, Ralph Gin-

gles and other Black voters claimed that the voting districts had been created to dilute their voting power. With the NAACP LDF as counsel, they
sued Lacy Thornburg, attorney general of North Carolina, under section
2 of the VRA. In *Thornburg v. Gingles,* the Supreme Court was unanimous
in finding "the legacy of official discrimination . . . acted in concert with
the multimember districting scheme to impair the ability of . . . cohesive
groups of black voters to participate equally in the political process and
to elect candidates of their choice."[16] The Supreme Court instituted a total-
ity of the circumstances, and took a dual-pronged approach to determine
whether voting districts were discriminatorily drawn.

In 1989 L. Douglas Wilder, a Democrat, became the first popularly
elected Black governor in American history. All others had been appointed by committees or legislatures. The Voting Rights Act had given
Black voters the power to elect candidates like Wilder. The act had also
given White voters the opportunity to judge a candidate by his or her
qualifications, instead of by race alone. Reprisals were immediate. Virginia held fast to its tradition of racial separation. The Wilder win came
some twenty years after Virginia was forced to end laws banning interracial couples. The Supreme Court had stricken down that Virginia law
in the famous case *Loving v. Virginia.*[17] Yet due to the Voting Rights Act
and challenges to voter suppression and terrorism, an African American
was the state's executive.

With each step forward, there were reprisals from those who would
take America back to a time when racial oppression created White superiority. In August 1989 a tear gas bomb exploded in the NAACP re-
gional office in Atlanta, Georgia. Civil rights attorney Robert Robinson
was martyred by a mail bomb in Savannah, Georgia, in December 1989.
NAACP president Benjamin Hooks led more than 100,000 protesters on a
Silent March on Washington, D.C., in August 1989. The march was reminiscent of the march down Fifth Avenue to protest lynching and White
mob violence on July 28, 1917. Despite obstacles of law and tradition, in
1992 Carol Moseley Braun, from Chicago, Illinois, became the first Black
woman to be elected to the US Senate and the first Black person to hold a
seat in the Senate since Reconstruction.

The Voting Rights Act's power was being restricted. In 1993 the Supreme Court struck down intentionally created majority Black voting
districts in *Shaw v. Reno.* Justice Sandra Day O'Connor, the first female
justice, called them "political apartheid."

Thurgood Marshall, a civil rights giant, had retired. His replacement
was the ultraconservative African American Clarence Thomas, appointee
of Republican president George W. Bush. *Shaw v. Reno* was the first voting rights case under this now decidedly conservative Supreme Court.
Thomas had come to court after damaging hearing on sexual harassment

charges by law professor Anita Hill, also African American, and questions regarding his qualifications to be on the high court by the National and American Bar Associations. The court invalidated the districts designed by the first female attorney general, Janet Reno.[18] Reno had approved the plan to reapportion districts in North Carolina in favor of historically disenfranchised Black voters, similar to the districting plan in Brooklyn. "Racial gerrymandering" was the new phrase used to negatively depict Black political power.

More disappointments followed. On the heels of the NAACP's defeat in *Shaw*, the court decided *Holder v. Hall* in 1994 and *Miller v. Johnson* in 1995.[19] In *Holder v. Hall*, Black residents of Bleckley County, Georgia, as well as the NAACP, challenged Holder, the county commissioner of a multimember commission that had replaced the single commissioner system.[20] The trial and appellate courts found in favor of the NAACP and the Black plaintiffs, but the Supreme Court reversed, implying Bakke-type "reverse discrimination."

Then the Supreme Court attempted to neutralize the Voting Rights Act with the strict scrutiny standard, which it had applied in *Miller v. Johnson* and *Shaw v. Reno*. The court determined that any case involving race as the overriding predominant factor must overcome this high hurdle. A history of race discrimination was no longer relevant. Under strict scrutiny, there must be a compelling state interest and a narrowly tailored plan to meet that interest, or the plan will be unconstitutional.

The era of voting rights reform had passed. The NAACP and the NAACP LDF were forced to put their differences aside and navigate a conservative wave in the country and the Supreme Court. Reverse discrimination lawsuits were filed on behalf of Whites by conservative, well-financed think-tanks intent on limiting Black progress. There was little concern for the brutality, discrimination, and disenfranchisement that had given birth to the NAACP. The core focus of many conservatives was the dismantling of civil rights protections. A prime target was the Voting Rights Act.

Since the *Miller* case, the Supreme Court has moved from being progressive to being moderate. With the addition in 1986 of Justice Antonin Scalia, a conservative, to a court led by Chief Justice William Rehnquist, an ultraconservative, it became dangerous to bring a civil rights case to the high court. A reversal might mean the loss of rights that had taken decades to achieve. The NAACP had always used political pressure, along with protest and litigation. But now it appeared that lobbying Congress and local politicians was its only major firepower. With each conservative nominee appointed to the court, the judicial door to racial justice was closing.

In 1989, President George Herbert Bush, who succeeded Ronald Reagan, was viewed as wealthy, sheltered, and out of touch. Those vulnerabilities might have made him open to showing the country that he could be liberal in civil rights where the Supreme Court was not. With few options, the battleground shifted to lobbying the White House, just as Congress was discussing limits on lobbying by nonprofit organizations and cutting funding for any legal services organizations that had the audacity to sue the federal government. The seeds of congressional division were planted.

TWENTIETH- TO TWENTY-FIRST-CENTURY BATTLES

In a war of attrition, the NAACP and the NAACP LDF both needed to maintain and define a message that reminded the public that a cold war involving voting rights still required vigilance. The battle was covert. A lack of vigilance could have consequences for generations. Then, in 1997, the success of Black candidates played a direct role in the court's ruling in a voting rights case. On June 14, 1997, in a 5–4 decision, the Supreme Court upheld a court-drawn redistricting plan that reduced the number of majority-minority Georgia congressional districts from three to one.

The case *Abrams v. Johnson* marked the second time the court had been asked to rule on the constitutionality of Georgia's congressional redistricting plan, drawn pursuant to the 1990 Census (the first case was *Miller v. Johnson*).[21] A deciding factor for the justices was the fact that Representatives Sanford Bishop Jr. and Cynthia McKinney, both Black Democrats, were reelected in Georgia, despite the fact that they were running in districts where Whites comprised the majority.[22] Their districts were referred to as racial gerrymandering.

In 2000 the nation faced a constitutional crisis watched by the world. Al Gore, a Democrat from Tennessee and vice president under Bill Clinton, was in a runoff for president in Florida against George W. Bush, the son of former president George H. Bush. The NAACP was on the ground during heated protests over the recount. States' rights as well as the purging of countless Black potential voters caused more controversy. A lawsuit was filed to halt the recount and declare George Bush the winner.

Florida objected. Chief Justice Rehnquist presided over a trial in the Supreme Court that resulted in a ruling in favor of Bush. John Roberts played a pivotal role in developing the arguments used in Rehnquist's opinion. Both conservatives had opposed intervention on state's rights until those beliefs conflicted with limiting voting rights. It was a perfect storm. Florida's recount was declared unconstitutional. The presidency was given to George W. Bush, a Republican conservative, in *Bush v.*

Gore.[23] This case brought to light the numerous Black voters purged from voting rolls or falsely accused of being former felons and prohibited from casting a ballot after waiting for hours to vote. These voters could have changed the outcome of this election. Preventing that pivotal Black vote from determining the fate of Whites was a cornerstone of supremacy politics postslavery.

After *Bush v. Gore*, Florida became the site of public hearings, revealing hundreds of complaints of voter irregularities and prompting a "Count Every Vote" rally. In 2001 the NAACP held "A Day of Moral Outrage: Count the Vote" rally to draw attention to voters purged from the rolls and disenfranchised in the national election. The NAACP lobbied Congress and, in 2002, President George W. Bush signed the Help America Vote Act (HAVA) to upgrade voting machines and improve elections.

In 2005 Indiana passed a driver's license photo identification law, *Crawford v. Marion County Board of Elections*, which required government-issued photo identification to vote. Similar to the 1890 Mississippi Plan, it was intended to undermine the vote of people of color, the elderly, poor, and any citizens who could not afford to pay the fees, take time off work, or travel to the government offices to obtain the specific photo identification required by law to vote. With each obstacle to the polls, a voter was less likely to vote. These voters were most often Democrats.

The NAACP and the NAACP LDF worked tirelessly to press Congress for the reauthorization of the Voting Rights Act in 2006. It was introduced by Rep. James F. Sensenbrenner, a Republican from Wisconsin. The bill was titled the "Fannie Lou Hamer, Rosa Parks, Coretta Scott King, Cesar E. Chavez, Barbara C. Jordan, William C. Velasquez, and Dr. Hector P. Garcia Voting Rights Act Reauthorization and Amendments Act of 2006." The Senate unanimously passed it. The House passed it with a vote of 390 to 33. Then, on July 27, 2006, President George W. Bush signed the Voting Rights Act reauthorization, with an extension of twenty-five years.

In 2008 the power of the Voting Rights Act was evidenced in the election of Senator Barack Obama from Chicago, Illinois, who became the first African American president of the United States. That same year, the Supreme Court upheld Indiana's driver's license photo identification requirement in *Crawford v. Marion County Board of Elections*.[24] In 2009 Congress passed the Military and Overseas Voter Empowerment Act to assist voting by members of the military overseas.

THE CIVIL DEAD

A civil death is the loss of the right to vote due to a criminal conviction. It is a punishment that was adopted from England during the colonial period. Disenfranchisement, considered a civil death, remains a part of American culture even though it is no longer practiced in England. The right to vote allowed a member of society to determine the future of the community. A criminal conviction meant the loss of good standing in the community as well as imprisonment.

After the Revolutionary War, states enacted provisions stripping away the right to vote upon conviction for bribery, perjury, or other infamous crimes demonstrating bad character. When the Thirteenth Amendment abolished slavery in 1865, the states enacted criminal laws referred to as "Black Codes" to unfairly convict African Americans, rendering them of bad character and thus disenfranchised.

The convict lease system was a criminal system that began after slavery and lasted for eighty years. The labor of incarcerated men and women was leased out to private businesses or municipalities. The prison wardens acted as businessmen. Their profits relied on a constant source of inmates, and the Black Codes fed the convict lease industry. The inmates were counted in the Census to determine the number of representatives in Congress and amount of governmental resources allotted to a political district. As under the two-thirds rule that had counted the enslaved in the population despite their having no voice in their representation, inmates have been counted in the population for political districts and provided the foundation for political power in rural communities.

Once released, the formerly incarcerated continue to be punished with disenfranchisement. They have served their time and debt to society, but civil death awaits many of them. In 1974 a group of formerly convicted felons in California challenged civil death. They attempted to register to vote and were turned away.

> Article XX, § 11 of the California Constitution has provided since its adoption in 1879 that "[l]aws shall be made" to exclude from voting persons convicted of bribery, perjury, forgery, malfeasance in office, "or other high crimes." At the time the respondents were refused registration, former article II, § 1 of the California Constitution provided in part that "no alien ineligible to citizenship, no idiot, no insane person, no person conflicted of any infamous crime, no person hereafter convicted of the embezzlement or misappropriation of public money, and no person who shall not be able to read the Constitution in the English language and write his or her name, shall ever exercise the privileges of an elector in this State."[25]

But in 1974 the Supreme Court ruled in *Richardson v. Ramirez* that states can pass laws disenfranchising convicted felons even if they had completed their sentences and paroles without violating their rights under the Equal Protection Clause.[26] The benefits of a prison are immense for communities with high unemployment and loss of population. The prison industrial complex is a combination of governmental interests, private businesses, and political expediency.[27] It provides jobs for local residents and supplements the population needed for political gain. There were an estimated 1.17 million people disenfranchised in 1976, 3.34 million in 1996, and over 5.85 million in 2010.[28] One out of every thirteen African American potential voters is disenfranchised.

In April 2011 a group of New York State senators challenged Part XX, which sought to restore prison-based gerrymandering in New York. Part XX of the New York State budget A9710-D was signed into law on August 11, 2010. The NAACP LDF, along with several other legal organizations, was allowed to argue on behalf of New Yorkers whose voting rights were directly affected by this challenge. The NAACP LDF successfully argued against the return to excluding inmates based on gerrymandering in New York. On March 13, 2012, the plaintiffs withdrew their notice of appeal, leaving the LDF and the other members of the coalition victorious in defending this important legal reform.

In *Little v. LATFOR*, the NAACP LDF, Center for Law and Social Justice, Dēmos, Latino Justice Puerto Rican Legal Defense and Educational Fund, New York Civil Liberties Union, the Prison Policy Initiative, and the Brennan Center successfully defended New York State's law requiring incarcerated persons to be counted in their home communities for state legislative redistricting purposes instead of at their prison addresses.[29]

Without this law, rural and usually non-Black communities had been given an oversized political presence and budgetary compensation for the presence of people within their population who received no viable representation of their issues. Inmate populations were used in a manner comparable to counting the enslaved for determining the number of representatives in Congress under the three-fifths rule of the Constitution. Similar laws against prison-based gerrymandering have been passed in Delaware, Maryland, and California.[30] In *Davidson v. City of Cranston*, voters pushed back against "prison gerrymandering" which would have counted the prison population within a voting district giving that district four times the political clout of the others there. Like under the three-fifths rule of slavery, inmates are not treated as constituents. Politicians are not representing the interests of the incarcerated. Yet, elected officials gain power from their numbers in the population.

In New York this practice had made a mockery of the principle of the "one person, one vote" and diluted the voting strength of communities of color. African Americans and Latinos in New York make up 30 percent of the general population but constitute 77 percent of the state prison population. Some 98 percent of all prisons are located in disproportionately white State Senate districts. Thus, counting incarcerated individuals where they are confined sapped the political power of African American and Latino

communities and instead provided political power to those who used
the inmate population to gain governmental resources by increasing the
census count of their districts. Part XX of this law was enacted to correct
this manifest injustice and ended that practice in New York State. On
March 13, 2012, the plaintiffs who were fighting to continue that practice
withdrew their notice of appeal, retreating from their attack on the law.[31]

An NAACP delegation testified about voting rights in the United States
at a human rights conference at the United Nations in Geneva, Switzerland, in 2014. America is the only nation that disenfranchises a person
for life based on a criminal conviction. Under the Constitution, states
can decide qualifications for electors. Disenfranchisement of Black voters
based on criminal convictions began with Black Codes and the convict
lease system following slavery. The American Civil Liberties Union, a
staunch ally in this war for voting rights, petitioned the Inter-American
Commission on Human Rights to investigate America's felony disenfranchisement laws. America can be found in violation of the Inter-American
Convention of Human Rights if the IACHR can be persuaded to stand up
to its most powerful member.

According to the Sentencing Project, about 15 percent of Black men in
America are disenfranchised. In Alabama, Delaware, Florida, Mississippi,
Nevada, Tennessee, Kentucky, Virginia, and Wyoming, formerly incarcerated persons with felony convictions lose their right to vote for life.
About 5.85 million Americans are denied the right to vote based on felony
convictions. In Iowa, residents lose their right to vote based on a single
felony conviction, even it is for a nonviolent crime. With the majority of
incarcerated persons serving sentences for nonviolent drug offenses and
the racial discrimination in the criminal justice system, millions of potential voters are among the civil dead—the poor who are without adequate
legal counsel and those who are the victims of America's War on Drugs.
The civil death of disenfranchisement is the last remaining scheme left
from the Mississippi Plan of 1890. The NAACP has launched a national
felony disenfranchisement campaign. The NAACP and the NAACP LDF
are continuing to attack America's civil death due to felony convictions.
Only America, Armenia, Chile, and Belgium consign their citizens to a
civil death.

SHELBY COUNTY V. HOLDER

In 2010 the Supreme Court ruled that corporations have free speech
rights. Contributing to a campaign became a form of free speech. In *Citizens United v. Federal Election Commission*,[32] the court held that congressional limits on the amount corporations could contribute to political cam-

paigns violated a corporation's right to free speech. A year later, photo identification laws similar to Indiana's were passed in Texas, Florida, and South Carolina, although there is scant evidence of voter fraud to support the rationale given for enacting strict photo identification laws.

The Supreme Court took a case challenging the heart of the Voting Rights Act in 2013. Section 5 of the act speaks to its authority to require certain states to seek preclearance from the federal government before making changes in their voting arrangements, in particular the power of the Justice Department, at that time led by Eric Holder, the first Black US attorney general. Holder is married to the sister of Vivian Malone, who had desegregated the all-White University of Alabama under armed military guard in 1963 as Governor George Wallace gave a speech proclaiming "segregation now, segregation forever." However, Section 4 is key. It provides the coverage formula.

The NAACP LDF was selected to argue as amicus at the high court's oral argument in *Shelby County, Alabama v. Holder*. Historically, Alabama had been awash in the blood of NAACP activists. Alabama was the site of the brutality in 1965 on the Edmund Pettus Bridge, in which hundreds of peaceful unarmed protesters were beaten unconscious by state troopers. The murders of Jimmy Lee Jackson by a state trooper, Reverend Reeb, Viola Liuzzo, and many others had led to passage of the Voting Rights Act in 1965. In the current case, evidence was presented of ongoing voter discrimination.[33]

So much was at stake. It was a setting reminiscent of Guinn v. United States nearly a hundred years before. This time the results were devastatingly different. Chief Justice John Roberts led the 5–4 decision, ruling that the formula that determined the states required to preclear changes to their voting laws was unconstitutional.

Justice Scalia referred to the Voting Rights Act as a "racial entitlement" program, similar to welfare or public housing. After decades of strikes being launched at the act, the conservatives finally gutted this extraordinary provision.

Chief Justice Roberts was a protégé of William Rehnquist, pall-bearer at his funeral, and the one called to replace him within days of that funeral. Roberts developed a plan to gut the Voting Rights Act as an attorney working in the Civil Rights Division. Now, as Chief Justice, Roberts can question its purpose given the great strides in race relations. During the *Shelby County* oral argument, he asked Solicitor General Donald Verrilli, "Is the South more racist than the North?" This means racism is so widespread there is no need to address it more in one particular region over another one. When it comes to America's systemic race problem, he believes, "The way to stop discrimination on the basis of race is to stop discriminating on the basis of race." As if centuries of race-based carnage was a product of unimaginative people, Roberts's remarks ending school desegregation in a 2007 Tennessee case reveal a need for him to read Justice Marshall's dissent in *Bakke*.

Justice Clarence Thomas, who wrote a concurring opinion, agreed with the conservative majority decision and complained that it did not go far enough. "Today, our nation is changed,"[34] he wrote. The Voting Rights Act was no longer needed, and he would find section 5 of the Voting Rights Act unconstitutional as well. Justice Ruth Bader Ginsberg dissented; reading from the bench, she said justice had been disserved by the *Shelby County* decision. Quoting Martin Luther King Jr., she reminded the devastated civil rights community: "The arc of the moral universe is long, but it bends toward justice."

Preclearance had placed civil rights attorneys like those from the NAACP and NAACP LDF in an offensive position, as opposed to a defensive one expending considerable time, money, and talent staving off attacks and bringing expensive lawsuits around the country to combat legislation intended to undermine the constitutional freedoms of Black Americans. When President Johnson signed the Voting Rights Act into law, he intended states like Alabama to bear the burden of proving that they were not discriminating against the voting rights of people of color. Now, within days of the court's decision in *Shelby County*, photo identification requirements were enacted in North Carolina.

Also in 2013, the NAACP LDF won a voting rights victory that was overshadowed by the *Shelby* decision. In *Arizona v. Inter-tribal Council of Arizona*, the Supreme Court ruled that states cannot require proof of citizenship to register to vote. The NAACP LDF was amicus on the side of the Inter-tribal Council of Arizona. Arizona had passed a law requiring government photo identification to register to vote.[35] However, federal law controls requirements to vote in federal elections, and photo identification was not a federal requirement.

In 2012 President Obama was reelected president of the United States. However, around the country, voters had waited hours in long lines to cast their ballots. Names had been purged from voting lists without explanation. In neighborhoods of color, voting machines failed. President Obama established the Presidential Commission on Election Administration under Executive Order 13639 in March 2013, which investigated the voting obstacles and presented recommendations: modernization of the registration process, improved access to polls, and state-of-the art polling places and voting technology.[36]

By this time the Congressional Black Caucus had grown to forty-six members.[37] In Louisiana, the home of the *Plessy* decision, more than 900,000 Blacks were registered to vote. The Black vote had become a determining factor in federal, state, and local elections. After slavery was abolished, there may have been more than seven hundred Blacks in elected offices nationwide. After *Plessy* that number plummeted, with scholars unable to find one Black elected official until the 1940s. In 2001 there were more than 9,000 Black politicians. In 1970, five years after passage of the Voting Rights Act of 1965, there were 1,469 Black elected officials.[38] Now there were more than 10,000. This number does not take into account high-ranking government policy makers or appointed officials and advisers.

Within weeks of when President Obama was reelected for a second term, a band of residents in Texas had signed a petition to secede from the Union. The NAACP brought a case against the state of Texas, challenging the Texas photo identification law that required a state driver's license, hunting license, passport, or military card to vote there. State university student identification cards were not acceptable. The NAACP challenged the law, and the NAACP LDF sought a role in the case as well, representing the Texas League of Young Voters Education Fund.

Texas congressman Marc Veasey stood with members of the NAACP in this action against Governor Rick Perry. In 2014 in the consolidated cases *Texas Conference of NAACP v. Steen, United States v. Texas,* and *Veasey v. Perry,* the court ruled in favor of these rigid photo identification requirements.[39] *North Carolina State Conference of the NAACP v. McCrory* challenged registration restrictions passed shortly after the Supreme Court gutted federal preclearance protections in the *Shelby County v. Alabama* case.[40] Thirty-six states have enacted photo identification laws.[41]

THE FUTURE

The Voting Rights Act was wounded by the *Shelby* decision, but it still stands. Voting rights cases are on the Supreme Court's docket and making their way to the court on appeal. Ohio is a battleground state. In *NAACP v. Husted,* the Ohio State Conference of NAACP Branches, joined by other organizations, successfully challenged Ohio laws SB 238 and Directive 2014-17 as a violation of the equal protection clause. The Ohio NAACP argued that the right to vote of African Americans was disproportionately burdened by limits on registration outlets, reducing voting days and voting hours.[42] A settlement was reached allowing Ohioans to vote on multiple days and during expanded evening hours.

On February 13, 2016, Associate Justice Antonin Scalia, age seventy-nine, died while on vacation at a Texas resort. Like Roberts, he was a protégé of Chief Justice William Rehnquist and his former law clerk. Justice Scalia carried the tradition of staunch conservativism into the court, now led by Chief Justice John Roberts. Scalia's derision of the Voting Rights

Act in the *Shelby* case garnered national rebuke. His death left the court with the possibility of a 4–4 tie on cases involving civil rights. In cases of a tie, the lower court decision stands without creating precedent for the nation.

In 2016 the court was presented with a challenge to urban voting power in *Evenwel v. Abbott*. The attack was against established protections won by the NAACP decades earlier in *Reynolds v. Sims* (1964). In the new case, Sue Evenwel and Edward Pfenninger claim that urban communities should only count eligible voters in determining the number of representatives in Congress. They argued against relying on the Census and asserted that instead the count should exclude those disenfranchised adults with felony convictions, children, the mentally ill, and immigrant nonvoters in the population when drawing voting districts. They claim that counting these people violates the equal protection clause because there are significant disparities between dense populations and districts that are not as densely populated, such as suburban and rural communities. The NAACP LDF was amicus in this case. The court's ruling, 8–0, written by Justice Ruth Bader Ginsberg, unanimously upheld the right of states to count everyone, the total population, when drawing voting districts.[40] Hilary Shelton, the NAACP's Director of the NAACP Washington Bureau and senior vice-president for advocacy, is leading the efforts to pass the Voting Rights Advancement Act (VRAA), which would not only reinstate the Section 4 coverage formula but strengthen it.

On March 6, 2015, President Barack Obama and Representative John Lewis stood at the foot of the Edmund Pettus Bridge in Selma, surrounded by some twenty thousand people attending the fiftieth commemoration of "Bloody Sunday" in Selma and remembering the hundreds of Black Americans beaten by Alabama state troopers for peacefully protesting the denial of their right to vote. President Obama was joined by civil rights activist Amelia Boynton Robinson, 103 years old. She was the first Black person to run for Congress in Alabama.

In 1915 Mrs. Boyton was three years old, and the NAACP had achieved its first voting rights victory in the US Supreme Court. Boynton Robinson, a lifelong NAACP member, was nearly beaten to death on the Edmund Pettus Bridge on "Bloody Sunday" in 1965. She witnessed the gutting of the Voting Rights Act in 2013 and championed congressional legislation to reinstate the vital preclearance provision. Mrs. Boynton Robinson passed away months after the historic fiftieth anniversary march across the Edmund Pettus Bridge in 2015. She leaves us a model of courage as well as marching orders for future battles.

Like a sergeant addressing her troops, Boynton Robinson had made herself clear. "For those who say they stand on my shoulders, I say get down and get to work." For over one hundred years, the NAACP has engaged in the battle for equal rights for African Americans. Their success has benefited all Americans. There is still a great deal of work to do. Racial injustice remains a fact of life in America.

Nine Killed in Shooting at Black Church in Charleston

CHARLESTON, S.C.—A white gunman opened fire Wednesday night at a historic black church in downtown Charleston, S.C., killing nine people before fleeing and setting off an overnight manhunt, the police said.

At a news conference with Charleston's mayor early Thursday, the police chief, Greg Mullen, called the shooting a hate crime.

"It is unfathomable that somebody in today's society would walk into a church while they are having a prayer meeting and take their lives," he said.

The police said the gunman walked into the historic Emanuel African Methodist Episcopal Church around 9 p.m. and began shooting.

Eight people died at the scene, Chief Mullen said. Two people were taken to the Medical University of South Carolina, and one of them died on the way.

New York Times, June 17, 2015.

There are those who cannot accept Black Progress. Whether it is a matter of photo identification laws or disenfranchisement, "We must fight as hard today as those before us fought fifty years ago," said NAACP president Cornell William Brooks.

The NAACP and the NAACP LDF, with their organizational allies across the country and local counsel, are marching toward an inclusive vision of democracy. They ill afford apathy, for the opposition believes only certain people deserve the type of self-determination that comes with the voting ballot. As political power increases among people of color, so will the creativity and obstinacy of those who believe America's democracy belongs only to certain Americans. The war for voting rights has been fought across every state, North and South. The battleground is wherever the challenge lies. The struggle is ongoing.

A lesson for all American citizens can be learned from voting rights activist Vernon Ferdinand Dahmer. This Mississippi NAACP leader lost his life to a Klansman's firebomb thrown into his home. He accepted the danger and sacrifices, giving the ultimate sacrifice. Because he understood the far-reaching importance of his work, Dahmer chose these words for his tombstone:

IF YOU DON'T VOTE
YOU DON'T COUNT

Appendix A

President Lyndon Baines Johnson
Addresses Congress on Passage
of the Voting Rights Act

[As delivered in person before a joint session at 9:02 p.m., March 15, 1965]

Mr. Speaker, Mr. President, Members of the Congress:

I speak tonight for the dignity of man and the destiny of democracy.

I urge every member of both parties, Americans of all religions and of all colors, from every section of this country, to join me in that cause.

At times history and fate meet at a single time in a single place to shape a turning point in man's unending search for freedom. So it was at Lexington and Concord. So it was a century ago at Appomattox. So it was last week in Selma, Alabama.

There, long-suffering men and women peacefully protested the denial of their rights as Americans. Many were brutally assaulted. One good man, a man of God, was killed.

There is no cause for pride in what has happened in Selma. There is no cause for self-satisfaction in the long denial of equal rights of millions of Americans. But there is cause for hope and for faith in our democracy in what is happening here tonight.

For the cries of pain and the hymns and protests of oppressed people have summoned into convocation all the majesty of this great Government—the Government of the greatest Nation on earth.

Our mission is at once the oldest and the most basic of this country: to right wrong, to do justice, to serve man.

In our time we have come to live with moments of great crisis. Our lives have been marked with debate about great issues; issues of war and peace, issues of prosperity and depression. But rarely in any time does an issue lay bare the secret heart of America itself. Rarely are we met with a challenge, not to our growth or abundance, our welfare or our security, but rather to the values and the purposes and the meaning of our beloved Nation.

The issue of equal rights for American Negroes is such an issue. And should we defeat every enemy, should we double our wealth and conquer the stars, and still be unequal to this issue, then we will have failed as a people and as a nation.

For with a country as with a person, "What is a man profited, if he shall gain the whole world, and lose his own soul?"

There is no Negro problem. There is no Southern problem. There is no Northern problem. There is only an American problem. And we are met here tonight as Americans—not as Democrats or Republicans—we are met here as Americans to solve that problem.

This was the first nation in the history of the world to be founded with a purpose. The great phrases of that purpose still sound in every American heart, North and South: "All men are created equal"—"government by consent of the governed"—"give me liberty or give me death." Well, those are not just clever words, or those are not just empty theories. In their name Americans have fought and died for two centuries, and tonight around the world they stand there as guardians of our liberty, risking their lives.

Those words are a promise to every citizen that he shall share in the dignity of man. This dignity cannot be found in a man's possessions; it cannot be found in his power, or in his position. It really rests on his right to be treated as a man equal in opportunity to all others. It says that he shall share in freedom, he shall choose his leaders, educate his children, and provide for his family according to his ability and his merits as a human being.

To apply any other test—to deny a man his hopes because of his color or race, his religion or the place of his birth—is not only to do injustice, it is to deny America and to dishonor the dead who gave their lives for American freedom.

The Right to Vote

Our fathers believed that if this noble view of the rights of man was to flourish, it must be rooted in democracy. The most basic right of all was the right to choose your own leaders. The history of this country, in large measure, is the history of the expansion of that right to all of our people.

Many of the issues of civil rights are very complex and most difficult. But about this there can and should be no argument. Every American citizen must have an equal right to vote. There is no reason which can excuse the denial of that right. There is no duty which weighs more heavily on us than the duty we have to ensure that right.

Yet the harsh fact is that in many places in this country men and women are kept from voting simply because they are Negroes.

Every device of which human ingenuity is capable has been used to deny this right. The Negro citizen may go to register only to be told that the day is wrong, or the hour is late, or the official in charge is absent. And if he persists, and if he manages to present himself to the registrar, he may be disqualified because he did not spell out his middle name or because he abbreviated a word on the application.

And if he manages to fill out an application he is given a test. The registrar is the sole judge of whether he passes this test. He may be asked to recite the entire Constitution, or explain the most complex provisions of State law. And even a college degree cannot be used to prove that he can read and write.

For the fact is that the only way to pass these barriers is to show a white skin.

Experience has clearly shown that the existing process of law cannot overcome systematic and ingenious discrimination. No law that we now have on the books—and I have helped to put three of them there—can ensure the right to vote when local officials are determined to deny it.

In such a case our duty must be clear to all of us. The Constitution says that no person shall be kept from voting because of his race or his color. We have all sworn an oath before God to support and to defend that Constitution. We must now act in obedience to that oath.

Guaranteeing the Right to Vote

Wednesday I will send to Congress a law designed to eliminate illegal barriers to the right to vote.

The broad principles of that bill will be in the hands of the Democratic and Republican leaders tomorrow. After they have reviewed it, it will come here formally as a bill. I am grateful for this opportunity to come here tonight at the invitation of the leadership to reason with my friends, to give them my views, and to visit with my former colleagues.

I have had prepared a more comprehensive analysis of the legislation which I had intended to transmit to the clerk tomorrow but which I will submit to the clerks tonight. But I want to really discuss with you now briefly the main proposals of this legislation.

This bill will strike down restrictions to voting in all elections—Federal, State, and local—which have been used to deny Negroes the right to vote.

This bill will establish a simple, uniform standard which cannot be used, however ingenious the effort, to flout our Constitution.

It will provide for citizens to be registered by officials of the United States Government if the State officials refuse to register them.

It will eliminate tedious, unnecessary lawsuits which delay the right to vote.

Finally, this legislation will ensure that properly registered individuals are not prohibited from voting.

I will welcome the suggestions from all of the Members of Congress—I have no doubt that I will get some—on ways and means to strengthen this law and to make it effective. But experience has plainly shown that this is the only path to carry out the command of the Constitution.

To those who seek to avoid action by their National Government in their own communities; who want to and who seek to maintain purely local control over elections, the answer is simple:

Open your polling places to all your people.

Allow men and women to register and vote whatever the color of their skin.

Extend the rights of citizenship to every citizen of this land.

The Need for Action

There is no constitutional issue here. The command of the Constitution is plain.

There is no moral issue. It is wrong—deadly wrong—to deny any of your fellow Americans the right to vote in this country.

There is no issue of States rights or national rights. There is only the struggle for human rights.

I have not the slightest doubt what will be your answer.

The last time a President sent a civil rights bill to the Congress it contained a provision to protect voting rights in Federal elections. That civil rights bill was passed after 8 long months of debate. And when that bill came to my desk from the Congress for my signature, the heart of the voting provision had been eliminated.

This time, on this issue, there must be no delay, no hesitation and no compromise with our purpose.

We cannot, we must not, refuse to protect the right of every American to vote in every election that he may desire to participate in. And we ought not and we cannot and we must not wait another 8 months before we get a bill. We have already waited a hundred years and more, and the time for waiting is gone.

So I ask you to join me in working long hours—nights and weekends, if necessary—to pass this bill. And I don't make that request lightly. For from the window where I sit with the problems of our country I recognize that outside this chamber is the outraged conscience of a nation, the grave concern of many nations, and the harsh judgment of history on our acts.

We Shall Overcome

But even if we pass this bill, the battle will not be over. What happened in Selma is part of a far larger movement which reaches into every section and State of America. It is the effort of American Negroes to secure for themselves the full blessings of American life.

Their cause must be our cause too. Because it is not just Negroes, but really it is all of us, who must overcome the crippling legacy of bigotry and injustice.

And we shall overcome.

As a man whose roots go deeply into Southern soil I know how agonizing racial feelings are. I know how difficult it is to reshape the attitudes and the structure of our society.

But a century has passed, more than a hundred years, since the Negro was freed. And he is not fully free tonight.

It was more than a hundred years ago that Abraham Lincoln, a great President of another party, signed the Emancipation Proclamation, but emancipation is a proclamation and not a fact.

A century has passed, more than a hundred years, since equality was promised. And yet the Negro is not equal.

A century has passed since the day of promise. And the promise is unkept.

The time of justice has now come. I tell you that I believe sincerely that no force can hold it back. It is right in the eyes of man and God that it should come. And when it does, I think that day will brighten the lives of every American.

For Negroes are not the only victims. How many white children have gone uneducated, how many white families have lived in stark poverty, how many white lives have been scarred by fear, because we have wasted our energy and our substance to maintain the barriers of hatred and terror?

So I say to all of you here, and to all in the Nation tonight, that those who appeal to you to hold on to the past do so at the cost of denying you your future.

This great, rich, restless country can offer opportunity and education and hope to all: black and white, North and South, sharecropper and city dweller. These are the enemies: poverty, ignorance, disease. They are the enemies and not our fellow man, not our neighbor. And these enemies too, poverty, disease and ignorance, we shall overcome.

An American Problem

Now let none of us in any sections look with prideful righteousness on the troubles in another section, or on the problems of our neighbors. There is really no part of America where the promise of equality has been fully kept. In Buffalo as well as in Birmingham, in Philadelphia as well as in Selma, Americans are struggling for the fruits of freedom.

This is one Nation. What happens in Selma or in Cincinnati is a matter of legitimate concern to every American. But let each of us look within our own hearts and our own communities, and let each of us put our shoulder to the wheel to root out injustice wherever it exists.

As we meet here in this peaceful, historic chamber tonight, men from the South, some of whom were at Iwo Jima, men from the North who have carried Old Glory to far corners of the world and brought it back without a stain on it, men from the East and from the West, are all fighting together without regard to religion, or color, or region, in Viet-Nam. Men from every region fought for us across the world 20 years ago.

And in these common dangers and these common sacrifices the South made its contribution of honor and gallantry no less than any other region of the great Republic—and in some instances, a great many of them, more.

And I have not the slightest doubt that good men from everywhere in this country, from the Great Lakes to the Gulf of Mexico, from the Golden Gate to the harbors along the Atlantic, will rally together now in this cause to vindicate the freedom of all Americans. For all of us owe this duty; and I believe that all of us will respond to it.

Your President makes that request of every American.

Progress through the Democratic Process

The real hero of this struggle is the American Negro. His actions and protests, his courage to risk safety and even to risk his life, have awakened the conscience of this Nation. His demonstrations have been designed to call attention to injustice, designed to provoke change, designed to stir reform.

He has called upon us to make good the promise of America. And who among us can say that we would have made the same progress were it not for his persistent bravery, and his faith in American democracy.

For at the real heart of battle for equality is a deep-seated belief in the democratic process. Equality depends not on the force of arms or tear gas but upon the force of moral right; not on recourse to violence but on respect for law and order.

There have been many pressures upon your President and there will be others as the days come and go. But I pledge you tonight that we intend to fight this battle where it should be fought: in the courts, and in the Congress, and in the hearts of men.

We must preserve the right of free speech and the right of free assembly. But the right of free speech does not carry with it, as has been said, the right to holler fire in a crowded theater. We must preserve the right to free assembly, but free assembly does not carry with it the right to block public thoroughfares to traffic.

We do have a right to protest, and a right to march under conditions that do not infringe the constitutional rights of our neighbors. And I intend to protect all those rights as long as I am permitted to serve in this office.

We will guard against violence, knowing it strikes from our hands the very weapons which we seek—progress, obedience to law, and belief in American values.

In Selma as elsewhere we seek and pray for peace. We seek order. We seek unity. But we will not accept the peace of stifled rights, or the order imposed by fear, or the unity that stifles protest. For peace cannot be purchased at the cost of liberty.

In Selma tonight, as in every—and we had a good day there—as in every city, we are working for just and peaceful settlement. We must all remember that after this speech I am making tonight, after the police and the FBI and the Marshals have all gone, and after you have promptly passed this bill, the people of Selma and the other cities of the Nation must still live and work together. And when the attention of the Nation has gone elsewhere they must try to heal the wounds and to build a new community.

This cannot be easily done on a battleground of violence, as the history of the South itself shows. It is in recognition of this that men of both races have shown such an outstandingly impressive responsibility in recent days—last Tuesday, again today.

Rights Must Be Opportunities

The bill that I am presenting to you will be known as a civil rights bill. But, in a larger sense, most of the program I am recommending is a civil rights program. Its object is to open the city of hope to all people of all races.

Because all Americans just must have the right to vote. And we are going to give them that right.

All Americans must have the privileges of citizenship regardless of race. And they are going to have those privileges of citizenship regardless of race.

But I would like to caution you and remind you that to exercise these privileges takes much more than just legal right. It requires a trained mind and a healthy body. It requires a decent home, and the chance to find a job, and the opportunity to escape from the clutches of poverty.

Of course, people cannot contribute to the Nation if they are never taught to read or write, if their bodies are stunted from hunger, if their sickness goes untended, if their life is spent in hopeless poverty just drawing a welfare check.

So we want to open the gates to opportunity. But we are also going to give all our people, black and white, the help that they need to walk through those gates.

The Purpose of This Government

My first job after college was as a teacher in Cotulla, Texas, in a small Mexican-American school. Few of them could speak English, and I couldn't speak much Spanish. My students were poor and they often came to class without breakfast, hungry. They knew even in their youth the pain of prejudice. They never seemed to know why people disliked them. But they knew it was so, because I saw it in their eyes. I often walked home late in the afternoon, after the classes were finished, wishing there was more that I could do. But all I knew was to teach them the little that I knew, hoping that it might help them against the hardships that lay ahead.

Somehow you never forget what poverty and hatred can do when you see its scars on the hopeful face of a young child.

I never thought then, in 1928, that I would be standing here in 1965. It never even occurred to me in my fondest dreams that I might have the chance to help the sons and daughters of those students and to help people like them all over this country.

But now I do have that chance—and I'll let you in on a secret—I mean to use it. And I hope that you will use it with me.

This is the richest and most powerful country which ever occupied the globe. The might of past empires is little compared to ours. But I do not want to be the President who built empires, or sought grandeur, or extended dominion.

I want to be the President who educated young children to the wonders of their world. I want to be the President who helped to feed the hungry and to prepare them to be taxpayers instead of taxeaters.

I want to be the President who helped the poor to find their own way and who protected the right of every citizen to vote in every election.

I want to be the President who helped to end hatred among his fellow men and who promoted love among the people of all races and all regions and all parties.

I want to be the President who helped to end war among the brothers of this earth.

And so at the request of your beloved Speaker and the Senator from Montana; the majority leader, the Senator from Illinois; the minority leader, Mr. McCulloch, and other Members of both parties, I came here tonight—not as President Roosevelt came down one time in person to veto a bonus bill, not as President Truman came down one time to urge the passage of a railroad bill—but I came down here to ask you to share this task with me and to share it with the people that we both work for. I want this to be the Congress, Republicans and Democrats alike, which did all these things for all these people.

Beyond this great chamber, out yonder in 50 States, are the people that we serve. Who can tell what deep and unspoken hopes are in their hearts tonight as they sit there and listen. We all can guess, from our own lives, how difficult they often find their own pursuit of happiness, how many problems each little family has. They look most of all to themselves for their futures. But I think that they also look to each of us.

Above the pyramid on the great seal of the United States it says—in Latin—"God has favored our undertaking."

God will not favor everything that we do. It is rather our duty to divine His will. But I cannot help believing that He truly understands and that He really favors the undertaking that we begin here tonight.

Source: National Archives and Records Administration, The Lyndon B. Johnson Library and Museum. http://www.lbjlib.utexas.edu/johnson/archives.hom/speeches.hom/650315.htm.

Appendix B

Memorandum for Mr. Shillady on Negro Suffrage and Disfranchisement

From Mr. Morton May 26, 1919

1. A vote is the formal declaration or expression of the will or preference of a person in regard to a question or issue submitted to him together with others for action.

(a) The term, vote, in derived from the Latin; end the act to which such term in applied was an absolute right inherent in every freeman centuries before the fabled exploit of Romulus.

1- Thus we find the ancient Hebrews deciding important questions by the casting of lots, that being their method of voting. See, Members 26:55, Leviticus 16:8, [P]salms 22:18, I Chronicles 24 and 25. So also, the dikasts in Greece voted by means of shells; and we have likewise the tabellae, or tickets, of the Romans.

2- To vote, that is to declare one's opinion or preference upon some issue, would seem ever to have been an every-day occurrence among mankind; but to vote as a political right is a privilege exercised only in the popular governments. Nothing of the sort is to be found in the ancient despotisms of the East, The Mosaic Code, however, recognized the right to vote, to cast lots, as a necessary function in successful government. Says Dr. Lord of Moses. "He gave dignity to the people by making them the ultimate source of authority, next to the authority of God." And so of the Athenian Democracy, when officials were not chosen by lot, they were elected from the entire body of citizens; and every citizen had some active part in the management of the State. So also, of the Roman people in that happy era between the time of the Gracchi and the rise of the first Caesar, their liberties were guarded in their possession of the right to vote.

(b) The principle of the government based in the consent of the governed, a consent obtained by means if votes, was not unknown during the Middle Ages.

1. Witness the free cities of the Hans[e]atic League, the Italian republics, the Swiss Confederation, and even the larger municipalities of France.

11. But it was in England that the idea of a free, representative was by gradual evolution brought into being. The ecclesiastical synods so well organized by Theodore of Tarsus paved the way to the Witenagernot, and through after the Conquest, the Council of the Magnates of the realm superseded the old Saxon congregation of wise men, yet in the Hundred leets and the shire moots was preserved the right to the exercise of the suffrage. And with the advent of parliaments came suffrage absolutely unrestricted in the shires, and in the boroughs the right of all freemen settling therein and paying their dues. J.R. Greed, History of the English People, Chapt. VI. By the ancient constitution of England all free-men who for twelve months (sometimes the old common law period of the year and a day) previous to the election resided within the corporate town, etc., paying scot and lot, could vote. Letter to the Duke of Richmond (1430) the "great disfranchising statute," the country franchise by the oligarchic tendencies of the great trade companies. And this restriction of the suffrage was soon followed by its corruption in the "management" of elections. Not until the Reform Bill of 1832 was there any extension of the elective franchise.

111. Consequently, the English colonists in the America held very conservative views as to popular participation in government, although the qualifications for suffrage varied greatly in the different colonies. There were all sorts of tests, principally as to property and religion. The religious tests were first to be abolished, the last survival of the kind existing in South Carolina from 1778 to 1790.

IV. The Federal Constitution recognized the right of each state to regulate the suffrage within its own borders. Thus it was that during the early part of the nineteenth century, a free-holder qualification was required in several of the states, the payment of taxes alone being required in Pennsylvania, Delaware, and Georgia.

(a) But the Negro Question complicated that of suffrage even before the Civil War.

1. States both North and South limited the suffrage to white males, although free Negros voted in North Carolina until the promulgation of the reactionary Constitution of 1835. Until the

Revolution, they were allowed to vote in every state except Georgia and South Carolina. Thereafter Delaware, Maryland, Virginia, and Kentucky, as well as North Carolina excluded them from the suffrage. So also in many Northern States. The Tennessee Constitution of 1834 limited the right to those Negroes who were competent as witnesses against white persons. See Stephenson, Race Distinctions in American Law, pp. 283–4. Yet it would seem that free Negroes did vote to some extent even in those states where they were excluded by law.

2. But the agitation over Negro suffrage prevented an extension of suffrage to the non-properties classes among the whites. See Porter, Suffrage in the United States, Chapts. 111 and IV.

3. It is worthy of note that Maine, Massachusetts, New Hampshire, Rhode Island, and Vermont appear not to have had any race distinctions in suffrage, Stephenson, Race Distinctions in America Law, p. 282.

(b) In 1865, the only states that permitted Negroes to vote on the same footing as white persons were the New England states mentioned, supra, and Wisconsin. New York and Tennessee permitted a restricted Negro Suffrage. Race Distinctions in America Law, p. 285. And the states, North as well as South, appeared at this time not to have progressed in their opinions regarding Negro Suffrage.

V. A readjustment of the suffrage was undertaken immediately following the Civil War.

(a) Everywhere in the South was reaction. Provisional legislatures elected by and composed of white men only convened, and forthwith promulgated the notorious Black Laws. See, John W. Burgess, Reconstruction and the Constitution. Chapt. IV. There seems also to have been a leak of loyalty to the Federal Government. Report of Carl Schurz to the President, 1865. And so there came the Reconstruction Acts of 1867, enfranchising Negroes in the District of Columbia and in the territories. Then came the earlier Civil Rights Act, then the Fourteenth Amendment. Porter, Suffrage in the U.S., Chapt. VII. The Fourteenth Amendment was proposed to the legislatures of the several states by the Fortieth Congress, on the twenty-seventh of February 1869 and was, on the thirtieth of March 1870, proclaimed to have been ratified by the legislatures of twenty-nine of the thirty-seven states.

(b) The last of the War Amendments provides that "the right of citizens of the United States to vote shall not be denied or abridged by the United States or by any State on account of race, color, or previous condition of servitude"; and Congress is given power by its terms to enforce the Article by appropriate legislation, thus rendering the Amendment

self-executing to the extent that all laws and all provisions of state constitutions in conflict therewith are thereby null and void. It can be seen,
of course, that the Amendment does not confer the right to vote upon
anyone, but invests citizens of the United States with an exemption from
discrimination in elections because of race, color, or previous condition of
servitude. So held in U.S. vs. Reese et al., 92 U.S. 214 and in U.S. vs. Harris,
106 U.S. 629. See also, Minor vs. Happersett, 21 Wall 162.

    *1. Thus an educational test, or a poll tax requirement, or a limitation to
a single sex is no denial of the suffrage within th[e] purview of the Amendment.
Minor v. Happersett, supra, and cases there cited.*

    *2. It would seem also that a property qualification is perfectly valid,
although this, an eminent authority, deems open to doubt. Cooley, General Principles of Constitutional Law.*

VI. *In the South the mandate of the Federal Constitution regarding suffrage was
speedy set at n[a]ught.*

    (a) *Disfranchisement of Negroes began even during Reconstruction, and,
after the fall of the Reconstruction governments, went merrily on space.
First the colored vote was suppressed by fraud and violence; and the
period between 1879 and 1890 reeks with tales of shot-gun outrages,
tissue ballots. Eight Ballot Box Laws, etc. see Hart, Negro Suffrage; and
Haworth, Reconstruction and Union.*

    (b) *Finally, tired of disfranchisement based on intimidating, the southern
whites sought to make secure the obliteration of Negro suffrage by
positive enactment. Constitutional changes in the suffrage requirements
were made by Mississippi in 1890, South Carolina in 1895, Louisiana
in 1899, North Carolina in 1900, Alabama and Virginia in 1901, and
Georgia in 1908.*

      1. The Mississippi Constitution of 1890 provides that a person
in order to vote must be a male citizen of the United States,
twenty-one years of age, and have resided in the state two
years, in the county, one year, and also one year in the precinct, and all poll taxes must have been paid for the two preceding years. The prospective voter must be able to read the
Constitution of the State; or, if he cannot read, he may vote if
he can understand or responsibly interpret the Constitution.
Idiots and insane persons, Indians not taxed, and felons are
excluded the suffrage. Sec. 4117 (3611) Chapt. 119. Miss. Code
(Ann.) 1906 reads: The registrar shall register in the registration book of the election district of the residence of such persons any one appearing before him, and being upon examination, by him adjudged entitled to be registered as an elector,
upon such person taking and subscribing the oath required by
section 242 of the Constitution. This vesting of judicial discre-

tion in the registrar is a feature common to all disfranchising acts, and is the chief weapon used in suppressing the Negro vote. See Brawley, Short History of The American Negro, p. 181, and Porter, p. 210.

2. Thus in the South Carolina Civil Code, sec. 182; After the first of January 1896, the Board of Registration to be appointed under section 176 shall judge of the legal qualifications of all applicants for registration.

3. In 1898, Louisiana invented the Grandfather Clause. By its provisions, one might permanently register before September 1, 1898, if he was entitled to vote in any state Jan. 1, 1867, or the son or grandson of such a one and twenty-one years old or over in 1898, or a foreigner naturalized before Jan. 1, 1989, resident in State five years before application for registration.

4. In Alabama, there was the usual poll-tax requirement. Also up to 1903, three defined classes of persons were to be permitted to register as permanent voters. They were (1) Those who had served in any of the wars of the United States from the Revolution to the Spanish War, including Confederate soldiers. (2) All legal descendants of the foregoing. (3) All persons who were of good character and who understood the duties and obligations of citizenship under a republican form of government. After 1903 only those could vote who were able to read and write any article of the constitution in English and who had worked the greater part of the preceding year, with alternatives, of course, said alternatives being property tests. Criminals were excluded the suffrage, each and every crime being specifically enumerated. And the legislature provided that on challenge a voter must take oath declaring himself qualified to vote, in the minute details, and that he is not guilty of any of the long list of crimes mentioned. Ala. Code (1907) Vol. 1, section 408.

5. In Georgia any male person of legal age who has paid his poll-tax may register and vote if he can read accurately or write accurately a paragraph of the state constitution that may be read to him. Any person owning or paying taxes on $500.00 worth of property may register and vote whether literate or illiterate. The Georgia Grandfather clause permitted permanent registration at any time before January 1, 1915.

(a) The Mississippi Constitution was never submitted to the people. But the state Court held in Sproule vs. Frederick, 74 Miss. 271, that ratification of the Constitution by the people was unnecessary to its validity, as well as declaring the Constitution not to violate the

War Amendments. In Williams vs. Mississippi, 170 U.S. 213, the literacy test came up for review, and was adjusted constitutional. It was also asserted that a law could not be invalidated merely because abuse was possible under it, when such abuse was not apparent on its face. In Giles vs. Harris, 189 U.S. 474 and Giles vs. Teasley, 193 U.S. 146, the Supreme Court decided against Federal intervention. These cases concerned the Alabama constitution. None of these cases were decided on the merits.

VII. On August 2, 1910, Oklahoma passed by forty thousand majority a constitutional amendment containing a Grandfather Clause. The words "For the Amendment" were printed at the botto[m] of the ticket, and unless they were marked out the ballot was counted affirmatively.

(a) Negro citizens being denied their right to vote by state election officials acting under the amendment. The Federal Government commented a prosecution against the said officials under U.S. Penal Code, section 19. The defendants were convicted, and upon appeal (see Guinn vs. United States, 238 U.S. 347) the conviction was sustained. By this case, in which Moorfield Storey appeared for the N.A.A.C.P., it was laid down that state election officials who conspire to deprive Negro citizens of their right to vote secured by the Fifteenth Amendment are indictable, that the repeal in 1894 of certain statues relating to suffrage did not withdraw offenses by election officers from the operation of U.S. Penal Code, section 19, and that Grandfather Clauses are subterfuges designed to defeat the express intent of the Fifteenth Amendment, and therefore unconstitutional.

(b) And in the three Maryland cases (238 U.S. 368), it was held that state election officials who, even though conforming to a state statute, deprive Negro citizens of their right to vote secured by the Fifteenth Amendment, are liable to such Negro citizens for the resulting damages, and also that the right to vote secured by the Fifteenth Amendment extends to municipal elections.

(c) In 238 U.S. 383, another Oklahoma case, it was decided that a conspiracy of state election officials to omit the returns from certain precincts at an election for member of Congress from their count and from their return to the state election board is indictable, and that the right to have one's vote counted at an election for a member of Congress is as open to protection by Congress as is the right to vote itself.

VIII. On February 12, 1919, the Atlanta Branch of the N.A.A.C.P. launched a Registration Drive. Prior to that date the registration books in Atlanta rarely had listed thereon the names of more than 600 colored persons, and in some years the number was low as 400. In one month, there were registered more that one thousand Negro voters, who immediately made their power felt by defeating a much desired bond issue. And the Branch intends to keep up the work.

On the other hand, it would appear from a letter published in the Southern Indicator of Columbia, S.C. on March 22, 1919, that recently in Greenwood, S.C. no inconsiderable number of colored men well able to meet literacy and property requirements were refused the right to register. The actual information set forth in the letter is meager, but if the facts are as implied, it would seem to be a case for the Federal Courts in accordance with the rulings in the cases in 238 U.S. At all events, an appeal is possible in the state courts, a hearing de novo being granted in the Court of Common Place under section 180 and 182 of the South Carolina Civil Code.

Both of these instances are steps in the right direction. No one is going to hand out the ballot on a platter. Says Porter, p. 266. "If the Negro lacks the ambition to take advantage of the law which is on his side and is vastly superior in numbers, it is a question whether he really desires the ballot." And again, "Until the Negro develops a real honest, deep desire to vote and is willing to assert himself and take that power which the law holds out to him, his cause, as it were, it almost hopeless." To obtain the vote the Negro must with continuous insistence seek the vote.

An expert from the Ballot Catechism, Oct. 20, 1871, and English publication issued in support of the Ballot Bill of 1871 is interesting in this connection. It follows:

98. What steps must be at once taken to give the liberal Party the necessary prestige, enabling them to go the whole length which the solemn necessity of the time requires?

1. By holding public meetings in favor of the ballot. Invite members of Parliament to be present, and request them to support the desires and resolutions on all these points. 111. Every city, town, and village, every political association of Liberals and others interested, should forward a properly prepared petition playing the passing of a Ballot Bill. IV. The petition should be in duplicate, one to the House of Commons, and the other to the House of Lords.

99. Why is all this action necessary?

Because it has been very frequently said that the nation exhibits no strong inclination for the Ballot, and that no pressure has been put upon members of Parliament by the People.

IX. And yet the Southern whites out for the sake of themselves by highly desirous that the Negro be no longer disfranchised.

   (a) Even as proven by events in Fourteenth Century England, corruption follows disfranchisement. Said John Hope (Occasional Papers, No. 11, American Negro Academy, p. 57), "For instance,

I know of a city election where the voter in one ward were so evenly divided and the candidates had calculated their strength so accurately, that one candidate felt safe in buying three white voters at the rate of one hundred and ten dollars. Large corporations may now operate easily in state and city; and some of the most flagrant cases of political jobbery that have been charged against Reconstruction rule are easily equaled by the bare-faced graft and bribery by which large business interests win their way through the assistance of white voters."

(b) Disfranchisement makes for an ignorant citizenry, and an ignorant citizenry, weakens both state and nation.

1. Only by participation in government on the part of the people can their interest in that government be aroused, and the government strengthened thereby. Witness the difference between ancient Athens and ancient Persia, between Rome and Republic, and Rome the Degenerate Empire, or between modern England and Russia.

2. And in the South, the actual disfranchisement and political apathy as to both races is very extensive. In one county in Mississippi, with a population of about 8,000 whites and 11700 Negroes in 1900, there were only twenty-five or thirty qualified Negro voters. In another county of Mississippi, with 8,000 whites and 12,000 Negroes only 400 white men and about 30 Negroes were qualified electors. Says Stephenson: In Iowa four out of five possible voters have actually voted in the last four elections; in Georgia a State of nearly the same population, the proportion is one to six. In Mississippi in 1906 only one out of eighteen males of voting age actually votes, in Georgia one out of fifteen. In a district in Mississippi with a population of 190,885, 2,091 voters were cast for the representative, John Sharp Williams, in 1906; in a district in Connecticut with a population of 247,875, 46,425 voters were case for Representative Litchfield. And it would appear that many who are capable of satisfying the qualifications in the South do not register, or, if they register, do not vote.

3. Comparison of 1918 Congressional vote.

X. It is to the interest of the North that the Negro have the vote. Present conditions not only disfranchise the Negro and a large number of the Southern whites but also disfranchise the Northern voter.

XI. And it is to the best interest of the entire nation that the Negro have the vote.

(a) The Negro is in law a citizen. To raise an extra-legal color distinction breeds disrespect for all law in the collective mind of the entire nation.

(b) The Negro in law has certain rights inherit to citizenship. To raise an extra-legal color distinction as to his right to vote deprives him of those rights; and if his color can operate against the exercise of his rights under the law, then is he less than a citizen, as there is operating against him that which it is beyond his power to change. Thus the Negro is born without rights; and without rights enforceable by the power of the vote, he will receive no benefits, the lesson of history being that only those receive consideration from governments who possess the power to force it to be accorded them. And the best governments have ever been those which accord every right under the law to the citizens thereof.

(c) As long as the Negro is deprived the suffrage, so long will lynchings continue to disgrace the nation. Who cares anything about an animal shorn of all power?

(d) Disfranchisement injures the country economically. The present labor system of the South is oppressive, an oppression impossible of being had the oppressed the power of striking back by means of the ballot. White workers and black workers both suffer, as with the price of black labor forcibly kept down, white labor cannot successfully demand its just due. And with cheap labor in the South, labor in the North, and capital in the North are injured.

(e) Disfranchisement is highly impolitic. No people, not even a wonderfully patient people, can remain forever hopeful and happy beneath continued injustice. To have millions of dissatisfied people in our midst, deprived of the vote, and because of such depravation, deprived of education advantages, of freedom from restraint in moving from one place to another, stigmatized as a race apart, as pariahs, and deprived of life, liberty, and property without due process of law, is a greater danger. From the mere standpoint of policy, it may be safe to treat with injustice an alien and a conquered people. But when people have imbi[b]ed for centuries the spirit of the land in which they live, they will not forever submit to having the blessings which that spirit teaches them to be their due, roughly denied them.

XII. Disfranchisement at present is almost as rife as ever in the South. Though the Grandfather Clause is now a thing of the past, literacy and property tests exist in most of the Southern states, a poll tax requirement in all of them, and a judicial discretion in the registrars in all, a discretion used to suppress the Negro vote. The decisions in 238 U.S. render the exercise of such a discretion for such a purpose dangerous in a fairly orderly community; but in the worst of the lynch-ridden communities, in the small places, actual intimidation would appear to be comparatively easy. It is that lawlessness which must be suppressed. The Federal Courts afford a remedy, both on the Criminal side of the Court and on the Civil side. 238 U.S. & U.S. Rev. Stats.

To a literacy test impartially administered no one can object. It is within the power of every man to acquire an education. To a property test, no one can legally object; and the Negro seeks only that which is his right under the law. But a property test is an undemocratic thing, no true believer in popular government can stomach it; nor would the South stand for this undemocratic thing were it not that its oligarchs seek thus to hold their power, it being the easier with such a test to cut down the Negro vote.

Albert Bushnell Hart sums up the matter thus; First, the system is really, although not openly, a discrimination between men on the ground not of their character or their acquisitions, but of the color; secondly, it means the permanent disfranchisement of the greater part of the Negro race, and their consequent relegation to a position in which one of the most effective springs of thrift and ambition is removed.

And in truth, the Negro's whole salvation would seem to hinge upon him exercising his right to vote, it having long been held that he who has no vote is less than free and arbitrarily governed. See John Winthrop. Arbitrary Government Described and the Government of Massachusetts Vindicates from That Aspersion (1644).

Notes

INTRODUCTION

1. *Dred Scott v. Sandford*, 60 U.S. 393 (1857).

CHAPTER 1

1. *NAACP: Celebrating a Century 100 Years in Pictures* (Layton, UT: Gibbs Smith, 2009), 12–15.

2. William English Walling, "The Race War in the North," *The Independent* 65 (September 3, 1908): 529–34. For more on the Springfield Riot see Robert L. Zangrando, *The NAACP Crusade Against Lynching, 1909–1950* (Philadelphia: Temple University Press, 1980).

3. Ibid., 529–34.

4. Ibid.

5. See Carolyn Wedin, *Mary White Ovington and the Founding of the NAACP* (New York: John Wiley & Sons, 1998).

6. Gilbert Jonas, *Freedom's Sword: The NAACP and the Struggle Against Racism in America, 1909–1969* (New York: Routledge, 2005).

7. Walling, "The Race War in the North," 529–34.

8. *Pace v. Alabama*, 106 U.S. 583 (1883).

9. Ala. Crim. Code § 4189 (1876).

10. See Manfred Berg, *The Ticket to Freedom: The NAACP and the Struggle for Black Political Integration* (Gainesville: University Press of Florida, 2005).

11. See *Plessy v. Ferguson*, 163 U.S. 537 (1896).

12. David L. Lewis, *W.E.B. DuBois: Biography of a Race* (New York: Henry Holt, 1993), 314–19.

13. Mary W. Ovington, *Half a Man: The Status of the Negro in New York* (Norwood: The Plimpton Press, 1911).

14. See Paula Giddings, *Ida: A Sword Among Lions: Ida B. Wells and the Campaign Against Lynching* (New York: HarperCollins, 2009).

15. Patricia Sullivan, *Lift Every Voice: The NAACP and the Making of the Civil Rights Movement* (New York: The New Press, 2009), 2–3.

16. Lewis, *W.E.B. DuBois: Biography of a Race*, 322–23.

17. Mary W. Ovington, *Black and White Sat Down Together: The Reminiscences of an NAACP Founder* (New York: The Feminist Press, 1995), 58.

18. Ibid., 59.

19. Charles F. Kellogg, *NAACP: A History of the National Association for the Advancement of Colored People* (Baltimore, MD: Johns Hopkins University Press, 1967), 297–99.

20. Berg, *Ticket to Freedom*, 11.

21. See *Black Americans in Congress, 1870–2007* (Washington, DC: US Government Printing Office, 2008).

22. See Michael Newton, *The Ku Klux Klan in Mississippi: A History* (Jefferson, NC: McFarland, 2010), p. 253–54. For more on James K. Vardaman's racism, see William F. Holmes, *The White Chief: James Kimble Vardaman* (Baton Rouge: Louisiana State University Press, 1970).

23. See Newton, *Ku Klux Klan in Mississippi*, 253–54.

24. *North Carolina Democratic Handbook* ([Chapel Hill]: Academic Affairs Library, University of North Carolina at Chapel Hill, 2002), 35.

25. "Statement of Carter Glass," in *Report of the Proceedings and Debate of the Constitutional Convention, State of Virginia* (1906), 3076. Glass went on to explain, in the debate about the 1902 suffrage amendments, that the entire purpose of the constitutional revision was "to discriminate to the very extremity of permissible action under the limitations of the Federal Constitution, with a view to the elimination of every negro voter who can be gotten rid of, legally, without materially impairing the numerical strength of the white electorate." Ibid., 3076–77.

26. Walling, "The Race War in the North," 529–34.

27. Ovington, *Black and White Sat Down Together*, 57–59.

28. Joyce B. Ross, *J. E. Spingarn and the Rise of the NAACP* (New York: Atheneum, 1972).

29. William B. Hixson, *Moorfield Storey and the Abolitionist Tradition* (New York: Oxford University Press, 1972), 123.

30. See ibid.

31. Ibid., 118.

32. *NAACP: Celebrating a Century*, 28.

33. Moorfield Storey to Charles E. Ward, March 30, 1906, in ibid., 122.

34. Clement E. Vose, *Caucasians Only: The Supreme Court, the NAACP, and the Restrictive Covenant* (Berkeley: University of California Press, 1967), 32.

CHAPTER 2

1. U.S. Const. art. I, § 2, cl. 2.

2. Ibid., cl. 1.

3. Roi Ottley and William J. Weatherby, *The Negro in New York: An Informal Social History* (Dobbs Ferry, NY: Oceana Publications, 1967), 62–63.

4. *Dred Scott v. Sandford*, 60 U.S. 393 (1857).

5. *Prigg v. Pennsylvania*, 41 U.S. 539 (1842).

6. *Dred Scott v. Sandford*, 60 U.S. 393 (1857).

7. Ibid., 412.

8. *The Liberator*, September 5, 1856, quoted in Herbert Aptheker, *A Documentary History of the Negro People in the United States: From Colonial Times through the Civil War* (New York: Citadel, 1960), 388.

9. Ottley and Weatherby, *The Negro in New York*, 65.

10. U.S. Const. amend. XIV, § 2.

11. www.archives.gov/education/lessons/blacks-civil-war/.

12. *Ex parte Yarbrough*, 110 U.S. 651 (1884).

13. http://history.house.gov/People/Listing/R/RAINEY,-Joseph-Hayne-(R000016)/.

14. Ibid.

15. See Jaqueline L. Harris, *History and Achievement of the NAACP* (New York: Franklin Watts, 1992), 11–15.

16. http://history.house.gov/People/Listing/R/RAINEY,-Joseph-Hayne-(R000016)/.

17. See John H. Franklin, *Reconstruction after the Civil War* (Chicago: University of Chicago Press, 1994).

18. *Black Americans in Congress, 1870–2007* (Washington, DC: US Government Printing Office, 2008), 65. For information on Rep. Joseph H. Rainey, see pages 62–67.

19. http://history.house.gov/People/Listing/R/RAINEY,-Joseph-Hayne-(R000016)/.

20. Richard M. Valelly, *The Two Reconstructions: The Struggle for the Black Enfranchisement* (Chicago: University of Chicago Press, 2004), 48–49.

21. See "Negro Suffrage: Should the Fourteenth and Fifteenth Amendments Be Repealed?" Speech presented by Hon. Edward De V. Morrell of Pennsylvania to the US House of Representatives, April 4, 1904, https://memory.loc.gov/cgi-bin/query/r?ammem/murray:@field(DOCID+@lit(lcrbmrpt2609div1)).

22. See ibid.

23. *Independent*, March 31, 1877. See also James M. McPherson, *The Abolitionist Legacy: From Reconstruction to the NAACP* (Princeton, NJ: Princeton University Press, 1975), 86–91.

24. David Walker, *Walker's Appeal, in Four Articles: Together with a Preamble, to the Coloured Citizens of the World, but in Particular, and very Expressly, to Those of the United States of America* (Written in Boston, State of Massachusetts, September 28, 1829).

25. Aptheker, *Documentary History of the Negro People*, 92.

26. *Dred Scott v. Sandford*, 60 U.S. 393 (1857).

27. Herbert Aptheker, *American Negro Slave Revolts* (New York: International Publishers, 1963), 75.

28. "The Ballot and the Bullet," *The Life and Writings of Frederick Douglass*, Volume 2 (4 volumes), edited by Philip S. Foner, 457–58. (New York: International Publishers, 1950–.

29. Frederick Douglass, "What the Black Man Wants," speech in Boston, Massachusetts (1865).

30. *The Civil Rights Cases*, 109 U.S. 3 (1883).

31. W. E. B. DuBois, "The Freedmen's Bureau," *Atlanta Monthly* 87 (1901): 354–65.

32. "Booker T. Washington Delivers the 1895 Atlanta Compromise Address [September 18, 1895]," History Matters: The U.S. Survey course on the Web, http://historymatters.gmu.edu/d/39/.

33. Booker T. Washington, *Up From Slavery: An Autobiography of Booker T. Washington* (New York: Doubleday, Page, 1901).

34. "Booker T. Washington Delivers the 1895 Atlanta Compromise Address."

35. Ibid.

36. *Plessy v. Ferguson*, 163 U.S. 537 (1896).

37. *Williams v. Mississippi*, 170 U.S. 213 (1898).

38. *Giles v. Harris*, 189 U.S. 475 (1903).

39. See Bruce L. Mouser, *For Labor, Race and Liberty: George Edwin Taylor, His Historic Run for the White House, and the Making of Independent Black Politics* (Madison: University of Wisconsin Press, 2011).

40. See Clay J. Smith Jr., *Emancipation: The Making of the Black Lawyer, 1844–1944* (Philadelphia: University of Pennsylvania Press, 1999), which examines the vital role of the Black lawyer in detail.

41. Wilson Record, *Race and Radicalism: The NAACP and the Communist Party in Conflict* (Ithaca, NY: Cornell University Press, 1964).

CHAPTER 3

1. See *Plessy v. Ferguson*, 163 U.S. 537 (1896).

2. *Bailey v. Alabama*, 211 U.S. 452 (1908) (challenging denial of writ of habeas corpus after being imprisoned for failing to working under conditions of slave-like peonage); and *Bailey v. Alabama*, 219 U.S. 219 (1911) (on appeal to the Supreme Court, challenging Alabama's violation of federal antipeonage laws).

3. *Yick Wo v. Hopkins*, 118 U.S. 356 (1886).

4. *Plessy v. Ferguson*, 163 U.S. 537 (1896).

5. Okla. Const. art. III, § 1 (1910).

6. *Guinn v. United States*, 228 F. 103, 108 (8th Cir. 1915).

7. Ibid.; *Guinn v. United States*, 238 U.S. 347 (1915).

8. *Guinn v. United States*, 228 F. 103, 108–9 (8th Cir. 1915).

9. Robert B. Highsaw, *Edward Douglass White: Defender of the Conservative Faith* (Baton Rouge: Louisiana State University Press, 1981).

10. *Myers v. Anderson*, 238 U.S. 368 (1915).

11. Carolina Mora, "NAACP: Foundation, Niagara Movement, Participation in *Guinn v. United States* and Prominent Personalities; Biography of Chief Justice Edward Douglass White" (unpublished research paper, August 21, 2013).

12. Ibid.

13. http://www.naacp.org/pages/naacp-history-charles-hamilton-houston.

14. Ibid.

15. See Albion W. Tourgée Papers, Chautauqua County Historical Society, Westfield, NY.

16. *Plessy v. Ferguson.*

17. Ibid.

18. Ibid.

19. http://www.pbs.org/wgbh/amex/garvey/peopleevents/e_estlouis.html.

20. *Buchanan v. Warley*, 245 U.S. 60 (1917).

21. Ibid.

22. Ibid.

23. Ibid.

24. Ibid.

25. *Williams v. Mississippi*, 170 U.S. 213 (1898).

26. Manfred Berg, *The Ticket to Freedom* (Gainesville: University of Florida Press, 2005), 28.

27. William B. Hixson, *Moorfield Storey and the Abolitionist Tradition* (New York: Oxford University Press, 1972), 142.

28. NAACP Records Legal Department, 1842–1997, Library of Congress.

29. *NAACP: Celebrating a Century*, 33.

30. NAACP.org/pages/washington-bureau-about.

CHAPTER 4

1. Myrlie Evers-Williams and Manning Marable, *The Autobiography of Medgar Evers: A Hero's Life and Legacy Revealed Through His Writings, Letters, and Speeches* (New York: Basic/Civitas Books, 2005).

2. H. W. Brands, *Woodrow Wilson* (New York: Henry Holt, 2003), 133–34.

3. John M. Cooper, *Woodrow Wilson: A Biography* (New York: Alfred A. Knopf, 2009), 271–73.

4. http://historymatters.gmu.edu/d/5719/.

5. W. E. B. DuBois, *The Souls of Black Folk* (Chicago: A. C. McClurg, 1903).

6. Trotter.Umich.edu/timeline/219/lifeoftrotter/13 (retrieved June 2016).

7. *Moore v. Dempsey*, 261 U.S. 86 (1923).

8. Kenneth Robert Janken, *Walter White: Mr. NAACP* (Chapel Hill: University of North Carolina Press, 2006), 49.

9. Richard C. Cortner, *A Mob Intent on Death: The NAACP and the Arkansas Riot Cases* (Middletown, CT: Wesleyan Press, 1988), 30.

10. Walter White, *A Man Called White* (New York: Viking, 1948).

11. Ibid.

12. Quoted in "The Real Causes of Two Race Riots," *The Crisis*, December 1919, 56–62.

13. *Ware v. State*, 146 Ark. 321, 324–25 (1920).

14. *Moore v. Dempsey*, 261 U.S. 86 (1923).

15. Ibid.

16. *Plessy v. Ferguson*, 163 US 537 (1896).

17. NAACP, "Shame of America," *New York Times*, November, 23, 1922.

18. Mark Perry, *Lift Up Thy Voice: The Sarah and Angelina Grimké Family's Journey from Slaveholders to Civil Rights Leaders* (New York: Penguin, 2002).

19. US Const., Nineteenth Amendment, August 18, 1920.

20. President Warren G. Harding, speech delivered October 26, 1921, in Woodrow Wilson Park in Birmingham, Alabama. See Samuel Hopkins Adams, *Incredible Era: The Life and Times of Warren Gamaliel Harding* (New York: Houghton Mifflin, 1939).

21. Phyllis Vine, *One Man's Castle: Clarence Darrow in Defense of the American Dream* (New York: HarperCollins, 2004).

22. Kevin Boyle, *Arc of Justice: A Saga of Race, Civil Rights, and Murder in the Jazz Age* (New York: Henry Holt, 2004).

23. *Buchanan v. Warley*, 245 U.S. 60 (1917).

24. *Guinn v. United States*, 238 U.S. 347 (1915).

25. *Plessy v. Ferguson*, 163 U.S. 537 (1896).

26. *West v. Bliley*, 33 F.2d 177 (1929).

27. *Robinson v. Holman*, 181 Ark. 428 (1930), 26 S.W. 2d 66 (Ark. 1930).

28. *Nixon v. Herndon*, 273 U.S. 536, 541 (1927).

29. Ibid.

30. Manfred Berg, *The Ticket to Freedom* (Gainesville: University of Florida Press, 2005), 78.

31. In *Nixon v. Condon*, 286 U.S. 73 (1932). Supreme Court opinion refers to previous Texas statute creating all-White primaries ruled unconstitutional in *Nixon v. Herndon*, 273 U.S. 536 (1927).

32. *Nixon v. Condon*, 286 U.S. 73 (1932).

33. *Nixon v. Herndon*, 273 U.S. 536, 541 (1927).

34. *Nixon v. Condon*, 286 U.S. 73 (1932).

35. *Grovey v. Townsend*, 295 U.S. 45, 55 (1935).

36. *Nixon v. Herndon*, 273 U.S. 536, 541 (1927).

37. Kenneth W. Goings, *The NAACP Comes of Age: The Defeat of Judge John J. Parker* (Westport, CT: Greenwood Press, 1990), 11; *Charlotte Observer*, April 18, 1920.

38. In 1930, the confirmation hearing before the US Senate on the nomination of Judge John Parker of North Carolina to the US Supreme Court resulted in a vote of 41–39 against him due to the lobbying efforts of the NAACP. Clement E. Vose, *Caucasians Only: The Supreme Court, the NAACP, and the Restrictive Covenant Cases* (Berkeley: University of California Press, 1967).

39. *Plessy v. Ferguson*, 163 U.S. 537 (1896).

40. *Guinn v. United States*, 238 U.S. 347 (1915).

41. *Lane v. Wilson*, 307 U.S. 268 (1939).

42. Ibid.

43. *University v. Murray*, 169 Md. 478, 182 A. 590 (1936).

44. *Mitchell v. United States*, 313 U.S. 80 (1941).

45. See *Smith v. Allwright*, 321 U.S. 649, 663 (1944).

46. Ibid.

47. Ibid.

48. "The Historical Origins of the Run-off Primary," *The Crisis* 91, no. 8 (October 1984): 20–22.

49. *Elmore v. Rice*, 72 F. Supp. 516 (1947).

50. http://scafricanamerican.com/honorees/view/2014/6/.

51. Ibid.

52. Ibid.

53. Ibid.

54. http://scafricanamerican.com/honorees/view/2014/6/.

CHAPTER 5

1. *Smith v. Allwright*, 321 U.S. 649 (1944).

2. Gloria J. Browne-Marshall, *Race, Law and American Society: 1607 to Present* (New York: Routledge, 2013), 261.

3. *Brown v. The Board of Education of Topeka, Kansas*, 347 U.S. 483 (1954).

4. *Davis v. Schnell*, 81 F. Supp. 872 (1949).

5. "Negro Disenfranchisement—A Challenge to the Constitution," *Columbia Law Review* 47 (1947): 76.

6. *Hodge v. Tulsa County Election Board*, 335 U.S. 889 (1948).

7. *Mills v. Green*, 159 U.S. 651 (1895).

8. *Perry v. Cyphers*, 186 F.2d 608 (1951).

9. *Perry v. Cyphers*, 186 F.2d 608-610.

10. Ibid.

11. *NAACP: Celebrating a Century 100 Years in Pictures* (Layton, UT: Gibbs Smith, 2009).

12. *Browder v. Gayle*, 142 F. Supp. 707 (1956) (the NAACP lost the trial court case); *Browder v. Gayle*, 352 U.S. 903 (1956) (the NAACP won at the Supreme Court).

13. *NAACP v. Patty*, 159 F. Supp. 503 (D.C.E.D. Va. 1958) (on appeal to the US Supreme Court the case was renamed *NAACP v. Button*, 371 U.S. 414 [1963]).

14. *Bryant v. Zimmerman*, 278 U.S. 63 (1928).

15. *Bates v. Little Rock*, 361 U.S. 516 (1960).

16. *NAACP v. Button*, 371 U.S. 414 (1963).

17. *Darby v. Daniel*, 168 F. Supp. 170 (1958).

18. Ibid., 190–91.

19. *Gomillion v. Lightfoot*, 364 U.S. 339 (1960).

20. *Colegrove v. Green*, 328 U.S. 549 (1946).

21. *Gomillion v. Lightfoot*, 364 U.S. 339 (1960).

22. *Baker v. Carr*, 369 U.S. 186 (1962).

23. *Reynolds v. Sims*, 377 U.S. 546 (1964).

24. John Wertheimer, *Law and Society of the South: A History of North Carolina Court Cases* (Louisville: University of Kentucky, 2010).

25. *Lassiter v. Northampton County Board of Elections*, 360 U.S. 45 (1959).

26. *Williams v. Mississippi*, 170 U.S. 213 (1898).

27. *Lassiter v. Northampton County Board of Elections*, 360 U.S. 45 (1959).

28. *Breedlove v. Suttles*, 302 U.S. 277 (1937).

29. Wayne Dawkins, *Emanuel Celler: Immigration and Civil Rights Champion* (Jackson: University of Mississippi Press, 2016).

30. *Hearings on Abolition of Poll Tax in Federal Elections, before Subcommittee No. 5 of the House Committee on the Judiciary,* 87th Cong. (March 12, 1962, and May 14, 1962) (statement of William Higgs), 48–53.

31. "Congress Recommends Poll Tax Ban," *CQ Almanac* (1962), https://library.cqpress.com/cqalmanac/document.php?id=cqal62-1326629#H2_1.

32. *Breedlove v. Suttles.*

33. "Congress Recommends Poll Tax Ban."

34. *Hearings on Abolition of Poll Tax in Federal Elections,* 27–28.

CHAPTER 6

1. Gilbert Jonas, *Freedom's Sword: The NAACP and the Struggle Against Racism in America, 1909–1969* (New York: Routledge, 2005), 226 (quoting Frank R. Parker, author of *Black Votes Count: Political Empowerment in Mississippi after 1965* [Charlotte: University of North Carolina Press, 1990]).

2. Jack Greenberg, *Crusaders in the Courts: How a Dedicated Band of Lawyers Fought for the Civil Rights Revolution* (New York: HarperCollins, 1994), 304.

3. *Anderson v. Courson,* 204 F. Supp. 806 (M.D. Ga. 1962).

4. *Anderson v. Martin,* 375 U.S. 399 (1964).

5. Jack Greenberg, arguing for the petitioners in the US Supreme Court oral argument, in *Anderson v. Martin,* November 21, 1963; decided January 13, 1964.

6. *NAACP v. Alabama,* 377 U.S. 288 (1964).

7. See William P. Jones, *The March on Washington: Jobs, Freedom, and the Forgotten History of Civil Rights* (New York: W. W. Norton, 2013).

8. See Faith S. Holsaert, Martha P. N. Noonan, Judy Richardson, Betty G. Robinson, Jean S. Young, and Dorothy M. Zellner, eds., *Hands on the Freedom Plow: Personal Accounts by Women in SNCC* (Urbana, Chicago, and Springfield: University of Illinois, 2012).

9. Greenberg, *Crusaders in the Courts.*

10. See Bruce Watson, *Freedom Summer: The Savage Season That Made Mississippi Burn and Made America a Democracy* (New York: Viking Press, 2010).

11. *Detroit News,* December 4, 1964.

12. The Civil Rights Act of 1964 (Pub. L. 88-352, 78 Stat. 241, enacted July 2, 1964).

13. "President Lyndon B. Johnson's Radio and Television Remarks Upon Signing the Civil Rights Bill, July 2, 1964" [Broadcast from the East Room at the White House at 6:45 p.m.], in *Public Papers of the Presidents of the United States: Lyndon B. Johnson, 1963–64* (Washington, DC: Government Printing Office, 1965), II: 842–44, entry 446.

14. "Martin Luther King Jr. Acceptance Speech," [December 10, 1964], NobelPrize.org, http://www.nobelprize.org/nobel_prizes/peace/laureates/1964/king-acceptance_en.html.

15. Greenberg, *Crusaders in the Courts.*

16. See Hasan K. Jeffries, *Bloody Lowndes: Civil Rights and Black Power in Alabama's Black Belt* (New York: New York University Press, 2009).

17. Ibid., 44.

18. C.T. Vivian, *Black Power and the American Myth* (Philadelphia: Fortress Press, 1970).

19. "Tear Gas, Clubs, Halt 600 in Selma March, State Trooper Beat and Injure Many Negroes," *Washington Post*, Monday, March 8, 1965.

20. Jeffries, *Bloody Lowndes*, 44.

21. Robert A. Caro, *The Years of Lyndon Johnson: The Passage of Power* (New York: Alfred A. Knopf, 2012), 564–65.

22. Robert A. Caro, *The Years of Lyndon Johnson: The Path to Power* (1982); *The Years of Lyndon Johnson: Means of Ascent* (1990); *The Years of Lyndon Johnson: Master of the Senate* (2002); and *The Years of Lyndon Johnson: The Passage of Power* (2012).

23. Pub. L. 88–352, 78 Stat. 241, enacted July 2, 1964.

24. Caro, *Years of Lyndon Johnson: The Passage of Power*, 546–47.

25. "Lyndon B. Johnson Addresses Congress on Voting Rights (March 15, 1965)," http://millercenter.org/president/speeches/speech-3386.

26. *South Carolina v. Katzenbach*, 383 U.S. 301, 327–28 (1966).

27. http://www.justice.gov/crt/history-federal-voting-rights-laws.

28. Ibid.

29. Ibid.

30. Ibid.

31. Ibid.

32. *South Carolina v. Katzenbach*, 383 U.S. 301, 327–28 (1966).

33. Ibid., 310n9 (1966).

34. *Katzenbach v. Morgan*, 384 U.S. 641 (1966).

35. *Harper v. Virginia Board of Elections*, 383 U.S. 663 (1966).

36. Ibid.

37. *Louisiana v. United States*, 380 U.S. 145 (1965).

38. *United States v. Mississippi*, 380 U.S. 128 (1965).

39. Martin Luther King Jr., *Quotations of Martin Luther King, Jr.* (Bedford, MA: Applewood Books, 2004).

40. Maegen Parker Brooks and Davis W. Houck, *The Speeches of Fannie Lou Hamer* (Jackson: University of Mississippi Press, 2010).

41. *Powell v. McCormack*, 395 U.S. 486 (1969).

42. Ibid.

43. *Allen v. State Board of Elections*, 393 U.S. 544, 553 (1969).

44. Ibid., 571.

45. *Cooper v. Power*, 282 F. Supp. 548 (1968).

46. Jonas, *Freedom's Sword*, 226 (quoting Parker).

CHAPTER 7

1. "High Court Nominee Hit for Racist Remarks," *Jet Magazine*, February 5, 1970, 3.

2. Denton L. Watson, *Lion in the Lobby: Clarence Mitchell, Jr's Struggle for the Passage of Civil Rights Laws* (New York: William Morrow, 1990).

3. *Oregon v. Mitchell*, 400 U.S. 112 (1970).

4. *Regents of the University of California v. Bakke*, 438 U.S. 265 (1978).

5. *National Association for the Advancement of Colored People v. Claiborne Hardware Co.*, 458 U.S. 886 (1982).

6. *United Jewish Organizations v. Carey*, 430 U.S. 144 (1977).

7. *United Jewish Organizations v. Carey*, 430 U.S. 144 (1977).

8. *Board of Regents v. Bakke*, 438 U.S. 265, 390 (1978).

9. *Regents of the University of California v. Bakke*, 438 U.S. 265 (1978).

10. Ibid.

11. *Regents of the Univ. of Cal. v. Bakke*, 438 U.S. 265, 399 (1978).

12. *Swann v. Charlott-Mecklenberg Board of Education*, 402 U.S. 1204 (1971); *Roe v. Wade*, 410 U.S. 52 (1973); *New York Times v. U.S.*, 403 U.S. 713 (1971); *Oregon v. Mitchell*, 400 U.S. 112 (1970); *Furman v. Georgia*, 408 U.S. 238 (1972).

13. *Mobile v. Bolden*, 446 U.S. 55 (1980).

14. Ibid.

15. *NAACP v. NAACP LDF*, 753 F.2d 131 (1985).

16. *Thornburg v. Gingles*, 478 U.S. 30 (1986).

17. *Loving v. Virginia*, 388 U.S. 1 (1967).

18. *Shaw v. Reno*, 509 U.S. 630 (1993).

19. *Holder v. Hall*, 512 U.S. 874 (1994); *Miller v. Johnson,* 515 U.S. 900 (1995).

20. *Holder v. Hall*, 512 U.S. 874 (1994).

21. *Abrams v. Johnson*, 521 U.S. 74 (1997); *Miller v. Johnson*, 515 U.S. 900 (1995).

22. Ibid.

23. *Bush v. Gore*, 531 U.S. 98 (2000).

24. *Crawford v. Marion County Board of Elections*, 553 U.S. 181 (2008).

25. *Richardson v. Ramirez*, 418 U.S. 24, 28 (1974).

26. Ibid.

27. "Taking into account the structural similarities and profitability of business-government linkages in the realms of military production and public punishment, the expanding penal system can now be characterized as a 'prison industrial complex.'" Angela Davis, in *Masked Racism: Reflections on the Prison Industrial Complex*, September 10, 1998, http://www.colorlines.com/articles/masked-racism-reflections-prison-industrial-complex.

28. http://sentencingproject.org/wp-content/uploads/2016/01/State-Level-Estimates-of-Felon-Disenfranchisement-in-the-United-States-2010.pdf.

29. *Little v. LATFOR*, Supreme Court for Albany County (NY), Case No. 3210-2011.

30. *Prison Legal News* reports on criminal justice issues and prison and jail-related civil litigation, mainly in the United States, and is a project of the Human Rights Defense Center, a 501c nonprofit organization. https://www.prisonlegal-news.org/news/2012/oct/15/new-york-court-upholds-law-requiring-census-count-to-use-prisoners-pre-incarceration-address/.

31. *Little v. LATFOR*, Supreme Court for Albany County (NY), Case No. 3210-2011.

32. *Citizens United v. Federal Election Commission*, 558 U.S. 50 (2010).

33. *Shelby County, Alabama. v. Holder*, 133 S. Ct. 2612 (2013).

34. Ibid.

35. *Arizona v. Inter-tribal Council of Arizona*, 570 U.S. __ (2013).

36. Executive Order 13639, supportthevoter.gov.

37. Congressional Black Caucus, cbc-butterfield.house.gov/members.

38. Joint Center for Political and Economic Studies.org

39. *Texas Conf. of NAACP v. Steen, United States v. Texas,* and *Veasey v. Perry,* 574 U.S. __ (2014).

40. *North Carolina State Conference of the NAACP v. McCrory,* 997 F. Supp. 2d. 322 (2014).

41. Wendy Underhill, "Elections: Legislative Update 2015," National Conference of State Legislatures, October 6, 2015.

42. *NAACP v. Husted,* No. 14-3877 (6th Cir. Sept. 14, 2014) (settlement announced April 17, 2015).

43. *Evenwel v. Abbott,* 578 U.S. __ (2016).

Bibliography

LETTERS AND PUBLISHED CORRESPONDENCE

Filson History Quarterly, published by The Filson Historical Society. Special Collections, University of Kentucky.

Johnson, James Weldon, and Grace Nail Johnson Papers. Yale University, Beinecke Rare Book and Manuscript Library, Yale University.

National Association for the Advancement of Colored People (NAACP), Papers. Library of Congress.

National Association for the Advancement of Colored People (NAACP), Legal Defense and Educational Fund, Inc., Papers. Library of Congress.

National Association for the Advancement of Colored People (NAACP), Visual Materials. Prints & Photographs Division. Library of Congress.

Tourgée, Albion W., Papers. Chautauqua County Historical Society, Westfield, NY.

Yale Collection of American Literature, Beinecke Rare Book and Manuscript Library.

BOOKS

Adams, Samuel Hopkins. *Incredible Era: The Life and Times of Warren Gamaliel Harding*. New York: Houghton Mifflin, 1939.

Aptheker, Herbert. *American Negro Slave Revolts*. New York: International Publishers, 1963.

Aptheker, Herbert. *A Documentary History of the Negro People in the United States: From Colonial Times through the Civil War*. New York: Citadel, 1960.

Archer, C. Leonard. *Black Images in the American Theatre: NAACP Protest Campaigns: Stage, Screen, Radio & Television.* Nashville, TN: Pageant-Poseidon, 1973.

Baker, Jean H. *Sisters: The Lives of America's Suffragists.* New York: Hill and Wang, 2005.

Baldino, Thomas J., and Kyle L. Kreider. *U.S. Election Campaigns: A Documentary and Reference Guide.* Documentary and Reference Guides. New York: Greenwood, 2011.

Bell, A. Derrick, Jr. *Constitutional Conflicts, Part 1.* Cincinnati, OH: Anderson Publishing Co., 1997.

Berg, Manfred. *The Ticket to Freedom: The NAACP and the Struggle for Black Political Integration.* Gainesville: University Press of Florida, 2005.

Bergman, Peter M. *The Chronological History of the Negro in America.* New York: Harper & Row, 1969.

Black Americans in Congress, 1870–2007. 3rd ed. Prepared under the direction of the Committee on House Administration of the US House of Representatives, by the Office of History and Preservation, Office of the Clerk. Washington, DC: US Government Printing Office, 2008.

Boyle, Kevin. *Arc of Justice: A Saga of Race, Civil Rights, and Murder in the Jazz Age.* New York: Henry Holt, 2004.

Brands, H. W. *Woodrow Wilson.* New York: Henry Holt, 2003.

Brooks, Maegen Parker, and Davis W. Houck. *The Speeches of Fannie Lou Hamer.* Jackson: University of Mississippi Press, 2010.

Brophy, Alfred. *Reconstructing the Dreamland: The Tulsa Race Riot of 1921, Race Reparations, and Reconciliation.* Foreword by Randall Kennedy. New York: Oxford University Press, 2002.

Browne-Marshall, Gloria J. *Race, Law, and American Society.* 2nd ed. New York: Routledge, 2013.

Bynum, Thomas. *NAACP Youth and the Fight for Black Freedom, 1936–1965.* 3rd ed. Knoxville: University of Tennessee Press, 2013.

Caro, Robert A. *The Passage of Power: The Years of Lyndon Johnson.* MP3 UNA ed. New York: Brilliance Audio, 2014.

Caro, Robert A. *The Years of Lyndon Johnson: The Passage of Power.* New York: Alfred A. Knopf, 2012.

Carr, Robert K. *Federal Protection of Civil Rights: Quest for a Sword.* Ithaca, NY: Cornell University Press, 1947.

Clayborne, Carson, and Myrlie Evers-Williams. *Civil Rights Chronicle: The African-American Struggle for Freedom.* New York: Publications International, 2003.

Cooper, John M. *Woodrow Wilson: A Biography.* New York: Alfred A. Knopf, 2009.

Cortner, Richard C. *A Mob Intent on Death: The NAACP and the Arkansas Riot Cases.* Middletown, CT: Wesleyan University Press, 1988.

Dawkins, Wayne. *City Sun: Andrew W. Cooper's Impact on Modern-Day Brooklyn.* Jackson: University Press of Mississippi, 2012.

Dawkins, Wayne. *Emanuel Celler: Immigration and Civil Rights Champion.* Jackson: University of Mississippi Press, 2016.

DuBois, W. E. B. *The Souls of Black Folk.* Chicago: A. C. McClurg & Co., 1903.

Ducat, R. Craig. *Constitutional Interpretation.* 10th ed. Boston: Wadsworth Publishing, 2012.

Elinson, E., and S. Yogi. *Wherever There's a Fight: How Runaway Slaves, Suffragists, Immigrants, Strikers, and Poets Shaped Civil Liberties in California*. Berkeley, CA: Heyday Books, 2009.

Evers-Williams, Myrlie, and Marable Manning. *The Autobiography of Medgar Evers: A Hero's Life and Legacy Revealed Through His Writings, Letters, and Speeches*. New York: Basic/Civitas Books, 2005.

Farber, Daniel A., and Suzanna Sherry. *A History of the American Constitution*. St. Paul, MN: Thomson/Vest, 2005. (For discussion of the debates leading to passage of the Fifteenth Amendment, see pages 455–87.)

Flexner, Eleanor. *Century of Struggle*. New York: Atheneum, 1970.

Franklin, John H. *Reconstruction after the Civil War*. Chicago: University of Chicago Press, 1994.

Giddings, Paula. *Ida: A Sword Among Lions: Ida B. Wells and the Campaign Against Lynching*. New York: HarperCollins, 2009.

Gilbert, Jonas. *Freedom's Sword: The NAACP and the Struggle Against Racism in America*. London and New York: Routledge, 2005.

Girardeau, A. Spann. *Race Against the Court*. New York: New York University Press, 1993.

Goings, Kenneth W. *The NAACP Comes of Age: The Defeat of Judge John J. Parker*. Westport, CT: Greenwood Press, 1990.

Goodwin, Doris K. *No Ordinary Time: Franklin and Eleanor Roosevelt: The Home Front in World War II*. New York: Simon & Schuster, 1994.

Greenberg, Jack. *Crusaders in the Courts: How a Dedicated Band of Lawyers Fought for the Civil Rights Revolution*. New York: HarperCollins, 1994.

Harbaugh, William H. *Lawyer's Lawyer: The Life of John W. Davis*. New York: Oxford University Press, 1973.

Harris, Jaqueline L. *History and Achievement of the NAACP*. New York: Franklin Watts, 1992.

Haskins, James. *Pinckney Benton Stewart Pinchback*. New York: Macmillan, 1973.

Higginbotham, Michael F. *Race Law: Cases, Commentary, and Questions*. Durham, NC: Carolina Academic Press, 2010.

Highsaw, Robert B. *Edward Douglass White: Defender of the Conservative Faith*. Baton Rouge: Louisiana State University Press, 1981.

Highsaw, Robert B., and Edward Douglass White. *The Supreme Court Under Edward Douglass White, 1910–1921*. Baton Rouge: Louisiana State University Press, 1981.

Hines, Darlene. *Black Victory: The Rise and Fall of the White Primary in Texas*. Columbia: University of Missouri Press, 2003.

Hixson, William B. *Moorfield Storey and the Abolitionist Tradition*. New York: Oxford University Press, 1972.

Holsaert, Faith S., Martha P. N. Noonan, Judy Richardson, Betty G. Robinson, Jean S. Young, and Dorothy M. Zellner, eds. *Hands on the Freedom Plow: Personal Accounts of Women in SNCC*. Urbana, Chicago, and Springfield: University of Illinois Press, 2012.

Janken, Kenneth Robert. *Walter White: Mr. NAACP*. Chapel Hill: University of North Carolina Press, 2006.

Jeffries, Hasan K. *Bloody Lowndes: Civil Rights and Black Power in Alabama's Black Belt.* New York: New York University Press, 2009.

Jones, William P. *The March on Washington: Jobs, Freedom, and the Forgotten History of Civil Rights.* New York: W. W. Norton, 2013.

Keyssar, Alexander. *The Right to Vote.* New York: Basic Books, 2009.

King, Gilbert. *Devil in the Grove: Thurgood Marshall, the Groveland Boys, and the Dawn of a New America.* New York: Harper Perennial, 2012.

King, Martin Luther, Jr. *The Measure of a Man.* New York: Fortress Press, 1988.

King, Martin Luther, Jr. *Quotations of Martin Luther King, Jr.* Bedford, MA: Applewood Books, 2004.

Lawson, Steven F. *In Pursuit of Power: Southern Blacks and Electoral Politics, 1965–1982.* New York: Columbia University Press, 1985.

Lawson, Steven F. *Running for Freedom: Civil Rights and Black Politics in America since 1941.* Chichester, UK: Wiley-Blackwell, 2009.

Lewis, David L. *W.E.B. DuBois: Biography of a Race, 1868–1919.* New York: Henry Holt, 1993.

Ling, Peter J., and Sharon Monteith. *Gender and the Civil Rights Movement.* New York: Rutgers University Press, 1999.

Madison, James H. *A Lynching in the Heartland: Race and Memory in America.* New York: Palgrave Macmillian, 2001.

Manfred, Berg. *The Ticket to Freedom: The NAACP and the Struggle for Black Political Integration.* New Perspectives on the History of the South. Gainesville: University Press of Florida, 2007.

May, Gary. *The Informant: The FBI, the Ku Klux Klan and the Murder of Viola Liuzzo.* New Haven, CT: Yale University Press, 2005.

McPherson, M. James. *The Abolitionist Legacy: From Reconstruction to the NAACP.* New York: Princeton University Press, 1976.

Micheaux, Oscar. *The Life of America's First Black Filmmaker.* London, New York: HarperCollins, 2007.

Miller, C. Craig. *Roy Wilkins: Leader of the NAACP.* New York: Morgan Reynolds, 2005.

Milton, John Cooper, Jr. *Woodrow Wilson: A Bibliography.* New York: Vintage, 2011.

Mouser, L. Bruce. *For Labor, Race, and Liberty: George Edwin Taylor, His Historic Run for the White House, and the Making of Independent Black Politics.* Wisconsin: University of Wisconsin Press, 2011.

NAACP: Celebrating a Century 100 Years in Pictures. Layton, UT: Gibbs Smith, 2009.

Newton, Michael. *The Ku Klux Klan in Mississippi: A History.* Jefferson, NC: McFarland, 2010.

North Carolina Democratic Handbook. [Chapel Hill]: Academic Affairs Library, University of North Carolina at Chapel Hill, 2002.

Ottley, Roi, and William J. Weatherby. *The Negro in New York: An Informal Social History.* Dobbs Ferry, NY: Oceana Publications, 1967.

Ovington, Mary W. *Black and White Sat Down Together: The Reminiscences of an NAACP Founder.* New York: The Feminist Press, 1995.

Ovington, Mary W. *Half a Man: The Status of the Negro in New York.* Foreword by Franz Boas. New York: Longmans Green, 1911.

Papers of the Presidents of the United States: Lyndon B. Johnson, 1963–64. Washington, DC: Government Printing Office, 1965.

Perry, Mark. *Lift Up Thy Voice: The Sarah and Angelina Grimké Family's Journey from Slaveholders to Civil Rights Leaders.* New York: Penguin, 2002.

Pfaelzer, Jean. *Driven Out: The Forgotten War Against Chinese Americans.* New York: Random House, 2007.

Record, Wilson. *Race and Radicalism: The NAACP and the Communist Party in Conflict.* Ithaca, NY: Cornell University Press, 1964.

Report of the Proceedings and Debate of the Constitutional Convention, State of Virginia. 1906.

Rhym, Darren. *The NAACP: African American Achievers.* New York: Chelsea House Publications, 2001.

Ross, J. Barbara. *J. E. Spingarn and the Rise of the NAACP: 1911–1939.* New York: Scribner, 1972.

Santella, Andrew. *The NAACP: An Organization Working to End Discrimination.* Journey to Freedom: The African American Library. New York: Child's World, 2003.

Saunders, Robert W. *Bridging the Gap: Continuing the Florida NAACP Legacy of Harry Moore.* Tampa: University of Tampa Press, 2000.

Schechter, Patricia A. *Ida B. Wells-Barnett and American Reform, 1880–1930.* Chapel Hill: University of North Carolina Press, 2001.

Shockley, Megan Taylor. *"We, Too, Are Americans": African American Women in Detroit and Richmond, 1940–54.* Urbana and Chicago: University of Illinois Press, 2004.

Sinnette, H. Calvin. *Forbidden Fairways: African Americans and the Game of Golf.* Chelsea, MI: Black Classic Press, 2015.

Smith, Clay J., Jr. *Emancipation: The Making of the Black Lawyer, 1844–1944.* Philadelphia: University of Pennsylvania Press, 1999.

Staff of the *Washington Post.* Landmark: *The Inside Story of America's New Health Care Law and What It Means for Us All.* Washington, DC: Public Affairs, 2010.

Sullivan, Patricia. *Lift Every Voice: The NAACP and the Making of the Civil Rights Movement.* New York: The New Press, 2009.

Tushnet, V. Mark. *The NAACP's Legal Strategy against Segregated Education, 1925–1950.* Chapel Hill: University of North Carolina Press, 2005.

Valelly, Richard M. *The Two Reconstructions: The Struggle for Black Enfranchisement.* Chicago and London: University of Chicago Press, 2004.

Vine, Phyllis. *One Man's Castle: Clarence Darrow in Defense of the American Dream.* New York: HarperCollins, 2004.

Vollers, Mayanne. *Ghosts of Mississippi: The Murder of Medgar Evers, the Trials of Byron De La Beckwith, and the Haunting of the New South.* New York: Little, Brown, 1995.

Vose, Clement E. *Caucasians Only: The Supreme Court, the NAACP, and the Restrictive Covenant Cases.* Berkeley: University of California Press, 1967.

Walker, David. *Walker's Appeal, in Four Articles: Together with a Preamble, to the Coloured Citizens of the World, but in Particular, and very Expressly, to Those of the United States of America.* Written in Boston, State of Massachusetts, September 28, 1829.

Washington, Booker T. *Up From Slavery: An Autobiography of Booker T. Washington.* New York: Doubleday, Page, 1901.

Waskow, D. Arthur. *From Race Riot to Sit-In, 1919 to the 1960s: A Study in Connections between Conflict and Violence.* New York: Doubleday, 1966.

Watson, Bruce. *Freedom Summer: The Savage Season That Made Mississippi Burn and Made America a Democracy.* New York: Viking Press, 2010.

Watson, Denton L. *Lion in the Lobby: Clarence Mitchell, Jr.'s Struggle for the Passage of Civil Rights Laws.* New York: William Morrow, 1990.

Wedin, Carolyn. *Inheritors of the Spirit: Mary White Ovington and the Founding of the NAACP.* New York: John Wiley & Sons, 1998.

Wertheimer, John. *Law and Society of the South: A History of North Carolina Court Cases.* Lexington: University Press of Kentucky, 2010.

White, Edward G. *Earl Warren: A Public Life.* New York: Oxford University Press, 1987.

White, Walter. *A Man Called White.* New York: Viking, 1948.

Wilkins, Roy, with Tom Matthews. *Standing Fast: The Autobiography of Roy Wilkins.* New York: Viking Press, 1982.

Williams, Michael Vinson. *Medgar Evers: Mississippi Martyr.* Little Rock: University of Arkansas Press, 2011.

Wilson, Sondra Kathryn. *In Search of Democracy: The NAACP Writings of James Weldon Johnson, Walter White, and Roy Wilkins (1920–1977).* New York: Oxford University Press, 1999.

Woodson, G. Carter. *Negro Orators and Their Orations.* Washington, DC: The Associated Publishers Inc., 1925.

Zangrando, L. Robert. *The NAACP Crusade Against Lynching, 1909–1950.* Philadelphia: Temple University Press, 1980.

MISCELLANEOUS

Patient Protection and Affordable Care Act of 2010 (Pub. Law 111-148). The Health Care and Education Reconciliation Act of 2010 (Pub. Law 111-152) was enacted to amend the PPACA; see http://www.healthcare.gov/law/ index. html (accessed December 2012).

ARTICLES

Current, G. B. "The Significance of the N.A.A.C.P. and Its Impact in the 1960s." *Black Scholar* 19, no. 1 (1988): 9–18. http://www.jstor.org.ez.lib.jjay.cuny.edu/stable/41068039.

DeMuth, Jerry. "Tired of Being Sick and Tired." *Nation,* June 1, 1964. Reprinted in *Reporting Civil Rights.* Part II, *American Journalism 1963–1973,* edited by Claiborne Carson. New York: Penguin, 2003.

"The Disenfranchisement of Ex-Felons: Citizenship, Criminality, and 'The Purity of the Ballot Box.'" *Harvard Law Review* 102 (1989): 1300.

DuBois, W. E. B. "The Freedmen's Bureau." *Atlanta Monthly* 87, no. 519 (March 1901): 354–65.

Emmons, C. "'Somebody Has Got to Do That Work': Harry T. Moore and the Struggle for African-American Voting Rights in Florida." *Journal of Negro History* 82, no. 2 (1997): 232–43. http://doi.org.ez.lib.jjay.cuny.edu/10.2307/2717518.

Franklin, V. P. "Introduction: Documenting the NAACP'S First Century—From Combating Racial Injustices to Challenging Racial Inequities." *Journal of African American History* 94, no. 4 (2009): 453–63. http://www.jstor.org.ez.lib.jjay.cuny.edu/stable/25653973.

Garrow, D. J. "The Voting Rights Act in Historical Perspective." *Georgia Historical Quarterly* 74, no. 3 (1990): 377–98. http://www.jstor.org.ez.lib.jjay.cuny.edu/stable/40582187.

Griffith, B. E. "Defense Strategies in Voting Rights Litigation after Shaw and Miller." *Urban Lawyer* 28, no. 4 (1996): 715–36. http://www.jstor.org.ez.lib.jjay.cuny.edu/stable/27895026.

Houston, R. "The NAACP State Conference in Texas: Intermediary and Catalyst for Change, 1937–1957." *Journal of African American History* 94, no. 4 (2009): 509–28. http://www.jstor.org.ez.lib.jjay.cuny.edu/stable/25653976.

Jones-Branch, C. "'To Speak When and Where I Can': African American Women's Political Activism in South Carolina in the 1940s and 1950s." *South Carolina Historical Magazine* 107, no. 3 (2006): 204–24. http://www.jstor.org.ez.lib.jjay.cuny.edu/stable/27570823.

Minchin, T. J. "Making Best Use of the New Laws: The NAACP and the Fight for Civil Rights in the South, 1965–1975." *Journal of Southern History* 74, no. 3 (2008): 669–702. http://doi.org.ez.lib.jjay.cuny.edu/10.2307/27650232.

"Negro Suffrage: Should the Fourteenth and Fifteenth Amendments Be Repealed?" Speech presented by Hon. Edward De V. Morrell of Pennsylvania to the US House of Representatives, April 4, 1904. https://memory.loc.gov/cgi-bin/query/r?ammem/murray:@field(DOCID+@lit(lcrbmrpt2609div1)).

Rustin, Bayard. "From Protest to Politics: The Future of the Civil Rights Movement." 1965. American Left Ephemera Collection, 1894–2008. AIS. 2007.11. Archives Service Center, University of Pittsburgh. http://digital.library.pitt.edu/u/ulsmanuscripts/pdf/31735066227830.pdf.

Shapiro, A. L. "Challenging Criminal Disenfranchisement under the Voting Rights Act: A New Strategy." *Yale Law Journal* 103, no. 2 (1993): 537–66. http://doi.org.ez.lib.jjay.cuny.edu/10.2307/797104.

Walling, William English. "The Race War in the North." *The Independent* 65 (September 3, 1908): 529–34.

Williams, D. "Reconstructing Section 5: A Post-Katrina Proposal for Voting Rights Act Reform." *Yale Law Journal* 116, no. 5 (2007): 1116–58. http://doi.org.ez.lib.jjay.cuny.edu/10.2307/20455751.

CASES

United States Supreme Court

Abrams v. Johnson, 521 U.S. 74 (1997).
Adarand Constructors, Inc. v. Peña, 515 U.S. 209 (1995).

Adderley v. Florida, 385 U.S. 39 (1966).

Afinor v. Ilantersett, 88 U.S. 162 (1875).

Allen v. State Board of Elections, 393 U.S. 544, 569 (1969).

Anderson v. Martin, 375 U.S. 399, 403–4 (1964).

Arlington Heights v. Metropolitan Development Housing Corporation (MHDC), 429 U.S. 252 (1977).

Arizona v. Inter-tribal Council of Arizona, 570 U.S. __ (2013).

Bailey v. Alabama, 211 U.S. 452 (1908).

Bailey v. Alabama, 219 U.S. 219 (1911).

Baker v. Carr, 369 U.S. 186 (1962).

Baman v. Parker, 348 U.S. 26 (1954).

Bartlett v. Strickland, 129 S. Ct. 1231 (2009).

Bates v. Little Rock, 361 U.S. 516 (1960).

Beer v. United States, 425 U.S. 130 (1976).

Berea College v. Kentucky, 211 U.S. 45 (1908).

Bob Jones University v. United States, 461 U.S. 574 (1983).

Bolling v. Sharpe, 347 U.S. 497 (1954).

Brandenburg v. Ohio, 395 U.S. 444, 446 (1969).

Breedlove v. Suttles, 302 U.S. 277 (1937).

Browder v. Gayle, 352 U.S. 903 (1956).

Brown v. Board of Education II, 349 U.S. 294 (1955).

Brown v. Texas, 443 U.S. 47 (1979).

Brown v. The Board of Education of Topeka, Kansas, 347 U.S. 483 (1954).

Bryant v. Zimmerman, 278 U.S. 63 (1928).

Buchanan v. Warley, 245 U.S. 60 (1917).

Burton v. Wilmington Parking Authority, 365 U.S. 715 (1961).

Bush v. Gore, 531 U.S. 98 (2000).

Bush v. Vera, 517 U.S. 952 (1996).

Campaign for Fiscal Equity, Inc. v. State of New York, 86 N.Y.2d 307 (1995).

Chambers v. Florida, 309 U.S. 227 (1940).

Chicago v. Morales, 527 U.S. 41 (1999).

Chisom v. Roemer, 501 U.S. 380 (1991).

Citizens United v. Federal Election Commission, 558 U.S. 50 (2010).

City of Richmond v. Croson Company, 488 U.S. 469 (1989).

City of Rome v. United States, 446 U.S. 156 (1980).

The Civil Rights Cases, 109 U.S. 3 (1883).

Clyatt v. United States, 197 U.S. 207 (1905).

Colegrove v. Green, 328 U.S. 549, 556 (1946).

Commonwealth v. Jennison, Rec. (Mass 1783); *Commonwealth v. Jennison, Proceedings of the Massachusetts Historical Society 1873–1875*, at 293, 294 (1783).

Cooper v. Aaron, 358 U.S. 1 (1958).

Crawford v. Marion County Elections Board, 553 U.S. 181 (2008).

Dred Scott v. Sandford, 60 U.S. 393, 406 (1857).

Easley v. Cromartie, 532 U.S. 234 (2001).

Edwards v. South Carolina, 372 U.S. 229 (1963).

Evenwel v. Abbott, 578 U.S. __ (2016).

Ex parte Yarbrough, 110 U.S. 651 (1884).

Franklin v. South Carolina, 218 U.S. 161 (1910).

Gainer v. Louisiana, 368 U.S. 157 (1961).

Gayle v. Browder and Owen Browder, 532 U.S. 203 (1956).

Georgia v. Ashcroft, 539 U.S. 461 (2003).

Georgia v. Stanton, 73 U.S. 50 (1867).

Georgia v. United States, 411 U.S. 526 (1973).

Giles v. Harris, 189 U.S. 475 (1903).

Gomillion v. Lightfoot, 364 U.S. 339, 341 (1960).

Gomperts v. Chase, 404 U.S. 1237 (1971).

Gratz v. Bollinger, 539 U.S. 244 (2003).

Grovey v. Townsend, 295 U.S. 45, 55 (1935).

Growe v. Emison, 507 U.S. 25 (1993).

Grutter v. Bollinger, 539 U.S. 306 (2003).

Guey Heung Lee v. Johnson, 404 U.S. 1215, 1216 (1971).

Guinn and Beal v. United States, 238 U.S. 347 (1915).

Hamm v. Virginia State Board of Elections, 379 U.S. 19 (1964), *aff'g Hamm v. Virginia State Board of Elections*, 230 F. Supp. 156 (1964).

Harper v. Virginia Board of Elections, 383 U.S. 663, 668–69 (1966).

Hansberry v. Lee, 311 U.S. 32 (1940).

Harper v. Virginia, 383 U.S. 663 (1966).

Hiibel v. Nevada, 542 U.S. 177 (2004).

Hills v. Gautreaux et al., 425 U.S. 284 (1976).

Hodge v. Tulsa County Election Board, 335 U.S. 889 (1948).

Holder v. Hall, 512 U.S. 874, 877–78 (1994).

Houston Lawyers' Association v. Attorney General of Texas, 501 U.S. 419 (1991).

Hudson v. McMillian, 503 U.S. 1 (1992).

Hunter v. Erickson, 393 U.S. 385 (1969).

Hunter v. Underwood, 471 U.S. 222 (1986).

Hurd v. Hodge, 334 U.S. 24 (1948).

Illinois v. William, 528 U.S. 119 (2000).

Jackie Holder et al. v. E. K. Hall Sr., Rev. E. K. Hall Sr., NAACP Chapter of Cochran, Bleckley County, et al., 512 U.S. 874 (1993).

James v. Bowman, 190 U.S. 127 (1903).

Johnson v. Bush, 126 S. Ct. 650 (2005).

Johnson v. California, 543 U.S. 499 (2005).

Johnson v. De Grandy, 512 U.S. 997 (1994).

Johnson v. Virginia, 373 U.S. 61 (1963).

Jones v. Alfred H. Mayer Company, 392 U.S. 409 (1968).

Katzenbach v. Morgan, 384 U.S. 641 (1966).

Lane v. Wilson, 307 U.S. 268 (1939).

Lassiter v. Northampton County Board of Elections, 360 U.S. 45 (1959).

League of United Latin American Citizens v. Perry, 548 U.S. 399 (2006).

Lee, Commissioner of Corrections of Alabama v. Washington, 390 U.S. 333 (1968).

Lombard v. Louisiana, 373 U.S. 267 (1963).

Lopez v. Monterey County, 525 U.S. 266 (1999).

Louisiana v. NAACP, 366 U.S. 293 (1961).

Louisiana v. United States, 380 U.S. 145 (1965).

Loving v. Virginia, 388 U.S. 1 (1967).
Lucy v. Adams, 350 U.S. 1 (1955).
McDaniel v. Barresi, 402 U.S. 39 (1971).
McLaughlin v. Florida, 379 U.S. 184 (1964).
McLaurin v. Oklahoma, 339 U.S. 637 (1950).
Meyer v. Holley, 537 U.S. 280 (2002).
Miller v. Johnson, 515 U.S. 900 (1995).
Mills v. Green, 159 U.S. 651 (1895).
Minor v. Happersett, 88 U.S. 162 (1875).
Mitchell v. United States, 313 U.S. 80 (1941).
Mobile v. Bolden, 446 U.S. 55, 72–75 (1980).
Monroe v. Board of Commissioners, 391 U.S. 450 (1968).
Moore v. Dempsey, 261 U.S. 86 (1923).
Myers v. Anderson, 238 U.S. 368 (1915).
NAACP v. Alabama, 377 U.S. 288 (1964).
NAACP v. Alabama ex rel. Patterson, 357 U.S. 449 (1958).
NAACP v. Button, 371 U.S. 415 (1963).
NAACP v. Harris, Case No. 01-CIV-120 (January 10, 2001).
National Association for the Advancement of Colored People, New York City Region of New York Conference of Branches, et al. v. New York et al., 413 U.S. 345 (1973).
Nixon v. Condon, 286 U.S. 73 (1932).
Nixon v. Herndon, 273 U.S. 536, 541 (1927).
North Carolina et al., Applicants v. League of Women Voters of North Carolina et al., 135 S. Ct. 6 (2014).
Northwest Austin Municipal Utility District v. Holder, 129 S. Ct. 2504 (2009).
Oregon v. Mitchell, 400 U.S. 112 (1970).
Pace v. Alabama, 106 U.S. 583 (1883).
Plessy v. Ferguson, 163 U.S. 537 (1896).
Powell v. Alabama, 287 U.S. 45 (1963).
Powell v. McCormack, 395 U.S. 486 (1969).
Prigg v. Pennsylvania, 41 U.S. 539 (1842).
Regents of the University of California v. Bakke, 438 U.S. 265 (1978).
Reitman v. Mulky, 387 U.S. 369 (1967).
Reno v. Bossier Parish School Board, 528 U.S. 320 (2000).
Reynolds v. Sims, 377 U.S. 533 (1964).
Richardson v. Ramirez, 418 U.S. 24, 27 (1974).
Schell v. Davis, 336 U.S. 933 (1949).
Shapiro v. Mack, 135 U.S. 2805 (2015).
Shaw v. Reno, 509 U.S. 630 (1993).
Shaw v. Hunt, 517 U.S. 899 (1996).
Shelby County, Alabama v. Holder, 133 S. Ct. 2612 (2013).
Shelley v. Kraemer, 334 U.S. 1 (1948).
Sipuel v. Board of Regents, 332 U.S. 631 (1948).
Slaughterhouse Cases, 393 U.S. 385 (1873).
Smith v. Allwright, 321 U.S. 649, 663 (1944).
Smith v. Tuner, 48 U.S. 283 (1849).
South Carolina v. Katzenbach, 383 U.S. 301 (1966).

State of Missouri ex rel. Gaines v. Canada, 305 U.S. 337 (1938).

Strader v. Graham, 51 U.S. 82 (1851).

Sullivan v. Little Hunting Park Inc., 396 U.S. 299 (1969).

Swann v. Charlotte-Mecklenburg, 402 U.S. 1 (1971).

Sweatt v. Painter, 339 U.S. 629 (1950).

Terry v. Adams, 345 U.S. 461 (1953).

Texas Conference of NAACP Branches et al. v. Steen (consolidated with *Veasey v. Perry*), No. 14-41127 (2014), *stay granted on appeal, Veasey v. Perry* and *North Carolina v. League of Women Voters* (consolidated with *North Carolina Conf. of NAACP Branches et al. v. Husted*), 574 U.S. (2014).

Thornburg v. Gingles, 478 U.S. 30 (1986).

Tillman v. Wheaton-Haven Recreation Association, 410 U.S. 431 (1973).

United Jewish Organizations v. Carey, 430 U.S. 144 (1977).

United States v. Cruikshank, 92 U.S. 542 (1876).

United States v. Harris, 106 U.S. 629 (1883).

United States v. Hays, 515 U.S. 737 (1995).

United States v. Johnson, 457 U.S. 537 (1982).

United States v. Mississippi, 380 U.S. 128 (1965).

United States v. Paradise, 480 U.S. 616 (1987).

United States v. Raines, 362 U.S. 17 (1960).

United States v. Reese, 92 U.S. 214 (1876).

University v. Murray, 169 Md. 478, 182 A. 590 (1936).

White v. Regester, 422 U.S. 935 (1975).

Williams v. Mississippi, 170 U.S. 213 (1898).

Wittman v. Personhuballah, 578 U.S. __ (2016).

Yick Wo v. Hopkins, 118 U.S. 356 (1886).

Federal Court

Guinn v. United States, 228 F. 103 (1915).

(F.3d)

Cleveland County Association for Government by the People, an Unincorporated Association v. Cleveland County Board of Commissioners, NAACP, United States of America, Amicus Curiae, 142 F.3d 468 (1998).

Hopwood v. Texas, 78 F.3d 932 (1996).

Johnson v. Bush, 353 F.3d 1287, 1292 (11th Cir. 2003).

Las Vegas Branch NAACP, et al. v. Cegavske, 800 F.3d 1032 (2015).

Pigford v. Glickman, 206 F.3d 1212 (D.C. Cir 2000).

(F.2d)

Dillenburg v. Kramer, 469 F.2d 1222, 1224 (9th Cir. 1972).

Gomillion v. Lightfoot, 270 F.2d 594 (1959).

Grisgby v. Harris, 27 F.2d 942 (SD Tex. 1928).

Kirksey v. Bd. of Supervisors, 544 F.2d 139 (5th Cir. 1977).
Lane v. Wilson, 98 F.2d 980 (1938).
League of United Latin American Citizens v. Clements, 999 F.2d 831 (5th Cir. 1993).
Mendez v. Westminster, 161 F.2d 774 (9th Cir. 1947).
NAACP v. NAACP LDF, 753 F.2d 131 (1985).
North Carolina State Conference of the NAACP v. McCrory, 997 F. Supp. 2d. 322 (2014).
Perry v. Cyphers, 186 F.2d (1951).
Smith v. Allwright, 131 F.2d 593 (1942).
United States v. Wyandotte County, 480 F.2d 969 (10th Cir. 1973).
West v. Bliley, 33 F.2d 177 (1929).
Zimmer v. McKeithen, 485 F.2d 1297 (5th Cir. 1973).

F. Supp.

Anderson v. Courson, 204 F. Supp. 806 (M.D. Ga. 1962).
Browder v. Gayle, 142 F. Supp. 707 (1956).
Brown v. Baskin, 78 F. Supp. 933 (1948).
Brown v. Baskin, 80 F. Supp. 1017 (1948).
Brown v. The Board of Education of Topeka, 98 F. Supp. 797 (1951).
Byrd v. Brice, 104 F. Supp. 442 (1952).
Colegrove v. Green, 64 F. Supp. 632 (1946).
Cooper v. Power, 282 F. Supp. 548 (1968).
Darby v. Daniel, 168 F. Supp. 170 (1958).
Davis v. Schnell, 81 F. Supp. 872 (1949).
Elmore v. Rice, 72 F. Supp. 516 (1947).
Gray v. Main, 309 F. Supp. 207 (1968).
Green v. Veneman, 159 F. Supp. 2d 360 (2001).
Hamm v. Virginia State Board of Elections, 230 F. Supp. 156 (1964).
Harper v. Virginia, 240 F. Supp. 270 (1964).
Lee v. Washington, 263 F. Supp. 327 (Md. Al. 1966).
Mississippi State Chapter, Operation PUSH v. Allain, 674 F. Supp. 1245, 1261 (N.D. Miss. 1987), *aff'd*, 932 F.2d 400 (5th Cir. 1991).
NAACP, DeKalb County Chapter v. Georgia, 494 F. Supp. 668 (N.D. Ga. 1980).
Pigford v. Veneman, 355 F. Supp. 2d 148 (2005).
Ventre v. Ryder, 176 F. Supp. 90 (1959).

State Court

Board of Education of Ottawa et al v. Tinnon, by His Next Friend, Elijah Tinnon, 26 Kan. 1 (1881).
Gomillion v. Lightfoot, 167 F. Supp. 405 (1958).
Gore v. Harris, 779 So. 2d 270 (2000).
Holfman v. Robinson, 213 So. 2d 267 (1968).
Johnson v. Bush, 126 S. Ct. 650 (2005) (*cert. denied*).
Lassiter v. Northampton County Board of Elections, 102 S.E.2d 853 (1958).
Little v. LATOR, Supreme Court for Albany County (NY), Case No. 3210-2011 (2012).

Mapp v. Ohio, 170 Ohio St. 427, 429 (1960).

Mott v. Cline, 200 Cal. 434, 253 P. 718 (1927).

Pace & Cox v. Alabama, 69 Ala. 231 (1881).

Rachel v. Walker, 4 Mo. 350 (1836).

Reynolds v. Board of Education of the City of Topeka, 66 Kan. 672 (1903).

Rice v. Elmore, 165 F. 2d 387, *cert. denied*, 333 U.S. 875, 68 S. Ct. 905 (1948).

Robinson v. Holman, 181 Ark. 428 (Ark. 1930), 26 S.W. 2d 66 (Ark. 1930).

Sipes v. McGhee, 316 Mich. 614, 25 N.W. 2d 638 (1947).

State v. Franklin, 80 So. Car. 332.

State of Ohio ex rel. Garnes v. McCann, 21 Ohio St. 198 (1871).

Thurman-Watts v. Board of Education of the City of Coffeyville, 115 Kan. 328 (1924).

Williams v. Board of Education of the City of Parson, 79 Kan. 202 (1908).

CONGRESSIONAL HEARINGS AND STATE CONSTITUTIONS

Extension of the Voting Rights Act of 1965: Hearings Before the Subcommittee on Constitutional Rights, Senate Committee on the Judiciary, 94th Cong., 1st sess. (1975). Okla. Const. art. III, § 1 (1910).

WEB SITES

"African American Women and Suffrage." Rights for Women: The Suffrage Movement and Its Leaders. National Women's History Museum. https://www.nwhm.org/online-exhibits/rightsforwomen/AfricanAmericanwomen.html.

Chronology of events leading to the Wilmington, NC, coup and race riot: http://www.ah.dcr.state.nc.us/1898-wrrc/report/Chapter3A.pdf.

"Guinn v. United States—Oklahoma's Grandfather Clause." http://law.jrank.org/pages/24874/Guinn-v-United-States-Oklahoma-s-Grandfather-Clause.html#ixzz3oNjkyFzC.

Journalists who reported on the civil rights movement: http://www.reportingcivilrights.org/.

"Missed Manners: Wilson Lectures a Black Leader." History Matters: The U.S. Survey Course on the Web: http://historymatters.gmu.edu/d/5719/.

Murder of Medgar Evers: https://vault.fbi.gov/Medgar Evers.

Murder of Viola Liussa: vault.fbi.gov.

"(1920) Archibald Grimke, 'The Shame of America, or the Negro's Case Against the Republic.'" BlackPast.org: http://www.blackpast.org/1920-archibald-grimke-shame-america-or-negro-s-case-against-republic#sthash.2fTEmEvP.dpuf.

University of Wisconsin-Madison Libraries. "Medgar Evers." http://search.library.wisc.edu/catalog/ocn236489242.

The White House Historical Association. "William Monroe Trotter Challenges President Wilson." http://www.whitehousehistory.org/william-monroe-trotter-challenges-president-wilson.

Acknowledgments

Thank you Rev. Dr. C.T. Vivian for your strength, sacrifice, and unwavering belief in the greater good.

The history of great work by the National Association for the Advancement of Colored People has made this book possible—and this nation a better place. Individuals, whether citizens, immigrants, or visitors, of every race and nationality, women and men of all ages, creeds, color, and political beliefs, benefit from the work of this illustrious organization. Freedom rings in America because of the NAACP.

It was such a pleasure to work with my editors, acquisitions editor Sarah Stanton and production editor Jehanne Schweitzer. I enjoy teaching. In this case, my students taught me to persevere with this project and see it through to fruition. I relied heavily on smart, dedicated young people who gave their time to this book under very unusual circumstances. Special appreciation must be given to Ruffa Espejon and my research assistant and former John Jay student Nataliya Gobenko, Spelman College student Aaliyah Connor, and researcher Bronwyn Zevallos. Without the persistence, optimism, and encouragement of my John Jay student Carolina Mora, this book would have been lost among so many competing projects. Thank you, Carolina. After learning about the struggle for voting rights in class, she insisted I complete this book so everyone would know of these sacrifices and injustices.

Thank you Ernie Marshall, my husband, for giving me the time I need to write. My friends are wonderfully supportive. Thank you for understanding my erratic schedule and frequent disappearances. My pet is truly a writer's cat. Words cannot fully describe my appreciation for the work of the late Jocelyn Clopton Cooper and Andrew Cooper, champions of voting rights in Brooklyn. They had the foresight and courage to be the first to challenge the political districts in Brooklyn, New York. Their case, *Cooper v. Power* (1968), resulted in the election of Rep. Shirley Chisholm, the first Black congresswoman. I miss my friend Jocelyn and will remain grateful for all she gave me and our Black community. I thank Dr. Teresa M. Brown for her encouragement. I thank members of the New York Democratic Lawyers Council, especially Debra S. Cooper, who is an excellent researcher, Lance Polivy, William Forni, Adeneiki Williams, and Sam Linn.

I am indebted to the librarians, staff, and researchers at the Library of Congress. Assistance was also given by the NAACP, National Archives, Schomburg Center for Research in Black Culture, John Jay College Library, and University of Massachusetts Amherst Libraries. I thank all those members of the Selma community who have provided years of the invaluable assistance and support to maintain the memory and lessons of Bloody Sunday, 1965. I am honored to know members of Elders' House in Selma, who work to pass the light on to future generations. My research was supported by funding from the Office for the Advancement of Research at John Jay College. I appreciate access to the Frederick Lewis Allen Room of the New York Public Library.

I am humbled by the sacrifices made by those who help create the voting rights enjoyed by all Americans. Their service must be acknowledged in general because it is impossible to list all of their names. Untold numbers were killed and assaulted in an attempt to halt the rise of Black political power. It is a privilege and our legal right to play a role in the political marketplace.

> May we forever stand,
> True to our God,
> True to our native land.
>
> —James Weldon Johnson, "Lift Every Voice and Sing" (1899)

Index

Mix, Robert, Sr., 142
Mobile v. Bolden (1980), 147–49
Moll, Lester, 77
Montgomery bus boycott, 97–99, 101, 105
Moore, Frank, 70
Moore, Harry and Harriette, 91, 96–97
Moore et al. v. Dempsey (1923), 65–66, 70
Moorer, Jacob, 41
Morehouse College, 83
Morgan, Clement G.. *See photo insert*
Moskowitz, Henry (Dr.), 11. *See also photo insert*
Motley, Joel, Jr., 107
Moton, Leroy Jerome, 62
mulattoes, 22, 25, 33
Mullen, Greg, 161
murder and mob violence: bombing of Birmingham Baptist Church, 123; Cheney, Goodman and Schwerner, 123, 124–25; Freedom Riders, 107; Harry and Harriette Moore, 91; maintenance of White power, 11–16, 24, 39, 48, 51, 150; march to Montgomery, 127–29, 157; Martin Luther King, Jr., 137–38, 143; Medgar Evers, 61; Red Summer of 1919, 92; Rev. George Lee, 96–97; Rev. James Reeb, 128; right of self-defense, 41, 75–77; Supreme Court rulings, 50, 82; Viola Liuzzo, 62, 128. *See also* lynching; race riots
Murphy, Frank, 77
Murray, Donald Gaines, 84
Myers v. Anderson (1915), 47

NAACP Legal Defense and Education Fund, Inc. (NAACP LDF): about the mission and goals, 3, 121–22, 152–53; challenging civil death, 153–56; conflict and tension with NAACP, 135–39, 144–45, 149, 150–51; Freedom Summer of 1964, 123–25; Greenberg as leader, 144; Selma to Montgomery march, 126–29; separation from NAACP, 122, 149;

Supreme Court rulings, 133–35, 143–45, 147–49; Voting Rights Act, 141, 150, 156–59
NAACP v. Alabama (1958), 103–4, 122
NAACP v. Button (1963), 104–5
NAACP v. Claiborne Hardware (1982), 143–45
NAACP v. Husted (2014), 159
NAACP v. NAACP LDF (1985), 149
NAACP v. Patty (1958), 99
NAACP Youth Council, 97–98
Nabrit, James, 83
National Association for the Advancement of Colored People (NAACP), about the birth, 1–3, 6, 7, 17–19; amicus support of *Guinn*, 47; Black Power programs, 138; challenging segregation in interstate travel, 84–85; challenging self-determination restrictions, 68–69; challenging the Grandfather Clause, 42–44; challenging voting restrictions, 1, 5, 12, 86–87; challenging White-only primaries, 78–80; congressional lobbying, 58–59, 114, 116, 124, 138, 152; defending right of self-defense, 75–77; *Elmore v. Rice* (1947), 87–88; Houston role in, 48–49; influence on Court nominees, 81–82; lynching and mob violence protests, 70–75; membership, growth/decline, 56, 58, 92, 100, 143–44, 148; membership disclosure, 102–4, 122, 143; money and time limitations, 56–58, 76, 137–38, 144–45; "Operation Suffrage," 92; presence in Texas, 78; proactive approach to cases, 82–89; struggle for voter registration, 70–75
National Association of Colored Women, 122
National Association of Colored Women's Clubs, 38
National Bar Association (formerly National Negro Bar Association), 69–70

85, 104–5; white violence to enforce, 67–68
Shaw v. Reno (1993), 150–51
Shelby County, Alabama v. Holder (2013), 156–60
Shepard, Sam, 96
Shillady, John R., 173–82
Sixteenth Street Baptist Church (Birmingham), 123
slavery: about the struggle before the Civil War, 31–35; Black self-determination and the end of, 2, 12–13, 30; continued struggle after the Civil War, 35–38; denial of right to vote, 21–22; *Dred Scott* decision and Fugitive Slave Act, 23–24; free Blacks during, 23–25; Freedman's Bureau, 29; manumission, 23, 25; post-war end of Reconstruction, 31; 13th Amendment, 54, 153–56; Vermont abolishment of, 22; White missionary efforts, 25; White supremacy efforts to maintain, 39–41, 59–60, 62, 153–54
Smith, B. S.. *See photo insert*
Smith, Howard W., 130
Smith, Lonnie (Dr.), 86
Smith, Mary Louise, 99
Smith v. Allwright (1944), 86–87, 91, 94–95, 96–97, 106, 129
Social Democratic League. *See* Walling, William English
The Souls of Black Folk (DuBois), 65
South Carolina: challenging the Voter Rights Act, 133; Constitutional Convention of 1895, 133; election of a Black to Congress, 28–30; Emanuel A.M.E. Church shooting, 161; Hamburg Massacre of 1876, 30; implementation of Mississippi Plan, 37; photo identification law, 157; school desegregation, 92; upholding Franklin murder conviction, 41; voter disenfranchisement, 87–88, 92; voter registration, 93; White-only primaries, 87–88
South Carolina v. Katzenback (1966), 133

Southern Christian Leadership Conference (SCLC), 101–2, 122, 124, 126–27
Southern Indicator (newspaper), 63
Southern Manifesto, 101
Spingarn, Arthur, 79
Spivey, Ed, 96–97
Springfield Race Riot of 1908, 66
Springfield Riot of 1904, 15–16, 19
Springfield Riot of 1908, 2, 5–9, 11–13, 26, 77
states' rights: influence on Supreme Court, 50; right to vote, 27, 46–47, 116, 141–42; 2000 Florida vote recount, 152–53; Voting Rights Act and, 133; White supremacy and, 16
Stennis, John, 116
Stephenson, C. W., 44
Stokes, Louis, 142
Storey, Moorefield: activism and reputation, 17–19, 63; challenging the Grandfather Clause, 46–47, 178; death of, 96–97; president of NAACP, 19, 42, 124–25; pursuing legal challenges, 47–48, 53–54, 65–68, 79. *See also photo insert*
Strunsky, Anna, 5
Student Non-Violent Coordinating Committee (SNCC), 107, 109, 122, 126–29
suffrage, 37–38, 43–46, 65, 92, 174–78, 181, 184n25. *See also* women's suffrage
Sumner, Charles, 18
Swann v. Charlotte-Mecklenberg Board of Education (1971), 146–47
Sweet, Gladys, 76–77
Sweet, Henry, 76–77
Sweet, Ossian (Dr.), 75–77
Sweet, Otis, 76–77
Sweet, T. L., 74

Taft, William Howard, 41, 44, 45–46
Talbert, Mary B., 58
Taney, Roger B., 3, 24
Tate, U. Simpson, 93
Taylor, George Edwin, 37–38